A Secret History,

The London Gay Men's Chorus

by

Robert Offord

A Secret History,

The London Gay Men's Chorus

by

Robert Offord

ISBN: 978-0-9955830-0-9

This book is produced by Robert Offord Publishing in conjunction with **WRITERSWORLD**, and is produced entirely in the UK. It is available to order from most bookshops in the United Kingdom, and is also globally available via UK based Internet book retailers.

WRITERSWORLD
2 Bear Close Flats, Bear Close, Woodstock
Oxfordshire, OX20 1JX, England
☎ 01993 812500
☎ +44 1993 812500

www.writersworld.co.uk

The text pages of this book are produced via an independent certification process that ensures the trees from which the paper is produced come from well managed sources that exclude the risk of using illegally logged timber while leaving options to use post-consumer recycled paper as well.

Dear Reader,

Twenty five years with the London Gay Men's Chorus has been the wildest rip-roaring ride. In this account I have attempted to be accurate and objective, but ultimately it can only be what I saw, heard and have managed to hold on to, not an approved official history. Please forgive any personal opinion that may have crept in, or any omission of significant people and important event that may have been left out.

Enjoy the telling, it's been an epic anecdote.

Huge thanks to Lesley Jordan for proof reading with patience, and constant constructive suggestion.

* * * * *

Robert Offord was born in 1951 and raised in North London. The teenage years were constructively derailed by psychedelic folk music, and in the 1970s a passion for pop-art and punk revolution arrived. After a brief diversion into scientific study, and some experimentation with existentialism and alienation, he gained a BA (Hons) from Middlesex University in 1981.

His career as a part-time art teacher was cut short by accidentally achieving international success as a graphic artist.

Freedom followed and in 1991 the London Gay Men's Chorus began; history continues to unfold.

Chapters

ONE
In the Beginning

Once upon a time... (it seems so long ago).

In the late nineteen eighties, a small group of gay men used to meet up at a do-it-yourself social club. The place was simply called 'London Friend', and something about it seemed to appeal to unconventional people. Those who managed to find their way there had usually noticed an inconspicuous advert in one of the gay newspapers. Those weekly papers were a vital component of gay life, and for many just about the only source of 'gay' information.

The group of volunteers who ran the London Friend organisation were attempting to provide an open, relaxed and free alternative to the still somewhat seedy and furtive gay club and pub scene. The venue for their idealistic enterprise was at the (then) derelict end of the Caledonian Road, behind Kings Cross Station, in an empty shop premises that had long since given up the hope of ever selling anything useful.

That particular era was a dark and difficult time for many people; crime, unemployment and poverty levels had all been going up steadily for the previous decade, yuppie greed was rampant and it felt as if society had become polarized. The country was gripped by the longest recession that had been experienced for sixty years. The police had been in the news for using particularly heavy-handed techniques to deal with angry pickets and 'stop and search' powers had been introduced in the mid-eighties. In the north of the country entire communities had been devastated by pit closures. A quarter of a million miners had lost their jobs and for school leavers, student grants had just been axed. Many young people were indignant at the establishment intolerance shown to spontaneous 'rave' events, and ludicrous attempts had been made to pass legislation banning techno music ('music characterised by a succession of repetitive beats'). The notorious Poll tax riots had taken place in March 1990, when Trafalgar Square had turned into a battlefield and 300 protesters were arrested. In the south-east nearly three-quarters of the population had refused to pay this tax, and it seemed that even the normally docile middle classes were becoming disaffected.

For gay men, homophobia in the media was making it an especially worrying time, and once a week, usually on a Wednesday night, a group of us gathered around the makeshift plywood coffee counter in the corner of our special little social club. There was always a surprisingly diverse collection of people; you could find yourself in conversation with a twenty-year-old gas fitter or a seventy-year-old retired teacher. It was a cross section of the community, and because the activities weren't focussed on dance music, drinking or cruising, the systems of social segregation that you would perhaps expect to find in a more conventional club didn't seem to apply.

Although the conversations were far reaching, we all had in common the fact that we were gay, so predictable topics could be our personal experiences of 'coming out', or the political and social repercussions of the current AIDS crisis. In 1986 the Health Secretary Norman Fowler had devised an alarmist public health campaign that resulted in the 'Don't Die of Ignorance' booklet being delivered through 23 million letter boxes. A lurid shlock-horror TV advert featuring dry-ice and shattered tomb stones reinforced the panicky message, and there seemed to be a widespread but unspoken implication that 'gay equals guilty'. In 1988 the Education Secretary, Ken Baker, had demanded that the "perverted" children's book 'Jenny lives with Eric and Martin' should be banned from schools and taken out of public libraries. There was a clear message that gay people were not acceptable members of society. At the Tory party conference Margaret Thatcher's declaration that 'children taught that they have an inalienable right to be gay are being cheated of a sound start in life' was greeted with rapturous applause.

At London Friend politicians were often criticised, and they sometimes seemed to be at the root of many of our problems. There was rarely a fixed agenda for our club night, and nothing was considered off-limits. Since most of those who attended London Friend were regulars and knew each other quite well, even the most private of secrets, such as of childhood abuse, could be shared. We bared our hearts, told our stories and spoke our minds. We talked about the way things were and of how they ought to be, and of how to change the prevailing attitudes of the general public and make our bit of the world a better place.

Every month or so one of us would make the effort to organise something that felt a bit more like a special event. Sometimes it was a video-tape recording of a relevant TV program that was shown, followed by a group discussion, and there were also quiz nights, when teams were drawn up and the prize box of chocolates passed round by the winners. Once or twice a year an author would be invited in to talk about their new book; they would get to sell a few signed copies, and we would get a sense that maybe we weren't quite so isolated after all. The stories they told encompassed other cities and cultures, and people like us who had lived their lives and found their own answers, though it was apparent that in the 1980's happy endings were not that common in gay literature.

Most of the time it was just the regular people who always turned up; the simple reassurance of being part of an informal group was enough of an incentive to draw us there. The tea urn was always steaming on the counter, and there was a cassette player in the corner where we could play our own choice of background music. Occasionally we listened to something cultured and classical, more often it was Elton, Bowie or maybe Queen; you could hum along, or join in if you knew the words and the mood and the moment felt right.

New and unfamiliar faces would drift into the group as the weeks slipped by, guarded individuals who stood at the back and self-consciously gulped at hot tea from chipped mugs. The lost or the lonely, refugees from ruthless cruising, outcasts from the in-crowd, would gradually realize that they could relax here. One could say exactly what one felt without fear of rejection; this tiny corner of the world was ours alone, and a thoughtful tolerance was one of our principles. You could chose to remain silent if you wished, just sit and bask in the safety of it all, or you could return a smile and engage in a conversation. Friendships would form, bonds developed. Sometimes wounded hearts were healed.

Although the atmosphere was informal, the emotions were often intense, and even on warm nights it seemed that the big plate-glass front window was always steamed up by the time we had to return to the isolation and darkness outside.

Our Wednesday evenings were an oasis of fellowship, safety and hope, a privilege that was denied to us for the rest of the week. For many that humble little social club became the central axis to our lives, the rest of the week span alarmingly out of control and beyond our grasp. Only London Friend felt like a secure home. For those who had been lucky enough to find it 'the club night' was always special, but there was one particular evening that stands out in my memory as being of extra significance.

Louis was making the tea that week. He was a big bloke, shaved head and a bit rough looking, originally from Cyprus and a trained actor. He was about forty then, and you got the impression he'd been around a bit. He turned down the tape player after one particularly loud and rowdy sing along, Abba, I think it was, and jokingly said, "You lot, honestly, you ought to form a choir". Those who heard the comment laughed and clapped at such an absurd idea, all except for me, I think my jaw might have dropped open; I'd been struck by a thunderbolt. As I heard the words my imagination flashed into life. It felt as if a door was slowly opening and I was dazzled by the potential of what I saw unfolding.

I gulped and simply said, "You're right. We must".

Outside the plate-glass window the traffic of the Caledonian road continued to rumble past; inside the club people carried on talking. Those nearest to where I sat looked at me strangely, perhaps a bit startled by the intensity and conviction with which I'd just spoken.

"Louis," I said, "Why don't we? Why can't we? It would be just great!" I could clearly see that an in-yer-face gay choir could challenge so much of the fear and prejudice that being whipped up. I was practically incoherent with the whirlwind of possibilities my mind was exploring.

There was a pause and then John, who was standing nearby said thoughtfully, "Yes, and I could play the piano". It was such a plain statement and he sounded so sincere; there was a smile on his face and his expression was confident, perhaps he had understood what I was thinking. We soon discovered that as well as playing the piano he could sing like an angel. He taught music in a school and knew how to go about organising a singing group.

John, Louis and I carried on exploring this unexpected diversion to the usual conversation. It turned out that Louis had tried doing a 'choir thing' before, but it had fallen apart after a few weeks without going anywhere much. I was teaching art to young adults at the local technical college, and knew just how hard it was to motivate people and overcome their inhibitions. All sorts of doubts and practical problems were raised, but I kept batting them away and returning to how satisfying and valuable it would be to actually do it. There was even a little room in the basement of the old building that wasn't used for anything. Being at London Friend meant there was potentially a big group of people available to engage with. We all enjoyed having a sing along. Some of us even had happy memories of singing in a school choir and knew how much fun it could be.

As we turned the ideas over and over, adding bits on, imagining the consequences, ignoring the difficulties, it gradually turned into the perfect project that absolutely demanded to be done. A gay choir! We needed to do it for ourselves, for our own sense of pride and self-worth and, with the appalling current perceptions about gay people, the general population of Great Britain needed to have it done to them. I optimistically and simplistically felt that people would not be able to reject and discriminate against a group that was singing to them. It would be a direct, non-violent, cultural attack against the very heart of all the problems concerning our acceptance. Since time immemorial the singing of meaningful songs of protest has always captured hearts, swayed emotions and been a significant part of every resistance movement.

The notorious 'section 28' had just been sanctioned by the government and passed into the laws of the land; it was time that we stood up and did something. It was now illegal for any local authority to do anything which might be interpreted as 'promoting a homosexual lifestyle'. Nobody knew where this bureaucratic homophobia was going to stop. Bigoted politicians were seriously proposing that gay people should be banned from teaching in schools and from working in the health service. The 'Sexual Offences Act' of 1967 had begun the process of granting some legal protection to gay people, now we were about to be re-criminalized. When the new bill was being debated one of the outrageous proposals was that "gatherings of more than three homosexuals would have to apply for a licence." There were suggestions in the tabloid press that HIV positive people could be rounded up, branded and isolated on some sort of prison-camp island. Were we going to have to start fighting just to be able to lead an ordinary everyday life? At that time I remember seeing a placard at a gay-organised anti-Thatcher demonstration in Parliament Square, the home-made lettering read: 'It's all going to get worse'.

The beautifully naive simplicity of standing up in public and singing felt just like the right sort of non-threatening, but subversive and confrontational action to take against all the guilt and shame that was being thrown at us. We could refuse to play the roles of diseased and perverted victims and criminals; we could challenge hatred, fear and ignorance by simply being unafraid and making music on our own terms and in public.

One casual comment, my spontaneous reaction, the coincidence of the right people hearing it, and all of us being in the empowering environment of London Friend, was the seed that eventually grew into The London Gay Men's Chorus. It was then the autumn of 1991, and we had a dream.

The use of the empty room in the basement was arranged, and at the next Wednesday gathering, we spread the word. "There's a choir starting, come along and have a sing, it'll be great". At the beginning of the week after that, we had our first meeting.

John had brought his Yamaha keyboard on the tube, walking rapidly through the streets of Kings Cross and trying to look inconspicuous. There were seven, or maybe eight, people in the room. Several of us had thought to bring along word sheets. We could choose from 'Somewhere Over The Rainbow', 'Pennies From Heaven', 'Spread A Little Happiness' or 'All Through The Night' in Welsh. We talked a bit more, and John showed off the pre-programmed facilities on the keyboard. Louis seemed to accept the role of being some sort of conductor for us. The only song we were all confident about doing was 'Somewhere Over The Rainbow', we tried it with a Bossa Nova backing, not very successfully. It was obvious that there was a very great deal to learn. After three hours we had to pack up and go home. It had been a strange evening, both frustrating and intriguing. We all agreed to meet up and try again the next week.

Somehow, despite the difficult start, the spirit and vision of the basic idea survived and slowly grew. Some of the original enthusiasts drifted away, but others joined in. As the weeks passed we began to find the right songs to sing, and that made all the difference. 'Something Inside So Strong' by Labi Siffre, was introduced early on, 'Every Time We Say Goodbye' by Cole Porter, 'If We Only Have Love' by Jacques Brell; these songs had a real and emotional significance for us. We needed this music; it was part of our lives and it was telling our stories. This was a form of therapy, instinctive and communal.

As the year drew to its close, the reality of what we were doing became more and more apparent. Meeting up once a week in the basement, enjoying ourselves for a few hours, occasionally speculating about what could happen, was not the whole picture. We had to perform somehow. Become bigger than just 'us'. This motley collection of people had work to do, and when it came down to it, the prospect was extremely intimidating. We talked about doing 'a show' for the other folk upstairs, part of the London Friend Christmas party. The idea was OK, we could do that, but it still wasn't enough. It was a safe option. Not quite 'the real thing'.

Louis got in touch with The Terrence Higgins Trust. The organisation had been founded as early as 1983, were recognised as the most significant AIDS charity, and had their phone number included in the 'Don't Die of Ignorance' booklet. They gave us permission to hold a street collection on their behalf, and supplied us with collecting boxes. I'm not sure they realised there was going to be any singing involved, we were hiding behind the 'London Friend' letterhead and not yet confident enough to call ourselves a choir. Someone suggested Angel tube station as a venue. There seemed to be a noticeably gay presence amongst the commuters there. London Transport had just opened up a shiny new booking hall, and seemed to be eager for 'community involvement'. We got in touch with a London Transport Community Liaison Officer and were offered a choice of times and dates. In a spirit of reckless defiance, we went for what we thought would be the busiest.

With ever mounting apprehension we continued to meet, week by week, and practise our repertoire. There was an on-going debate about what we should call ourselves. Various suggestions were thrown around and rejected; 'Rainbow Singers' was too coy, 'Triangle Gang', sounded ugly, 'Zoo Squad', just too weird. I was adamant that the word 'gay' should be upfront, out in the open and unambiguous. No decision was reached. The date of our debut drew closer. Eventually, on the afternoon of our big day, I painted the words 'Gay Men's Choir', on a big sheet of white paper, rolled it up, and set off for Angel station. The name described what we were, nothing more was necessary, and nothing less was acceptable.

It was a cold Friday evening at the beginning of December, 6.30pm.

Nine brave gay men stood in a cluster by the ticket machine, felt very foolish, and began to sing. We had all come directly from our various daytime activities; nurse, teacher, salesman. Patrick, very smart in a suit, Gordon in bike-courier Lycra, Stevie, six foot four and waist length hair, was in denim. Dennis, who was visually impaired and often carried a white stick, stood in the front and held our poster. Somebody else was in leathers; I was doing the 'country squire' look in a Barbour jacket. We must have looked a bit like a dysfunctional 'Village People', one of each type. Our little group clustered together and sang with a defensive energy, and people paused in their tracks, stood still and stared. Oh... how they stared.

We had assumed that commuters would see us, drop a coin in the box if we were lucky, and carry on by; but people seemed to want to stay and listen and an audience formed. Nobody had ever seen or even imagined anything as outlandish as 'a gay choir' before. After twenty minutes we had sung every song that had been rehearsed. We started at the beginning again, and the audience grew into a bit of a crowd.

I don't remember exactly how much money we raised for the Terrence Higgins Trust that evening, but the two plastic collecting boxes were pleasingly heavy. By the time we were starting our third repeat the station manager came over and told us that we had to stop. The station had become so crowded that the escalators had to be turned off and apparently there were people backed up on the platforms. Our first public performance had ended with us being told to move on, and it really felt like we had arrived. We all went off to the pub that night, and began to plot just exactly how we would 'move on'.

TWO

Manchester at Midnight

Although Louis, John and I had no definite plans we also had no doubts about the need to continue what we had started. As the next year began, our weekly meetings carried on. We knew that we had to have a bit more of a programme than just a regular but unstructured gathering in a borrowed basement; we needed to have properly organised rehearsals. There was also some vague intuition telling us it was now necessary for 'the choir' to become a separate group with its own identity. We intended to become something more than just 'those people from London Friend'. Louis made an announcement that 'the choir' would now be meeting every Monday and there seemed to be about fourteen of us interested in taking things further. We scouted round for a suitable location, had a whip round, and for thirty pounds a week rented an attic room in The Holborn Centre for the Performing Arts. It was cheap, near a tube station and there was a friendly looking pub just round the corner.

The Holborn Centre was a virtually derelict old building with a slick chromium and plate glass snack bar in the lobby; the rest of it was a Victorian ramble of dismal bare rooms and hairpin staircases. It was always disconcertingly deserted, and except for the showcase snack-bar, unheated. In the winter we had to sing in coats, with gloves if you'd remembered to bring them, and in the blaze of summer we gasped for air, sang flat and sweated.

In retrospect I can now see that the rehearsal procedure we evolved is absolutely standard choral practice, groups of singers behave in exactly the same way everywhere from Fiji to Finland. Someone stands at the front, makes musical noises, gestures rhythmically, and tries to inspire all the others.

If the musical director has enough charisma and is respected by the participants then the ritual works; communal music is made. With a newly formed group, not yet used to singing together and still somewhat inhibited, the procedure was rather less reliable, and we sometimes doubted the worth of what we were all doing.

It seemed so primitive and purposeless and was often embarrassing; to stand in a half circle and try to make musical noises, as if all common sense had been suspended. But luckily there would come a moment, as the light faded and our feet ached, when something about what was going on would feel inexplicably and instinctively right. We would rediscover why we had started this uncomfortable weekly ritual. A phrase that was being sung would trigger a memory and a meaning would become clear. A particular note would find its harmonic partner, and the results would ring in our ears and unite the group. An ancient tribal consciousness seemed to materialise, fleeting magic glittered in the air and our spines tingled. Futile questions and irrelevant answers fell away, we could not have explained why it was necessary, but we carried on anyway.

The Holborn Centre had a fragile future. The old building was ringed around by modern office blocks and it was clearly ripe for redevelopment.

At the end of the summer we were given notice to quit, and we thought for a while that our experiments with 'the performing arts' were coming to a close. We had enjoyed our rehearsals, and were now used to the routine of a Monday night, but there had only been one or two performances, and it didn't look as if there was a market for what we were doing. With nowhere to meet up, and no requests for the choir to perform, it was beginning to feel as if the show was over.

In 1992 Elton John announced the launch of The Elton John Aids Foundation. He had been so moved by the plight of a terminally ill American boy Ryan White, that he had decided to devote his considerable resources to improving the lot of those affected by AIDS. With all his wealth and celebrity behind the cause, some of us wondered if our unknown gay choir had any further purpose.

With only a couple of weeks to go before our impending eviction, somebody discovered that there was an empty basement at the London Lesbian and Gay Centre in Farringdon. It was only used once a week for the 'Sadie Masie' disco, was painted matt black and reeked of stale beer and damp earth. It was part of a 'gay space', and the fact that we could use it for free made us feel that perhaps we might continue a little longer.

We took a chance and moved our Monday meetings to Farringdon. Nobody knew if it was a sensible thing to do, but it was an opportunity, and there was a great bar upstairs. Sometimes we saw the film-maker Derek Jarman there, holding court like some eerie emperor with all his acolytes around him at the big table in the corner.

The existence of a gay choir took many people by surprise, and when we performed the audiences were usually fascinated and attentive. Even a small amateur outfit such as we then were, represented a group of people strongly united and making a loud noise in public. Given the right context and a receptive crowd, the effects could be powerful. Historical records reveal that years ago various European monarchs took singers into the battlefield with them, alongside their soldiers; they realised it could make a significant difference to the outcome of a conflict. 'Chapel Royal' the choir that still resides at Hampton Court Palace, is a direct descendant of the group of singers that accompanied the crusades in the eleventh century. A trained choir with a serious intent can manipulate emotions, inspire morale and effect a reaction.

The experience of group singing is a mutual process; the performer is affected by the spectator, as well as the other way round. Whilst performing a really committed singer is in a state of enhanced consciousness with all of their senses turned fully on. A direct communication of emotion occurs between transmitter and receiver that can sometimes feel like a two-way telepathic short circuit. Music can be a powerful magic.

One such moment happened to us a couple of months after we had moved to the Lesbian and Gay Centre.

John Harold, our pianist, was born and bred in Manchester, and one weekend whilst visiting his parents, he heard of a rather unlikely sounding night-time performance opportunity for us in a Manchester car park.

What was being planned was a midnight AIDS vigil; we had not done such an event before and were uncertain as to how we should handle such a powerful theme. At that time an AIDS diagnosis was perceived to be an unambiguous death sentence. Many of us had lost friends; all of us faced fear and felt shrouded by shadows. Sorrow and grief certainly had to be a part of the vigil, a degree of anger was appropriate, and we felt that a defiant celebration of life well lived must also be incorporated.

John got in touch with an old friend who worked at the Manchester Royal Infirmary; they knew of a nurse who would be willing to speak about working with AIDS patients. Then a bereaved partner heard of the plan and came forward; angered by his anonymity and rejection he wanted to read a poem in memory of his lover.

It was a small group of people from the local gay pub, The Rembrandt, who had first suggested the idea of a vigil. They had prepared some simple flyers, and during August, a couple of weeks before the proposed event, began distributing them around what was unofficially known as Manchester's gay village.

Louis took John and the keyboard up there in his car,

and the rest of us went on the train. I remember meeting the local vicar, and spent the night sleeping on the settee in his living room. I never asked him if he was gay; in that era the question would have been dangerously intrusive, but it was obvious he was sympathetic.

On the morning of the allotted day the Rembrandt crew met up at the back of the Sackville Street car park, and constructed a raised platform from a few borrowed scaffolding poles and planks; everything we could think of had been prepared.

As dusk descended and the area emptied out, two cars were positioned so that their headlights shone towards the makeshift stage. The keyboard was plugged in, covered by a plastic sheet, and then we stood around and waited, nobody knew how many people would turn up. At 10pm there seemed to be a couple of dozen, as midnight approached it was starting to look more like a couple of hundred.

We sang, hesitantly at first, and the silent crowd held candles in the darkness. A haze of light drizzle shimmered and sparkled in the damp night air. The hospice nurse spoke about the fear, shame and secrecy that surrounded AIDS patients, and the chosen poem was read by the bereaved partner. We sang again, and suddenly it seemed the candles were being held up higher.

The front of the crowd drew in closer, and we could see from the tiny stage that people held on to one another. Several right at the front, and one person standing poignantly alone, wept openly and without inhibition. We now sang with feeling and power and purpose, and it seemed to unleash a great wave of urgent and communal emotion. My eyes also brimmed with salty tears, and the blurry shining of hundreds of lit candles seemed to become a great shimmering and glittering sea of shared grief.

Our songs had acted as an emotional catalyst. Without our presence the event would have been unbearably sad, hollow and devoid of comfort. The addition of the right music had transformed it into a focussed, therapeutic and healing experience, and bought some defiant spirit, warmth and hope back into a damaged community.

The power of all that need, and the passions it awoke, swept us back to London and carried us deep into the winter months. Nine of us had got on the train to go to that car park in Manchester, and it proved to be a turning point. The newly formed gay choir had felt like a homeless, ragged tribe with little sense of direction, now we understood that in the right context we could be an empowered strike-force of storm troopers.

THREE
The Queer Concerts

When we appeared before an audience Louis conducted the group and John played the piano. It might have looked as though they were the leaders, but behind the scenes we were a very active democracy; everyone was united in driving the choir onwards. In retrospect I can see that there were very significant logistical advantages to being such a small group, but at the time we thought there weren't enough of us. We decided that with more people we would have a greater stage presence and make a larger sound; to fulfil our purpose, our little tribe had to grow.

We all agreed a plan of action, had a collection, and a small advert was put in the community weekly newspaper, Capital Gay. Louis had a personal computer, still a bit of a novelty in those (pre 'Windows 95') days, and we printed some little flyers and left them surreptitiously amongst the Aids information leaflets in a couple of gay pubs.

Some tiny fragment of information found its way to a person who would alter everything for us.

Richard was a 'homo-hippy'; he remembered the early days of the 'Gay Liberation Front' and still carried with him the aura of a radical outsider. He was vegetarian, thin as an antelopes bleached leg-bone, dressed in bright colours and lived illegally in a cavernous basement at the scruffy end of Islington. The idea of a gay choir had caught his imagination and vaguely seemed to coincide with his own plans. He had been thinking of doing a vocal techniques course, and then becoming some sort of alternative voice-coach for actors and singers. After a few weeks of coming along to our rehearsals at the Gay Centre he was hooked, and the choir would never be the same again.

The London Lesbian and Gay Centre had served us and the rest of the community well; it was constantly busy with people putting on events, going to courses, or just seeking a social oasis in the bustle of the city. Its organisation was chaotic, most of the staff being inexperienced but idealistic volunteers, and there was no sound financial plan to keep it afloat. Perhaps inevitably it gradually collapsed into a bitter ruin of bankruptcy and rumours of embezzlement, and sank without trace.

We had to move again but this time we were empowered with a sense of purpose, and moved straight into Richard's Islington squat. It was known as 'Voicespace', and the only way into it was down a narrow flight of unmarked steps at the back of the Finsbury Library.

The main area was a bare, low ceilinged hall. A long corridor led off from one corner, and gave access to a succession of rooms. The first one was Richard's living quarters, large and comfortably furnished with a collection of decent dumped furniture and Indian wall hangings. The room at the other end of the corridor, next to the toilets, was always locked, and a tatty sign on the door read 'Bulgarian Friendship Society'. Richard assured us that several times a year a small group would meet there, drink rough red wine and vodka, and sing along to an old gramophone. In all the years that we were at Voicespace, we never saw or heard this happening, and remained convinced that it was all a cover up for some sinister but cash strapped KGB operation. The addition of a gay choir to the premises created a wonderfully surreal juxtaposition, and contributed another layer of eccentricity to the decidedly odd atmosphere that surrounded our hidden basement.

The advert in Capital Gay and the pub flyers had bought in a few new members, and sometimes as many as 20 people would now turn up on a Monday night. The group was still small enough to meet and rehearse in Richard's room, and whilst John bashed out the notes on an old upright piano, Louis tried to beat time and keep the group together. An unconventional, and multi-cultural, collection of songs evolved, and every few months the odd opportunity to perform somewhere would come to our attention.

At that time the only hospital unit in the country specifically dedicated to AIDS treatment was at the Middlesex Hospital. We sang in the patients' ward a couple of times, but were more frequently asked to do something approximating to a funeral or memorial service in their chapel. On those occasions we would try to find something suitably sombre and dignified to perform. 'The Humanist Association' was another regular customer, and they usually got a brighter set of songs. We always tried to include something with political overtones and a banner-waving chorus. We rarely got paid and we always delivered an educational message whilst we entertained.

Pubs were often keen to try out what they thought might be an interesting cabaret act, but such venues always proved problematic for us. Cramped onto a shoebox stage in a corner, and shouting to overcome the background noise, all we could do was belt out a few old Motown hits to keep the customers' attention. One of our new members occasionally worked as a script writer for radio comedy shows, and since he very obviously had a talent for word play we asked him to try writing new lyrics to some of the musical classics. Keith Parke's version of 'Diamonds are a Girl's Best Friend' was reborn with a safer sex message as 'Condoms are a Boys Best Friend', and went on to become one of our standards for several years.

Amongst ourselves we tended to forget that we were an 'out gay choir', but it was frequently the novelty value of hiring a 'freak show' that got us our bookings. It was frustrating that we were never able to give any audience the whole picture of what we knew a gay choir could, and should, do. The obvious solution was to devise our own format and present our shows the way we wanted.

The big bare basement in Voicespace wasn't ideal, but it was free, and we could disguise it, construct a temporary platform to use as a stage and invite lots of people. The scenario could be some sort of communal party, with organised entertainment, and maybe even a jokey theme for everyone to participate in.

Inspired by the Manchester experience, John was devoting all his time and thought to the composition of an AIDS Requiem. It was to be a complex, multi-layered and serious piece of music. It couldn't be rushed, and we knew it wasn't a good idea to pull incomplete bits of this new work out of context and use them separately. It could be many months before it was finished, and then we would have to rehearse and polish it before it could be properly presented. Until the new requiem was ready we would just have to rely on our existing repertoire for our Voicespace shows. That motley collection of songs was strung together and turned into our first concert.

The photocopied flyer for it read: The London Gay Men's Choir presents 'Songs of Love and Lust Under the Library' (Tea and buns provided, minimum donation £2)

It sounded like a kitsch, camp Agatha Christie mystery, and we thought the intriguing combination of music and narrative would be interesting enough to draw people in.

We borrowed as many trestle tables, benches and chairs as we could, and placed them around the hall. A few pots of flowers, candles in bottles and bowls of nuts were set out. Sixty or so people turned up, and we stood at the front and sang through our set of songs. Some worked, others didn't; the whole event was just a bunch of mates having some fun.

All our friends came along. They'd been hearing us talk about the choir for over a year, but this was the first time that we were able to invite our own audience, and do exactly what we wanted without any restrictions.

People had bought along cans of beer, and the kettle in the corner was constantly on the go. It was a peculiar, laid back sort of party, with the choir as host, and the theme setting of a make believe theatrical café. We were to extend this idea in future events, when the entire choir dressed as waiters, or waitresses, and served plates of jelly and steaming soup to 'planted' audience members dressed as pastiche members of the public. 'Love and Lust' was a great success, and in the ensuing weeks we began to devise a sequel.

That first Voicespace concert occurred in July 1994, and it proved to be the start of an extraordinary sequence of shows that have influenced our style ever since. As each new performance party was invented we got more ambitious. The repertoire was deliberately chosen to complement the theme and the boxed-in corner of the hall became a proper little bar. At future events we would buy wholesale catering supplies at Macro and sell plastic cups of wine and cans of beer, at a pound a go. Suddenly we were running a business and earning an income, as well as developing our own eccentric version of an evening's entertainment.

New members would occasionally drift into our circle, and one of them was Alisdair, a recently graduated actor who was always getting involved in a whole variety of fringe theatre productions. He had previously worked with a rather unconventional married couple, Keith and

Lynn, who as well as bringing up two children, ran an adventurous theatre group called the Lansbury Players. One evening Alisdair bought Keith and Lynn along to see what we were getting up to. They were amazed by what they saw and had a hunch that interesting things could develop from it. Lynn and Keith were to get involved in all our future shows, taught us a lot about 'theatre skills' and traditions, and had an amazing talent for improvising their way around all the technical difficulties that would otherwise have grounded our madcap experiments.

Even when we weren't doing a show Lynn would come along to rehearsal nights. She would make cups of tea for everyone, keep us tidy and contribute constructive ideas. The kids on the local estate were often interested in what was going on in the basement, and would occasionally hammer on the door or drop things through the pavement grill windows, so she also acted as our unofficial bouncer and would chase them off so we could carry on rehearsing in relative peace.

For 'The Third Birthday Bash' Keith helped us to rig up lights, microphones, backing tracks and an amplifier. The space was filled with streamers and balloons, and we now thought of the whole hall, not just the stage in the corner, as an arena for performance. Well over a hundred people turned up to enjoy the fun and games. We had never expected to get to our third birthday, and it was the biggest and best party show that we had ever put on.

John Harold had now finished his AIDS Requiem. Although it was constructed around the traditional Latin text, it was an unmistakably modern piece of music, sometimes dissonant and disturbing, at others sweeping and majestic. It was a complex, and occasionally difficult, multi-part structure, and the more we rehearsed it the more it became obvious that a big production was needed. It felt like a good idea to return to the roots of where the idea had been born and we optimistically decided to hire The Free Trade Hall in Manchester. We would present the premiere concert with all the professional trimmings. It was to be called 'Undying Heart'.

The choir used all of the bar profits, and eventually all of John's savings as well, and hired six extra musicians, kettle drums, tubular bells, a grand piano and vans full of lighting and sound equipment. John, who was going to be the conductor holding everything together, had a gold-sequin evening jacket made. I contributed an elaborate twenty page illustrated programme and we printed 1000 copies; after months of rehearsal, when the long anticipated date eventually arrived, we set off in our chartered coach for a long weekend in Manchester.

Peter Tatchell came along, and a clutch of B list celebrities who had been rounded up to read out our poems set between each movement of the Requiem; we arranged a bank loan and paid for hotel rooms all round.

The Free Trade Hall is a venue with an amazing history. On the 17th of May 1966 it was where Bob Dylan held his notorious 'electric' concert, and someone in the audience shouted out their acerbic "Judas" rebuke. It was also where, on 4th of June 1976, the Sex Pistols staged their first, wild 'Anarchy in the UK' gig that launched punk onto the unsuspecting public.

We naively assumed it was such a well-known place that everyone paid attention to what was happening there, and that their publicity machinery would provide all the sales we would need. Our name was already known in the gay community of Manchester, and given the size of that community, filling the place wouldn't be a problem. The Free Trade Hall holds an audience of two thousand, and when we arrived on the night before the concert, we discovered that less than fifty tickets had been sold. Our operatic baritone soloist, Gerry, had such a bad cold that his voice had simply disappeared. Disaster descended upon us like a locomotive dropping in slow-motion from a viaduct, and it was too late to do anything much about it. The frantic night that we spent distributing leaflets around the city and giving away tickets resulted in an audience of about a hundred people.

The show was amazing, and went without a hitch. John knew his stuff and his Requiem was a wonderful suite of musical pieces, there were quotes from Verdi, references to Beethoven, and just a whisper of Mozart. Alan stepped in and did the baritone solo parts; the string section was perfectly in tune, the bells exactly on cue. The addition of poetry readings contributed a rhythm and gravitas just as we hoped they would. The resonant echoes of the great empty hall seemed to open up to infinity with the glory of it all. As tragedies go, this one was utterly magnificent.

We learned a lot of lessons that weekend, and came back to London with a £10,000 debt and a giddy feeling of elation. By leaving all the publicity up to the venue we had made a rudimentary and in retrospect, blindingly obvious mistake. More significantly for us, the musical achievement had been spectacular; we finally understood the enormous potential of a talented team that could work together around a shared ambition.

Several months later the poems that we had collected together for the concert were all published as a paperback anthology under the title 'How Can You Write a Poem When You're Dying of AIDS'. It was a moving memorial to all those affected, and an impressive souvenir of our enterprise, but since all the royalties had been donated to the Lesbian and Gay Bereavement Project, it did nothing to ease our debt. We had a significant problem.

A few days after our return from Manchester six of us met up at Louis's flat in Dalston. We brainstormed an avalanche of different ideas about finance and fantasy. Would a bungled bank robbery by a gay choir be a good publicity stunt? Were begging letters to possible benefactors in really poor taste? An urgent necessity was the mother of our invention.

The use of the hall in Islington allowed us to try out all sorts of alternative fundraising projects. Alisdair and I wanted to stage a series of Voicespace quiz nights and began elaborate preparations. For our research we distilled and then subverted the essence of every trashy TV game show we could think of. Over the next year we held a series of events where absurd prizes were awarded to bedazzled teams after preposterously surreal competitions.

There were dozens of resourceful ideas. Inspired by the Mothers Union we devised a beetle drive and then awarded a big bottle of cheap gin to the winner, and a jar of evil home-made jam to the loser. Raffles took place at every opportunity, the prizes becoming ever more peculiar as choir members slowly ran out of suitable possessions that could be given away. Every few weeks more flyers were distributed around the local pubs, each time advertising some new and strange event being staged in the basement.

For the next concert I took to heart the maxim that life is what you make it, and the seventeen members of the choir invented a new collective persona for ourselves. We became an understudy super-group whose plane had got lost in the middle of some bizarre journey; it was called 'The World Tour'. The location of the hall could be anywhere the song suggested; Bali one minute, New York the next. Paris lay beneath the tail fin; Bulgaria was set in the room at the end of the Voicespace corridor where the real Bulgarian Friendship Society held their mysterious meetings.

We arranged all the chairs in 'departure lounge' mode before the audience arrived. The 'passengers' had to pass through a homemade but impressive looking, metal-detector arch to gain access. Big Tony wore a security guard uniform, and with a hidden foot switch was able to buzz at any audience member that he fancied frisking. It was surprising how many of them happily revealed an assortment of metallic piercings. Visas were issued at random and a selection of cheap 'duty free' merchandise gave the supposed travellers a shopping opportunity. Whilst they awaited their departure they could inspect the deviously altered travel posters we had used to decorate the walls, and listen to ludicrously calm airport announcements. Each one starting with an authentic "bing-bong" and mentioning friends who we knew were going to be there. As 'departure' became imminent the messages about mislaid luggage and lost relatives escalated into ever more outrageous calamities. A mock 'celebrity', concealed behind dark glasses and bodyguards, arrived from the street outside and was ostentatiously ushered through a pack of camera-flashing paparazzi to the room at the back.

The performance gathered momentum with a pair of immaculate (drag) air-hostesses who demonstrated some very odd and beautifully synchronised security and safety procedures. The whole extravagant concept was completed by a rich sequence of exotic songs. Every detail was perfect, and by the time the three surprise gun-toting hijackers had forced the captain to land, the audience had been absolutely transported.

Without quite realising how radical we were being, we had accidentally launched ourselves into the arena of alternative performance-art events. Abbreviated versions of The World Tour show were put on a couple more times in other venues, evolving as they went, but the idea never worked quite as perfectly as it did for that first performance in our own Voicespace venue.

Although Louis was the character who stood in front and conducted, the ideas we were devising and producing were developed by a team of people. Such grand conceits as the World Tour were greater than the efforts of any one person; the richness of detail was achieved by combined imaginations working smoothly together. It was the lessons we had learned from the Manchester Requiem disaster being put into action.

It was late on a Friday night that the fates twisted our future around again.

Louis had spent all evening at some gay pub, and was staggering home, blind drunk, along Kingsland High Street in Dalston. A group of guys hanging around on the corner decided that they really didn't like the look of him, and were shouting insults. Louis, being proud, 'out', and a loud-mouth, answered back. He was punched and beaten by the gang till he fell over, and was then kicked unconscious and left. Sometime later he was spotted by passing strangers and an ambulance summoned to take him to hospital. When his condition was eventually stabilised he was put in a full body cast, and his jaw, broken in two places, was wired shut.

It was six weeks before his broken bones had healed enough for him to be able to stand unaided again. The damage to his broken spirit was somehow more traumatic. He didn't speak for a long time, and when eventually he did, it was in a shy mumble. As well as being a figurehead for the choir, Louis had become a friend; we felt that we had been through a lot together. The physical and psychological hurt he experienced had changed him, and he now seemed to want to impose a certain isolation upon himself. He decided to embark on a different journey after the incident, and none of us were able to dissuade him. He ceased to be our musical director and after some directionless drifting finally landed in Brighton, quietly running a health food café.

It was a disturbing and dramatic motivation for us to carry on being out and unafraid. We continued to rehearse with John half conducting us from behind the piano. The unruly joy of being in the choir was as strong as ever, but the dark colours that had always been in our palette were now perhaps more precious and poignant.

There was a steady trickle of bookings that seemed to keep us busy, sometimes, surprisingly, from the tattered fringes of the religious community. Dr Elizabeth Stuart asked us to sing at the launch party for her controversial gay prayer book 'Daring to Speak Loves Name' in Westminster Hall, and there was a lot of interest from the press. A Gay Humanist Association conference happened in the Conway Hall, and those present were inspired by our songs as much as we by their speeches.

Between 1993 and '95 we did a series of performances at the McKellen Hall in Notting Hill to raise money for the London Lighthouse. Fund raising events in pubs for all the needy AIDS charities and gay groups were continually being requested, and paid or not, it was our vocation to comply. It sometimes felt like shouting in the dark, but such evenings gave us a sense of purpose, and kept us in touch with the need to be instantly accessible and relevant to the embattled gay community.

In 1994 Edwina Currie attempted to introduce an amendment to get the gay age of consent reduced to 16, in line with that for heterosexual acts. The vote was solidly defeated, and all the accompanying press coverage indicated that many still assumed all gay men were evil paedophiles; equality for gay people was not an acceptable idea. A brave young man named Euan Sutherland decided to challenge the ruling, and with the help of the political pressure group Stonewall, took his case to the European Court. We invited Euan along to one of our concerts, presented him with a 'Voice of the Year Award' for his courage and asked our audience to sign a petition demanding equality. In 1997 the European Court ruled that the British government were violating our human rights, but it still took until 2001 before the law was changed to grant 'age of consent' equality. Every step of the way had been turned into a battle.

Each year we had participated in some sort of World Aids Day event at the beginning of December. Our very first performance, at Angel tube station in December 1991, had been a charity collection on behalf of the Terrence Higgins Trust. Three years after we had first made an association with the THT, Nic Partridge got back in touch to ask if we could do something for them at St Martin's in the Fields. There was a solemn 'reading of names' ceremony planned for Trafalgar Square. It was a disconcerting and haunted roll-call of all those who had died, and the Terrance Higgins Trust wanted a non-denominational service to be available in the church afterwards. Although this was a very high profile and public event, it wasn't show business, and as we sat together in a pew and waited for our section to start there were no nerves. It was an occasion that was much more important than our egos or vanity; we remembered our friends, and the twist of fate that had taken them away and left us behind. We just had to deliver our songs with clarity and sincerity, then step to one side and let the context carry the message.

Seasons rushed by, and all the time we were becoming more professional, adaptable and confident, conscious that we were often on show and being critically judged. The Voicespace concerts were still our favourite and most time consuming activity, and by the time we had done 'The Third Birthday Bash', 'Fairies in the Grotto', 'World Tour', 'Carry on up the Chorus' and 'After Eight Mince' they had become so well known that we had to start doing two or three night runs, and it became necessary to sell numbered tickets to accommodate everyone.

One of the ideas that we presented was a Christmas show set in a department store. There was no argument about the name we chose, our collective cynicism dictated that we had to call it 'Herods'. Half dismembered window dummies decorated the stage, and all of the various shop departments we invented were represented in different areas of the hall. 'Gentlemen's Requisites' was a particularly outrageous presentation of racks and harnesses, fetish wear and feathers. 'Household' was designer labelled buckets and brooms with sequin bows.

'Bridle Wear' was belts, straps and horse-brasses. Since it was a Christmas show there was a Santa's grotto; another role tailor-made for Big Tony. This time he was in a curtained-off alcove and wearing a Santa suit with nothing underneath. The store detective, 'inconspicuously' dressed in a ludicrously long mac and an outsize stick on moustache, followed audience members around. He would stand uncomfortably close behind them, take random measurements and occasionally disappear behind an opened newspaper with cut out eye-holes.

Before the show officially started we 'ran the shop' for half an hour, and small groups did sketches in each area to get the audience warmed up. The performance included a makeover demonstration by 'Madge' (Martin McGonnigle) from the 'Cosmetics Department' on a stooge we had planted in the audience. The results reduced the whole hall to tears of laughter and even on stage we were unable to keep straight faces during the show.

The traditional Christian festival celebrates the arrival of a great prophet, and in keeping with the modern spirit, our production also resulted in the appearance of a great profit. In spite of our all our cynicism, we were most profoundly grateful.

Another venture that earned us a much-needed chunk of income was party entertaining. There were now about twenty five members in the choir, and with our experience of mucking in and just making things happen, a group of us could easily become a well-oiled and seriously disciplined dinner-party catering-team for an evening.

We turned up at the venue early to help with cooking the food and decorating the space, and then changed into a uniform of pink bow ties and waistcoats to greet guests and run the coat-check. Another change into black ties, with a white napkin on the forearm, transformed us into slick and efficient waiters for the meal. When that was finished and the tables cleared we surprised everyone by forming into a group at the front and singing a set of well-prepared songs. The apparent serving staff had turned the tables on the guests, pulled a rabbit from the hat, and transmuted into the entertainment. We stayed to clear up afterwards as well, drank lots of wine and couldn't believe how much fun it was to play all these games together, and then get paid for it. We were earning enough income to put a dent in our huge Manchester debt, and getting to engineer and participate in some of the best parties any of us had ever been to.

In three short, mad years the choir had evolved beyond our wildest dreams. Life for those involved often felt like a wild ride, and so much was happening on so many different levels that the totality of it all was much too complicated for us to fully comprehend. Like multiple metaphors colliding confusingly on a page of prose, it didn't make sense. The memories of all the extraordinary events began to concertina together; crashing cars piling up on a surreal yellow-brick showbiz motorway. Images from unasked for adventures skidded and span, smashing into frozen cameos. Sparkling splinters seemed to hang in the air above our spot-lit stage and nobody knew where we were.

FOUR
Palladium and the Palace

When an organisation called Stonewall called our phone number it felt as if a volcano of startling events was suddenly erupting all around us. They were a group formed in 1989 by Michael Cashman, Ian McKellan and others specifically to lobby and campaign for gay rights. Stonewall were good at publicity and seemed to have connections with some of the right people in the establishment. That autumn they were secretly organising what was to become a high profile annual charity concert, and one evening we received a phone call: "Would we be interested in backing the Pet Shop Boys for the concert finale?"

The producer of the show wanted to achieve a big Busby Berkley effect, and would have liked a few more than our membership of twenty five or so. We rang around all our friends and tried to get hold of anyone who had ever been in any sort of choir. Three weeks later, when the musical arranger came along to a rehearsal, we had nearly forty singers who were up for it. The song was Go West, a re-release of the old Village People anthem. We tackle more complicated pieces without a second thought now days, but at the time it felt like deep water; rock and roll in six part harmony!

We laboriously note bashed our way through the five pages of sheet music each week, and after two months were familiar with all the clever chord structures it contained. The venue was confirmed as The London Palladium, and the event was to be on a Sunday night. We had done the 'big stage with lots of spotlights' experience in Manchester, but this was in a different league, it really felt like big-time showbiz.

The atmosphere was electric with excitement. The back-stage area at the London Palladium is an extraordinary maze of tiny rooms and dank brick corridors. The choir had a sound check on stage after lunch and then spent the entire afternoon fussing and fretting, shivering and tingling in our room. Everybody had done everybody else's make-up at least three times over. People wandered off to get bottles of water and promptly got lost in the labyrinth of numberless rooms on different levels. Celebrity spotting turned into a dressing-room competition, and there were so many disorientated 'stars' drifting around that eventually everybody won.

The Go West single had climbed up the charts during the previous weeks, and had just arrived at number one when the concert happened. It was the Pet Shop Boys only live appearance at that time, and when the familiar opening chords rang out, and we stumbled from the sheltering darkness of the wings out into the dazzling light, the audience erupted. I don't think our enthusiastic harmonies could possibly have been heard much above all the cheering, but the 'big production number' effect was achieved anyhow. The song ended, the curtain came down and the show was over. We all went along to the private celebrity party in Soho afterwards, confidently joining in the triumphal celebrations with all sorts of inebriated glitterati until very late. I remember perching on a bar-stool and talking to Stephen Fry for what seemed like hours. Nobody had really dared to hope that the first concert would be quite such a success. The Stonewall organisation had pulled off a real coup.

Our experiences with the choir had been a blurred journey of mayhem and joy, excitement and confusion. After the event at The London Palladium there was a strange feeling we had suddenly swerved round an unexpected corner; we couldn't begin to guess what lay ahead. It somehow felt as though both we, and the whole of the gay community, had subtly but significantly changed.

Throughout our time together individuals had constantly been joining or leaving the group. Some had come along simply to find a partner, others left when jobs or flats changed. Some found they couldn't take the pace of it all; the choir was such an intense, disruptive and non-stop activity. Inevitably people who had started out as 'other members' turned into close friends, for it was always an intensely bonding experience to live through all those extraordinary events together. Nobody from outside the group would ever really understand what it felt like to share all that stuff.

The time came for John Harold, one of the founders of the group, to leave. The pressure on him had been enormous, and he felt he had to get some of his own life back; spend an occasional evening at home, write that opera he'd been promising himself.

Once his personal decision had been reached he felt he had to act upon it, and his sudden departure felt like a very dramatic upheaval to us. One week he was in charge, the next he wasn't there. Some people felt that it was a selfish thing to do, and muttered about betrayal, but most of us realised it was a case of serious overload; he had the option of staying and facing an almost inevitable breakdown, or leaving and reclaiming the balance and stability of his life.

Richard Roberts, our original 'homo-hippy', was the nearest thing we had to a properly trained singer. Although he was willing to lead rehearsals for some of the time, he was not in any position to replace John and all that he had been doing for us. At this point Paul Hawley stepped forward, he had been living in the same shared house as Alisdair the actor, and had joined the choir at the same time, and so had been around for long enough to understand the ethos of the organisation. Paul was an attractive and energetic American with all the crucial self-confidence that was needed, and in addition had the experience of being a member of the gay men's chorus in Washington before he moved to London.

We realised there were going to have to be changes in

the way we did things, and most of us reckoned that Paul would know what to do. This was obviously going to be a turning point, and there were still doubts and arguments; strong words were voiced, and hurt feelings were apparent at the meetings. Eventually about a third of the choir left saying that they wanted to set up a more conventional choir that would do classical music, but most of us were confident and optimistic enough to carry on. Paul now stood at the front as musical director and Richard helped out.

The eight or nine people who left the choir carried on with their own rehearsals for a few months, and even managed to put on a performance at a church hall in Wanstead, but there wasn't enough energy in the group and it subsequently faded away.

The majority of the Gay Men's Choir remained and continued to meet up at Voicespace every Monday evening. We put an advert in the gay paper and from the trickle of replies that came in, began to compile a list of paid pianists who could come and note bash for us. This fundamental change in the structure and dynamic of our rehearsals had far reaching consequences for us.

A hard core of permanent members and helpers had developed within the choir; we met up and made things happen, like magicians. At one of our discussions we were at last forced to acknowledge that a regular, long term, financial commitment was necessary. We were not dealing with a one-off debt any more, this was a weekly wage bill, and it was going to be a permanent state of affairs.

David Batten worked in a housing trust and knew a lot about the structure and function of charities. He volunteered to investigate the issue of charitable status for the choir and whether it could be advantageous for us. It turned out to be more complicated than we had anticipated. You didn't just have to be of benefit to the community; you had to have a formally drawn up written constitution, and a chairman, secretary, treasurer and audited accounts. We felt it would be beneficial in the long term and 'annual general meetings' were added to our calendars amidst all the surreal anarchy of choir life. David became our first chairman, and in recognition of our more professional ambitions, I made us a proper logo design. It was nine different stylised 'block' faces inside a single square outline, and I hoped that the image symbolized diversity within a unified whole. We also changed our name from 'choir' to 'chorus'. The latter sounded less 'churchy' and indicated a new awareness of the community role we were playing. Another corner had been turned.

We found a succession of pianists, both from word-of-mouth recommendation and from occasionally repeated adverts, but they were seldom satisfactory. Neil was really keen and shared our ideological vision, but his fingers turned into a tangled knot when the sheet music became complicated. Old Fred was a real pro, his whole life had been spent in a succession of bars backing blues and jazz bands, and he could play anything we put in front of him. Unfortunately the lifestyle had left him with a very obvious alcohol problem, and sometimes he would drop off to sleep and snore gently during our rehearsals. He was a nice old bloke; it seemed unkind to wake him up. The Scots pianist we eventually found was great. He had come from the Royal College of Music and could do everything we asked except be reliable; he was always getting called away to do more highly paid work for other people.

The chorus carried on successfully earning an income from odd jobs, and sometimes they turned out to be very odd indeed. Richard knew a couple of dropped-out idealistic architects who had bought a bomb-damaged derelict church in Hackney. They were devoting their lives to rebuilding it as an Arts Centre; living in an old hall at the back and getting a succession of small local authority grants which left them free to make it up as they went along. They had been at it for over a year, and were slowly succeeding. Their own domestic accommodation was more or less habitable, but the main body of the church was still a roofless ruin; rats nested amongst the heaps of rubble and there was an almost unimaginable amount of work to do.

We were hired to put on a themed party there to mark the launch of the rebuilding project, but David and Beena, our architect clients, never quite clarified exactly what that theme was. It certainly needed to be mystical and spiritual, the resonant echoes of the venue's past demanded it, but the religion being celebrated was a bizarre mixture of faith and fear, Hammer horror movies and eastern exoticism. There were no restrictions as to what we could do, and everything that was decadent, bizarre and visually extravagant was encouraged. It was the perfect brief for a London Gay Men's Chorus event.

Old planks were laid across the muddy puddles, and fallen stones piled up to make abstract sculptural shrines. Rows of candles led off into dark corners and nightlights were spaced along broken beams, silhouetted against the starry sky that hung above the great roofless space. Loudspeakers were suspended from the rafters and concealed under heaps of rubble, and smoke machines planted at strategic points.

On the night of the launch party, the invited audience were well primed with mulled wine and then assembled at the back of the ruined church. We had prepared a dustbin full of strange costumes; as a solitary bell sounded an unearthly procession appeared from a concealed doorway. Masked monks carrying flaming torches led the group, and a cherub scattered tissue paper petals from a basket. Hollywood starlets and nuns accompanied Venetian carnival creatures wreathed in garlands and bearing banners. Axe men in leather hoods and loincloths appeared from the shadows and joined in the eerie chanting that started the evening's entertainment.

We used every trick in the book, invented a few more of our own and put on a really remarkable show. Wires had been laid so that we could throw a switch and illuminate a raised plinth, previously hidden in the pitch-black space at the far end of the old building. A 'virgin' statue was revealed on the platform, swathed in a vast gold lame robe, wearing a huge headdress and with a naked muscle-man laid at her feet. As the plainsong chanting became more complex and intense the statue began to levitate. It was Richard in white face makeup, and there was a seven-foot stepladder concealed beneath his robes. He had risen to a height of twelve feet before someone at the back of the astonished audience cheered and broke the spell. The levitating virgin statue stuck its tongue out and the ludicrous resurrection party signalled the birth of the Arts Centre project.

The whole place was a marvellously weird and funky building site for the next few years. During that time several chorus members became regular weekend navies, carrying bricks and mixing cement, laying tiles and getting involved in the endless succession of odd jobs that needed doing. It was such fun being involved that being paid fifty pounds for a day's work almost seemed unfair. I spent many happy hours there, balanced on the shaky scaffolding seventy feet above the nave like a renaissance old master, painting rows of lush Victorian lilies on the new ceiling.

Several years later it was declared finished and the chorus was invited to sing there again for the official opening night party. It's now a thriving enterprise enigmatically known as '291', and has an expensive gothic styled restaurant, state of the art projection facilities and hosts avant-garde art exhibitions. Looking at it today you wouldn't believe how it all began.

Sometimes a series of successes were leavened by an

absolute disaster. An event that had started out with good intentions would become horribly derailed; it was almost as if our 'karma' has to be brought back into equilibrium.

The chorus was invited to be top of the bill at a charity 'Variety Night' event being put on by the Hackney Pride committee at a pub called Chats Palace. The evening was poorly organised and too many well intentioned locals had been encouraged to participate; the schedule over-ran dramatically. We had to get there at 7pm to do our sound check, but it was twelve thirty at night before our slot came up, and by then we had all spent five hours waiting in the bar and most were very drunk, loud and tired.

Labi Siffre was also on the bill, he heard us doing a rowdy rendition of 'So Strong', the moving civil rights anthem he had written, didn't approve, and said so. The atmosphere was horrible, the audience were ready to go home, and so were we. When we had eventually staggered on to the stage nobody had paid any attention to the conductor or the pianist, and we somehow managed to forget all our words. We were unprepared and unprofessional, and the shame of what we knew was a disgraceful performance was a real shock. Luckily only a few dozen people had stayed around to see it, and we vowed that a fiasco like that would never happen again.

That unfortunate evening was significant for another reason. It was the first time that any of us had come across the amazing Lorraine Bowen. She lived nearby in Hackney, and had walked to the venue with all her stage equipment on a shopping trolley. Casio keyboard, crumhorn, glitter ball and ironing board, all piled up perilously and trundled through the streets. When we heard her performance there was an instant recognition of her surreal wit, musical skill and uncompromising attitude. After the Variety Night had ground down to its overdue end, we piled her gear into the back of my car, gave her a lift home and were subsequently invited to sing a couple of songs on her next CD.

A few weeks later David, Paul, Dan and I went over to the studio she used. It turned out to be a tiny soundproofed spare room in Edmonton, and we spent the evening singing, and then triple overdubbing, the backing tracks. Although we had initially been a bit disillusioned with the distinctly amateurish look of the studio, the four of us ended up sounding like a really big and professional choral group. We did a whole series of strange and inventive shows with her after that, and various groups of individuals from the chorus have been backing singers on all of her CDs ever since.

The chorus was in a constant state of flux, always being swept into new experiences, meeting different people and doing extraordinary things. All the time we were learning new skills and being influenced and altered by what was happening to us. It was gradually becoming apparent that no matter what occurred, the chorus would go on; somehow there was a stable foundation and a reliable continuity within this swirling whirlpool of activities. It was an absurd amount of fun, but it was worth taking seriously too. This anarchic development was all held together by the music that was being made, and we often felt a need to push forward; explore the possibilities and find out what a slicker presentation and a surer and more professional sound would feel like. It might just make things even more interesting if we could learn about proper singing techniques and musical theory.

We practised harder, and with a steady trickle of temporary pianists coming in to work for us, paid attention to what any passing musician might have to say about the way we sang and performed.

On the radio one evening in early 1996, Paul heard a mention of a national competition for choirs organised by Sainsbury's supermarkets. It sounded odd, like coming across a bust of Beethoven carved out of cheddar cheese on the dairy counter.

We knew nothing about the illustrious history of the Choir of the Year Competition, but filled in the application form anyway, and put together a ten-minute presentation with a bit of everything in it. There was a formal show-off piece, a trashy pop romp with comic choreography, and a banner waving gay anthem.

We should have suspected that the competition was a serious affair when we were asked to provide written confirmation of copyright permission for all the pieces we proposed to perform. We had never needed to do anything like this before, but realised we had to comply with this official requirement. The 'trashy pop song' we wanted to include was Da Doo Ron Ron, written by Phil Spector in the early 1960s. Paul found a publisher's address in a music catalogue and wrote him a letter explaining who we were and what we wanted to do. A month later we were surprised to receive a hand written reply from the man himself saying he was delighted we remembered his work and would be honoured to have it heard in the prestigious Choir of the Year Competition.

The London heat of the competition was held in the old Methodist Hall in Westminster. The singing was non-stop for a whole day and the packed audience was comprised of the other competing choirs. As we sat and watched it rapidly became apparent that this was a top-notch event. One choir after another got on to the stage and presented their ten minute sets, and each one was impeccably tight, trained and together. We realised we were out of our depth and felt horribly like a bunch of rough amateurs.

With only twenty singers the chorus was the smallest outfit there, and we weren't remotely polished. The only thing we had going for us was our self-righteous and indignant integrity. When we sang it was from the heart and our music was performed for significant and meaningful reasons. As we trooped off to the warm-up room, just before we went on, we all agreed that technically our set was going to be a lost cause. We certainly knew how to make a pub full of gay guys laugh out loud, and also how to make a midnight crowd in a Manchester car park cry; that sort of emotional communication and committed passion was the only thing that could pull us through this potentially embarrassing performance. We knew we couldn't compete in terms of musical prowess, but were nevertheless determined to deliver our social and political message.

Nobody in the hall had ever heard of a 'gay' choir before, and the idea of coming across one in a serious choral competition was outrageous. Serious singers did not perform pop songs in this context and the audience was buzzing with mockery, prejudice and cynicism. We had been openly wearing our London Gay Men's Chorus T-shirts throughout the day, and one tight lipped schoolteacher, sitting nearby and shepherding his junior flock of musical children, had been shooting looks of horror and hatred at us at every opportunity.

We filed on to the stage with an efficient military precision, and then just let rip.

To everyone's amazement, at the end of our ten minutes, the audience was whooping with delight and cheering out loud. We might have lacked finesse, but we made up for it with defiant courage and a shocking explosion of energy. We quietly went back to our seats and listened humbly to all the remaining choirs.

At the end of the evening when the results were read out, the panel of judges announced that we had been selected as 'Choir of the Day'. We were utterly dumbstruck. My heart leapt as I heard the words being said out loud, then my eyes filled with tears as I realised what it meant. We had earned respect, and we were being accepted. None of us, even in our wildest dreams, had ever expected that to happen.

FIVE
Busted and Being Big

Life with the London Gay Men's Chorus was endlessly surprising. Our sequence of shows in the 'Voicespace' basement had continued for three years; they were an extraordinary combination of outlandish invention and cunning planning. It seemed as if the more we did, the more fertile ideas were generated, and as the members of the group spent time together we passed them back and forth, adding structure and detail till they gained enough weight to fall to the ground and take root. Lynn, acting as our stage manager, was some sort of gardener who nurtured our ambitious schemes and made things flourish. Keith was our production manager, and it was he who spread light wherever he could. He did the technical wizardry, added the sound effects and several times tried to capture all of the magic on film for posterity. Our regular committee meetings served to plot the whole show procedure methodically onto charts three months in advance: Exactly when the repertoire had to be prepared and learned, when any costumes, fittings and props had to be finished, publicity circulated, catering supplies brought for the bar and programmes printed. By the time we got to the first night everything was running as smoothly as possible. One fateful evening however, we discovered that you could never predict absolutely everything.

It was the final, pre-show, dress rehearsal for a Christmas production called 'Eat, Drink and be Mary'. We had been rehearsing the songs for the previous four or five months and all the preparations were finished. The only things missing were an audience and our guest of honour, an outspoken bishop from Devon who had caused a scandal in the tabloids by coming out as gay. It was a brave thing to do, and we wanted to present him with our 'Voice of the Year' award, an idea we had invented both for our own publicity purposes, and also as a genuine recognition of courage and honesty. Other recipients of the honour had been a bus conductor who had refused to let the driver move the bus until some loud-mouthed homophobic bullies got off, and a radio producer from Greater London Radio who made a point of including gay interest news items.

It must have been right in the middle of the dress run for 'Eat, Drink and be Mary' when the Voicespace phone rang. Richard went off to answer it, and when he came back he looked a bit shaken. He stood in the middle of the stage and held up his hands. "Err, stop" he said. "I've just had a call from the Islington police. They've got some of our leaflets. They say they know what we're planning to do tomorrow night, and if we go ahead they'll bust us".

There was a silence, and then somebody said plaintively, "Is this for real?" but we could see that Richard wasn't joking. We called an early tea break and a group of us went off to the other room to sit down and talk. We drew up a long list of the things we were planning to do that were definitely illegal, and then another of things that were probably illegal, but with the section twenty eight laws you were never too sure. We knew that Voicespace wasn't licensed for public entertainment; we were definitely breaking all the health, safety, fire and overcrowding regulations. We certainly hadn't got a licence to serve liquor, and Lynn's son who was helping out behind the bar was underage. The Section 28 laws had made it an offence to 'promote a homosexual lifestyle', and with a show called 'Eat, drink and be Mary' we certainly hoped we were doing that, but had no idea how the ruling could possibly be defined.

I was all for going ahead and getting busted, and also getting an extra camera crew there and filming the whole thing. The start of the show, the arrival of the bishop, the bust, what a drama! Maybe we could tell the BBC and get a proper news team there.

David was more realistic, Richard would get evicted for sure and we could easily get ourselves arrested. The notorious 'operation spanner' case had happened in Yorkshire that year, and that group of men who had privately filmed their consensual sexual activities were still in prison. We wouldn't get away with our concert, and what's more there couldn't ever be any more shows in the Voicespace basement.

We went back into the main hall and lined up all the chairs, as if there was an invisible audience, and in a mood of futility and finality, completed the rehearsal for the show that would never happen. Then we went home and phoned the bishop and as many of our regular audience as we could to tell them not to come. A couple of us went along the next night, to stand outside and explain to the disappointed people who still turned up, that we wouldn't be doing a show, and sure enough, a police patrol car did arrive to check on what was happening.

It felt as though we had gone around in a great big circle and would now have to start all over again.

We carried on meeting up for rehearsals at Voicespace, furtively at first, but as no more phone calls came, the paranoia subsided and things gradually got back to normal.

We knew we were being watched and could no longer use the basement hall as a performance space, so turned to the listings magazine 'Time Out' for a guide to the enormous number of alternative spaces we would now have to begin investigating. There were now between twenty five and thirty people regularly coming to our rehearsals so the chorus was too big to fit in the back-room-of-a-pub type of fringe venue. It had to be something more like a proper theatre, and they were expensive, much less widespread, and frequently booked up for a year in advance.

We visited little theatres all around London, took copious notes and did a lot of wondering, trying to imagine what a suburban audience would make of one of our shows, and if we could persuade our mailing list of regular attendees to follow us. Eventually we booked up a week at the Oval House theatre for the middle of the next year, tried not to think about it and got on with rehearsals. There were still lots of other things happening and the summer looked as if it was going to be busy.

Stonewall had been in touch again. They were planning another big concert, this time at the Royal Albert Hall, and they wanted us on board. We were swinging from one extreme to the other. It was a huge stage and they wanted a big show. There was a suggestion that we join forces with the Pink Singers, and as many others choirs as we could get, and form a super-choir. We were to be performing in our own right this year, not as backing for some other act, so we started looking around for a suitably big production, grand opera piece to perform. Verdi's Chorus of the Hebrew Slaves was chosen, along with another classical standard, and our old Labi Siffre song, Something Inside So Strong, which had been specifically requested by the producer.

The whole thing escalated magnificently. Joint rehearsals were arranged, and the super-choir eventually included Velvet Fist, Diversity and the Pre-Madonnas as well as the Pink Singers and us. It was then that the Pride festival organisers heard about it. At short notice we were asked if the newly formed super-choir could open the main stage event in Victoria Park, Hackney. One last joint rehearsal was arranged for everyone at Voicespace, the only impromptu venue that was available, and just over a hundred singers turned up. We hoped that the Islington authorities would be looking in another direction that

Saturday, and got away with it.

Each of the three songs in our super-choir repertoire used a different conductor, and it was an immense education to see how their different techniques altered the results. One would be concentrating on breath control and enunciation; the next was more concerned with keeping the pitch up. The third, at this late stage, was only interested in dynamics and expressing the emotion. That one hurried rehearsal showed us the huge potential for learning more technique and gaining greater depth in our future work.

The performance at Pride ended up feeling more like a big open-air workshop. The vast audience was an anonymous mass beyond the crash barriers. We concentrated on the conductors and tried not to stare back at the cameras that kept zooming in for the big screen close-ups being projected behind us. It came as a surprise to hear a roar of applause happening as we finished.

The London Gay Men's Chorus members met up back stage and got changed out of formal wear into more lurid costumes for our next appearance. A month before the Pride invitation arrived, Toyah Wilcox had been in touch. She was going to be on the Pride stage in the late afternoon and wanted to do something special. She had come along to a Voicespace rehearsal and explained her plan to turn her old hit song 'I Wanna Be Free' into a huge crowd sing-along. Then and there we worked out some harmonies for the chorus line. It sounded so good that she decided that one of the other songs she was planning could also do with some additional backing. She was playing Puck at the Regents Park Open Air Theatre that month, so was able to visit our rehearsals easily. On her next visit a week later we ran through both songs and talked about the presentation. They were both 'over the top' songs and we felt the occasion warranted some extravagant costumes. That eventual directive was that everybody should wear the wildest things they'd got. There was a bondage master, a glitter elf, a ballroom princess, a Red Indian, a Regency dandy in a top hat and tails along with twelve others. We were meant to be a visual representation of the sentiments expressed in the song, but since many in the crowd were also wearing fancy dress for the Pride parade, the overall effect began to resemble a painting from Hieronymus Bosch.

Police estimates put the size of the 1997 Pride crowd at 250,000, about two and a half times the size of a Rolling stones stadium show, and when we came on stage with Toyah it sounded as though every single person there was cheering. Great clouds of smoke drifted across banks of coloured floodlights, and banners were waved high. We cheered back, and adopted suitably majestic poses.

It was the second time we had been on stage that afternoon, and it already felt like way past midnight.

We tumbled down the backstage steps as dusk was falling and got changed again. This time into chorus t-shirts, ready for the finale when all the performers were invited back on stage to join the headline act for the last song. It was Donna Summer doing the disco anthem 'I

Feel Love', and thanks to several hours spent in the backstage hospitality area, the whole park seemed to be shimmering and pulsing to the same urgent electromagnetic beat. There were fireworks glittering in the sky. What an unreal day.

The real purpose of setting up the super-choir had been for the Stonewall concert at the Royal Albert Hall, and by the time that arrived, we were a bit more prepared. A range of primary coloured t-shirts had been distributed. We organised ourselves into a spectrum, stood in front of a fifty foot rainbow banner, and sang as an integrated unit. The feeling of participating in a big trained chorus, doing a huge song, in a massive concert hall, is extraordinarily thrilling. The sounds coming from within your own body are magnified and complimented by all the people singing around you. The music expands inside your framework and holds you suspended in floating harmonic structure. When it all goes well an awesome grandeur is made manifest. A few precious seconds can seem to turn into a transcendental experience. It's no accident that organised religions use the power of music to inspire people.

The Albert Hall concert had a packed programme, and like that crazy day at the Pride festival, we kept on getting on and off the stage.

The combined might of the super-choir started the whole thing off, and then Jocelyn Brown wanted us to do a rousing gospel song with her at the end of the first half. Some of the super-choir singers objected to the blatant Christianity of it all and chose not to participate, but most of us changed into black t-shirts and joined in, the emotional charge inherent in the rock-gospel music overwhelming any irrelevant ethnic references that were contained in the lyrics.

For the big finale we stood in formation in the choir stalls and waited for Elton to come on. When he appeared in a blond wig and red sequin dress we did 'There Ain't Nothing Like a Dame', to the obvious delight of the huge audience. The choir had only rehearsed the song with him once before, but everyone seemed to know it, and from where we stood we could all see his auto-cue easily enough. The rehearsal that morning had been a great lesson in how to get through all the complicated paraphernalia and tension of a big production. Elton had been calm and friendly, his technical crew fiercely well organised and efficient, and he had been thoughtful enough to come over and graciously thank us all for helping him out.

After the show I witnessed a clamouring crowd of pushy photographers pouncing on him as he left via the stage door, and felt really sorry for all the media pressure that he has to put up with. It's as if with every wish there comes a curse; being an international mega-star might look glamorous, but sometimes it must feel like an epic nightmare.

Heaven, the infamous gay night club in Charing Cross had been hired for the after-show party, and when we arrived there I met a different side of celebrity. As I waited patiently in line for the coat check, I realised that Marc Almond, who had also been on stage earlier, was standing behind me. I was surprised that he had joined the queue, and after a while turned and asked him why he didn't just go to the front. "Yes, I suppose I could" he said and laughed, but he stayed where he was, and we talked animatedly about the big show for the next five minutes.

A few years later I bumped into him again at another of the big Albert Hall shows. The choir had grown a bit bigger by then, and we couldn't all comfortably fit into our bare little concrete box of a dressing room, so had spread out into the lower level corridor to do our practice scales and warm-up. We were blocking the corridor, lined up two deep all along one wall, and the conductor was facing us. Marc came out of his dressing room and didn't want to push through the middle and interrupt, so stood still at the end where I happened to be positioned, and waited for us to finish. He leaned in close and whispered "sounds great, it'll be a good one". Nice man, Marc Almond, he's often thought of as a bit of a left-field fringe pop star, but I learned later that he's sold over 30 million albums worldwide since the 1980s, and the 'Tainted Love' single went platinum.

You experience all sorts of strange things if you spend any time with the chorus, seeing how the music machine works, driving the entertainment industry. You get to go to unusual places you wouldn't normally visit, and you often do odd things there. Sometimes you witness esoteric and extreme behaviour patterns. It all adds up and gives you a much bigger picture, and the experience changes the way you think about the world and your own place in it. Knowing that it's what you are doing that is making everything else happen. The insight enlightens and empowers you, constantly increases your awareness of what's possible and enabling you to engage with the processes of change; zapping the zeitgeist. All the people who have spent a long time with the chorus have been profoundly changed by it. It may look as though being in the group is just standing in a crowd and singing, but the summation of everything that goes on invariably seems to be a life-altering experience.

The year ended with an invitation to appear on Channel Four's 'Big Breakfast' on Christmas day. The director of the show was, no doubt, courting controversy, wanting to appear cutting edge and a bit dangerous, and yet remain comfortable and Christmassy. We were told exactly what was wanted and which carols we could sing. They weren't going to take any risks; the guy with the clipboard was in control.

'Christmas special' programmes are always recorded in advance, so it was a very early morning in late November when we all assembled at Voicespace to board the coach to the big recording session/party at the studio. The apparently ordinary Big Breakfast house was in fact a purpose built stage-set. Removable ceiling panels were incorporated to allow for aerial shots into the set, and camera track was fitted on to the wall of the staircase. As there were about twenty of us we had been allocated the overflow dressing room, and were disappointed to discover that it was a portacabin in the car park. Since it was still only 7am, a cup of tea would have been welcome, but the only refreshment provided was an American retro bubble-gum vending machine that only took US quarters.

After a half hour wait we were led on to an upper balcony of the studio. A huge fake Christmas feast was laid out on a table directly below us. An impressively iced cardboard-box cake and a glazed and burnished rubber turkey languished amongst the sumptuous decorations; the champagne was tinted lemonade, only the peanuts were real.

The celebrity guests sat glumly around the fake feast below us waiting for the shoot to begin. The presenter, Vanessa Feltz, stood to one side and was having a loud and bad tempered argument with one of her team. When the continuity clapperboard snapped shut, she and all the guests joked, laughed, pulled crackers and burbled inanely. We sang twenty-five second extracts from carols, smiled, waved and dropped curly streamers artistically from the balcony. There were long unexplained pauses when cameras were turned off and pages of script were crossed out. The chorus was bored and tired, we don't do mornings well, and the Channel Four crew was sullen. We had been eager to see the special guest, Madonna, but it turned out that her interview had been videotaped in New York the previous week.

Vanessa's off camera argument, interrupted by the recorded blocks of enforced party jollity, continued until we left at 9.30am. As we got back on the bus she stood at the door, beaming and thanking us effusively. It might have been a 'gay special' for them, but for us it had been a really grim ordeal, and not many of us bothered to turn the TV on and watch when it was broadcast on Christmas morning.

SIX
Ripped Off and Roots

There had always been a steady turnover in the membership of the chorus. It was accepted that individuals came and went, for as many different reasons as there were different people. Two years after the choir started there were perhaps eighteen singers. Over the next three or four years overall numbers remained relatively steady, never more than thirty at any one time. In 1997 however, the membership started to grow. We had been getting a lot of publicity and had also become more organised. More people were joining and choosing to stay, and the increase in numbers caused many changes in our methods. We had to abandon the comfy old back room at Voicespace, and move out into the main hall for our rehearsals. I bought a load of office chairs came from a second hand furniture shop so that people could sit down, and then got hold of a tea urn from a man who did burgers from a van at football matches. Ensuring enough sheet music had been photocopied turned into a major job. Instead of running a few off for free during the lunch hour, somebody now had to devote time and money to sorting it out. Ultimately the size of stage that we could perform on became an issue, and long distance transport was to turn into a logistical nightmare.

It still tended to be the same group of people who organised things at the heart of the chorus. The extraordinary experiences that long term members had shared bonded us together, and taught us how to get things done. We understood and trusted one another, frequently met up and talked, and intuitively sensed what directions we should, and could, go. Sometimes one of the newer recruits would show a specific talent, or have skills that were relevant, and they would then join in with the organising and show everyone how their particular area should be managed. With the ever-increasing numbers, and escalating workload, we sometimes found ourselves desperate for additional help. One area that was always short of willing volunteers was finance.

A couple of years earlier we had gone through the motions of getting organised so that we could qualify for charity status. We soon realised that a bit of methodical bureaucracy actually made the organisation run more smoothly, so when a new Australian guy, named Andrew, said he could 'do the books' we were grateful.

None of us had ever exhibited any enthusiasm or skill at playing with the numbers. Andrew was keen to ingratiate himself and seemed eager to make new friends, perhaps he was feeling insecure, gay people can be like that sometimes. At one of our regular meetings he presented his first set of accounts. They seemed ridiculously complicated, but apparently that was the way that efficient businesses did it. He was a smooth talker, and the sum totals on the bottom line looked realistic, so we were reassured.

Chorus life was always busy, and we got on with sorting out the sea of details that constantly swirled about us. Nobody was unduly alarmed when a few meetings later Andrew didn't turn up; not everyone was always able to make every single meeting.

We'd just done something particularly well paid, and wanted to find out tactfully if the cheque had gone through yet, so David phoned up our bank, rather than the client, and asked for a statement. There was nine pounds left in our account, and nothing had been paid in for the last quarter.

Andrew wasn't at home. He didn't reply to any messages, or answer the door. A week later we got a letter, posted in England but with no address on it, explaining that his father had just died and he had to go back to Sydney and would be in touch. There was another brief letter eventually, saying he was sorry and that he would pay the money back in monthly instalments; they never came.

A succession of solicitors informed us of what could, and could not, be done. The 'evidence' we had was not specific enough, the exact amount of money that was missing was unclear, the possible courses of action prohibitively expensive.

We lived our lives as gay men knowing that the system was not always just, but we never expected to get stabbed in the back by 'one of our own'. We knew we'd been screwed, but it was our hearts, more than our pockets, that felt the hurt. I just felt sorry that someone should be so muddled up and miserable as to need to steal from his friends.

Paul, an ex-policeman from Leicester, took over the bookkeeping. The accounting procedures were tightened up and simplified. Another lesson had been learned, and a sadly stained page of our chorus history was turned over.

Sometimes changes happened as fast as a fuse blow, arriving with an alarming impact that altered our outlook instantly. Sometimes developments were so slow that they resembled glaciers, a gradual, gentle shifting of landscape that was so subtle it was almost imperceptible.

Shortly after the first Sainsbury's Choir of the Year competition, the chorus had run a small ad in one of the gay papers. We knew that we had to learn more about the formal techniques of choral singing, and that we weren't going to get there without some professional teaching. The advert was vague and open ended, it just asked for 'musicians and/or conductor with choral experience'. We didn't know exactly what we were after, only that we needed it. The result was two new people coming along to our rehearsal to check us out. One was Andrea, a twenty four year old lesbian from Chicago, studying in London for a year as part of her conducting course. The other was Jeremy, another Australian and, as it turned out, the slow moving glacier that inexorably shaped our future. Although he was only in his early twenties he had extensive experience of singing with various groups, and had already qualified as a conductor.

Andrea had impact. We respected her as a gender equal, liked her girly qualities, and understood that she was a musical authority. Her teaching technique was both exacting and tentative, which suited our newly discovered sensibilities, but there was also an underlying cocky confidence that we immediately recognised as our own. We paid attention to what she said; nobody had ever explained and demonstrated qualities of voice quite so clearly and patiently. She taught us all sorts of vocal tricks, and made us aware of the overall sound picture when she was conducting.

Jeremy was quite a shy person. I remember going over to talk to him at the end of his first rehearsal, I had picked up a strong impression that he needed befriending. We had a conversation about choirs he had sung with, and then talked about him being adrift in an alien city on the other side of the world to his homeland. He hadn't known what he wanted to find when he came to London, but some creative instinct told him it wasn't going to be available in Sydney. I admired his courage and confidence, but wondered about the wisdom of such a radical and drastic rootlessness.

Frequently Jeremy would just sit by the piano, quietly observing the dynamics of what was happening. Sometimes he'd join on the end of the bass section and sing with us, and occasionally he would stand out at the front and conduct. He reinforced everything that Andrea taught us, and then seemed to add an extra layer of intensity by encouraging us to express the feeling of what we were singing. When we were all in tune, both musically and emotionally, it would almost feel as if a lost chord was about to be found, he brought us to a higher level of consciousness. It might have been something intangible to do with the expression on his face, or the shine in his eyes, but he could communicate his passion when he conducted us.

The first time we felt this extraordinary and elusive quality during a public performance was on a December 1st 1996, at a World AIDS Day event at Gabriel's Wharf, on the south bank of the Thames.

Our stage was a tiny open-air bandstand standing in the middle of an empty paved area fifty feet from the old river wall. The temperature was zero degrees, and it seemed to have got dark extra early. We stood in a group next to the embankment bag-people's temporary caravan kitchen, and sipped scalding hot coffee to try to stop shivering. The event was a heavy combination of remembrance ceremony mixed with civil protest, and there was a small crowd of a couple of hundred earnest people gathered in the chilly shadows. The great river slid silently by, its oily surface glittering with city lights.

As the proceedings began we huddled in our coats at the back of the stage, and a succession of speakers were powerfully angry, or eloquently sad. There was a grim, Zen-like focus with the chorus that evening. We had done this type of event before, and were exactly tuned in to everything that was happening. Our music was woven carefully into the structure, and what we sang expressed all the hoping, and the hurting, that was the very real purpose of our being there. At events such as this there is no whooping and cheering during the songs, but you can always feel the effect you are having, an electric tingle that you can sense in your skin, and then push out towards the crowd. You make a sort of telepathic inner-eye contact with those who listen, and sometimes feel great waves of warm emotion radiating back at you.

It was a very intense experience for everyone who was there, but especially so for me. As I stood on that stage I was looking out over the dark river and into my own past. The Victorian-gothic façade of my old school stood exactly opposite Gabriel's Wharf. Its shadowed front door filled with memories of a painful adolescence. I was confronting my history, separated by a gulf of twenty-five years and a quarter of a mile of slowly moving water; the physical presence of the great river somehow symbolic of the gap between then and now. It felt as if I hovered suspended and apart from the moment, both absent from the picture and strangely, undeniably, present in the very heart of it. I was in the same location, but I was changed. I had not been defeated; I stood in the dark and sang. I was still defiant, and there was no going back.

That memorial ceremony was a river of no return for Jeremy also; but he wasn't confronting his past, he was standing at the front and facing into the chorus, and his own future. He devoted all his care, time and creative energy, into the organisation for the next four and a half years. He had been observing and measuring the chorus, and himself, for the last six months. When the time came for Andrea to return to Chicago, Jeremy Haneman took over.

It was a smooth transition; he knew what we could do best and how to persuade us to do it. He also knew our weaknesses and had the training to push us gently forward.

The chorus gradually grew deeper, stronger and much much larger during his years with us, and he, in turn, became more confident, and was able to develop a more stable personal foundation for himself. There were problems with visas and passports to deal with along the way, but with the network of chorus connections we eventually helped to sort out some officially sanctioned employment that necessitated him staying in this country, and some years later he became a legal UK citizen.

The next concert we put on was 'It's Just Not Cricket' at the Oval Theatre. It was the first of our own productions we had done since the ban on performing at Voicespace. The chorus now had to reach out to a wider audience and consider the general public. As well as becoming more technically polished, we had to consider being less controversial and confrontational, perhaps even toning down some of the outrageousness that always seemed to creep into our shows.

Rehearsals continued calmly and methodically. Jeremy insisted that we never use sheet music on stage, so we had to learn everything we sang by heart. The obvious result was that we all looked up and paid more attention to our conductor. He could now communicate tempo, dynamic and mood to us, and control the relative balance of each section with instant results. The more we worked with Jeremy the more we came to recognise his techniques. He didn't just conduct us with hand movements; he transmitted information with his every nuance and expression. He could signal a section to sing louder with the arching of his eyebrows. Clenching his jaw, gritting his teeth, pursing his lips, dropping his shoulders, every gesture and hint of body language could be read and translated into the appropriate reaction. Sometimes the messages he gave were so subconscious and subtle, and we were all tuned in to his techniques so well, that the mutual communications were practically subliminal. The chorus gradually developed a new and more polished sound.

Ever since we had been in Voicespace we had been using the old piano that Richard had bought for £50. No matter how many times it was tuned, it still sounded like a honky-tonk pub instrument, and we knew the coarseness of it was holding us back. Throughout the preceding years the chorus had had to develop a thrifty attitude, but with our new resolve to reach out to a greater audience, we knew the time had come for us to invest in the sound we were capable of making.

David had written a letter to the Elton John management asking if there was perhaps an old discarded keyboard we might have, but when we heard nothing back we began to investigate the cost of a new one. There were all sorts of elaborate instruments being manufactured, and we thought we ought to choose something sophisticated so that we wouldn't grow out of it in a few years; this was going to be an asset for our future. Everyone we asked had different opinions but we eventually decided on a computer controlled sampler costing nearly two and half thousand pounds. Paul went off to Chappels, the West End music store where the professionals shopped, and placed our order. The flight case and foot pedals added to the cost, and when the complete package arrived it was so heavy it took two people to lift it, and the only car it would fit in was Lynne's battered old estate. It sounded magnificent, at the touch of a button it could reproduce the sound of a single flute, a symphony orchestra or anything else, and with the floppy disc drive we would be able to record our own backing tracks.

It was a real boy's toy, and having something that sounded like a grand piano instantly made a difference to our rehearsals. Ironically, the Oval House theatre already had a perfectly good in-house instrument, so we didn't get to use it for the next concert, but we were very consciously sowing the seeds for interesting developments.

To give a bit more variety in our shows, we liked to include a few monologues or small group numbers, and at that time one of our really strong and confident solo singers was Stefan, a good looking young German with a frosted blond buzz-cut. He had already done a string of one-man shows in Berlin nightclubs, and asked if he could do a piece in our 'It's Just Not Cricket' show.

During rehearsal one evening he stood next to the keyboard and did an impromptu audition for us. He looked and sounded really professional and we all agreed a Stefan solo spot would be a good idea. He chose an old Marlene Dietrich standard to sing and we slotted it in as the opening number. Whenever we rehearsed the show in running order he sang his part well and we were pleased with the logical progression of ideas the programme presented. It wasn't at all scary, and felt as if it would all be very accessible to the general public. We were attempting to portray the more acceptable and commercial face of gay culture, clever but clean, bold but not really anything offensive.

It wasn't until the opening night that any of us saw Stefan in full costume and make up. He transformed into the most flamboyant drag diva any of us had ever seen. Our show opened with a frighteningly and fabulously beautiful cabaret creature, lewdly pouting and provocatively taunting the shocked audience. Lyrics that had previously seemed to be vaguely ambiguous were revealed as red-hot hard-core, and gender issues plus rampant, deviant sexuality were being rammed down their throats in the first few seconds. A wild atmosphere of danger, excitement and decadence hung in the air and flavoured everything that came after.

It's Just Not Cricket was another turning point; we never paid a great deal of attention to over-sensitive straight expectations again. If we wanted to do camp, then there were no holds barred; we would try and do it as well as we could. If we wanted to set spines tingling, then we would turn out the lights and nail the listeners to the floor with raw emotion. Music was our weapon, and we had earned the right to use its power for whatever purpose we chose; our gayness would not be compromised.

Now that we could only use Voicespace for rehearsal and not concerts, Paul the ex-policeman and I were continually on the lookout for additional places to perform.

I got hold of a list of potential venues from Haringey Arts Council, and we investigated all the possibilities. Most of them were the standard collection of back rooms in pubs, or dusty old church halls, but one of them was intriguingly listed as an open-air performance space in Highgate woods. It was leased for the summer months to an out-of-work actor who used it to put on Punch and Judy shows for local children. I phoned him and we all arranged to meet early one evening to go and see it.

The three of us walked through the trees down what appeared to be an old cart track for five minutes, and then turned off on to an overgrown muddy footpath. After a further ten minutes of hillocks, thickets and tangled tree-roots, the branches parted to reveal a wide open clearing. There was a shallow paddling pool, dug out during the 'back-to-nature' health conscious 1930s, then abandoned during the economic cut-back of the war years. It was a perfect circle of smooth concrete with a six inch rim and painted a luminous sun bleached blue. There was a gently sloping natural amphitheatre formed in the woods on one side, where our potential audience could sit, and a great colonnade of mature beech trees stood like a row of Greek columns at the back.

The blue pool must have been nearly a mile from the nearest road, and the atmosphere was amazingly peaceful. I stood in the middle of the circle and sang a couple of lines, the sound seemed to reflect off the smooth surface and carried clearly in the still evening. It was one of the most magical places we had ever seen in London, and we were determined to put on a summer show there, even though the potential problems were mind-boggling.

It wasn't difficult to convince the other people in the chorus, we were used to the idea of being unconventional and breaking rules, everything we did seemed to cross some boundary or other, and there was a powerful 'can do' attitude driving our activities.

A power supply was going to be difficult to arrange in the middle of Highgate woods. Petrol driven generators would have been offensively noisy in that perfect sylvan setting. I'd once heard an eco-friendly rock band in a fringe music festival set on a remote Scottish island. They had used a team of volunteers on a bicycle-powered generator. I tracked them down and was told that the electronic output fluctuated such a lot we really shouldn't plug our expensive keyboard into it.

The date was getting closer and flyers had to be printed. The show would be called 'Out in the Open', and we eventually decided to do it completely unplugged; just rely on a hired piano and lungpower. We prayed for a dry, sunny weekend, and on the morning of the concert it was beautiful.

One of the local residents had come across some of our flyers and tried to whip up a protest at the prospect of 'all these gay perverts in the neighbourhood.' We had already got council permission so he turned to the local paper, which ran features on it. There was an exchange of letters but luckily there didn't seem to be a strong public reaction. It was reassuring, but we didn't know what to expect and hoped we weren't going to be met by any angry demonstrations on the day.

The piano arrived in a van; we hoisted it onto a trolley, tied it securely down and set off along the bumpy track. A jogger ran past with an astonished look on his face, but was much too English to stop and ask what we were doing. By the time we had manhandled the piano through the woods it was so out of tune that the start of the show was delayed whilst it was radically readjusted.

At lunch time we had signposted a trail of arrows and leaflets on trees and lampposts all the way from Highgate station. They were all torn down during the afternoon but the audience drifted in anyway. A young couple with children and a picnic hamper settled down unselfconsciously right at the front. Middle aged mums with uneasy looking husbands stood back beneath the cover of trees. Groups of guys lay about on the grass with bottles of wine.

By the time the show started there must have been a couple of hundred people gathered by the old blue pool, and the whole afternoon was utterly glorious. It was so simple; a group of friends standing in a wood and singing songs on a summer afternoon, yet so amazingly strange and far removed from any normal reality.

The whole event is now a gauzy web of floating half remembered images, wonderfully studded with shining gems of a cinematic clarity that confirm one's suspicion we really did make such magic things happen.

The chorus can do that sometimes, suddenly jump the rails and generate the strangest of dreams and myths. It's one of the things that keeps us going; the never quite knowing what might be around the next corner.

The music is always leading us onwards; it's as if we are on a giddy journey through an unrolling landscape, the sky and the scenery like some wide open mouth, ever hungry for more mountains and further forests, and us always choosing to take the road less travelled by, and then suddenly finding ourselves within an expanded moment of perfect peace in a sunlit glade.

SEVEN

The Battle of Stratford and the First CD

Only a few weeks after we had shared our songs in idyllic summer woodland, the Chorus found an opposite extreme to explore.

The Theatre Royal Stratford East has had an interesting history; it was the home for Joan Littlewood and her company when they were inventing new ways to present social realism during the fifties and sixties. She hung out with Joe Orton and Lionel Bart, and devised the production 'Oh What a Lovely War' which rocked the establishment and ignited the resurgence of interest in musical theatre. The suburban area around it has since declined and it's now ruthlessly pierced with grim tower blocks and grinding poverty. The old theatre stands like a neglected aunty in a dirty nursing home. There are still faded velvet curtains, but the baroque plasterwork is tarnished and crumbling. Rats nest under the holes in the floor, and when one ran across the stage during a rehearsal our horrified and hilarious girly shrieks bought forth a stage hand with a broom who just shrugged and casually shooed it away.

We had been invited to participate in one of the

regular Variety Nights that are held there. The idea was based on the old music hall tradition of a whole collection of short acts all stitched together by a fast talking and extrovert compere. Our fellow novelty acts were a motley collection of fringe entertainers and agency eccentrics. There was a really clever female magician whose tricks always went riotously wrong, a ventriloquist with a menagerie of upholstered animals, an old man with only seven fingers who told the bluest jokes I've ever heard, and a group of four half-clad dancers who flung and posed and postured athletically.

Pat and Dave, two loud mouthed Irish jokers were acting as hosts, and they appeared in the bar before the show had even started, dressed in charity-shop old-lady drag outfits and warming up the audience for a rowdy night out. The crowd was a mixed bunch of locals who had obviously been to these nights before and knew the routine, getting tanked up in the bar, before during and after, was all a part of the ritual.

We were the big finale, so watched the show from the back of the stage and enjoyed all the wild fun, it was a non-stop fairground ride of sketches and show business anarchy, just the sort of thing we enjoyed doing in our own Voicespace concerts.

Pat announced our appearance and there was a hushed silence as thirty of us filed to the front and started our first song. We wanted to finish with a loud backing track and choreographed version of 'It's Raining Men' so had started with something quiet for contrast. It wasn't what the audience wanted, or expected, and there was only a brief ripple of claps when we finished the first song. Half way through the second number there was a loud drunken bellow from the back of the little auditorium, and somebody else shouted "get off poofters", a half-full can of beer flashed through the footlights, sprayed the chorus and landed with a clatter on the stage. There were answering shouts from all around the darkened theatre, more beer cans flew, some sideways across the auditorium and some on to the stage; it was impossible to know who was in support of the hecklers or what was aimed at the chorus. It suddenly felt frightening.

Jeremy was conducting us, he didn't turn around, miss a beat or falter in any way, but we could see that his jaw was clenched shut and his eyes were blazing with anger. We carried on singing and this time there was more obvious applause when we finished.

Jeremy glanced over his shoulder at the crowd, then turned back and mouthed the word "loud" to the sound man who was waiting in the wings with our backing track.

The bass beat at the beginning kicked in fast and the front row hunkered down into their choreography start positions urgently; as the verse picked up energy we slowly rose to standing position and then leapt up as high as we could for the big "WOOW" at the end of the verse. Jeremy was grinning like a maniac and the pounding beat was madly empowering everyone to sing more loudly and fiercely than we had ever done before.

As if one person, the entire group of us moved forward to the very front of the stage and suddenly it was the audience's turn to feel apprehensive. Our punching fists were raised in violent defiance and the angrily bellowed vocal line of "It's Raining Men" became transformed into a threatening war cry. The song ended with a tremendous crescendo and the audience instantly exploded into a deafening drunken riot of cheering and booing, whooping and shouting; it felt as if the roof was being blown off.

There was supposed to be a 'thank you and goodnight' speech from Pat and Dave, but they just stood in the wings looking stunned, there was no way that mob was going to sit down and shut up. The curtain started to come down and most of us managed to step back behind it. Suddenly left isolated and awestruck on the darkened stage, we all shook with the freaky emotions of everything that had just happened. Whatever the bizarre battle had actually been about, we knew that with our volume, energy, anger and a stubborn determination to stay out there, we had somehow won.

At the next rehearsal several people said things like 'we're not going to do that again', but in fact two years later we were invited back to do another Variety Night at The Theatre Royal Stratford East, and we did. It was still being hosted by Pat and Dave, and there was an equally odd collection of alternative performers. Our set of songs at the end of the show was enthusiastically received by the crowd, and we felt able to stay and meet up with some of the locals in the bar afterwards.

That sounds like a happy ending, except that like so many other small theatres it has since suffered a funding crisis and Pat and Dave are now no longer able to put on

Variety Night shows there.

Since it was a year old the chorus had always been busy, now that there were more members, and we were doing more things outside the shelter of our own gay community, we got a lot busier.

We still continued to meet up and rehearse in Voicespace, but it many ways it wasn't all that suitable for us. The ceiling of the main hall was low and the acoustic was awful. The corridor that led off from the hall actually ran underneath the tower block next door, and when their main drain got blocked we were flooded with raw sewage. There were several rehearsals when we turned up expecting to sing, but ended up spending the night baling out buckets full of the stuff from Richards bedroom.

In spite of the problems, Voicespace provided us with stability and security and felt like our home. We had developed our style there, and the inherent problems of the place caused us to evolve an adaptable template for doing our events. We found that we could now do shows in all sorts of other spaces that were available to us.

The chorus used theatres, pubs, clubs, churches, bar-rooms and ballrooms. Each venue posed its own set of problems, and we were always inventing ways to get round them. If there was no stage we would hire a van and turn up with our own set of four homemade10 by 8 foot plywood platforms. For lights we often had to use our 'gardening equipment' halogen security floods, tied to a handy pillar with a length of cable. If there were no curtains, and we couldn't put up a screen, we just rewrote the 'entrances and exits' parts of the program so that we didn't need curtains.

Outdoor events were common, there seemed to be a constant stream of Pride parades, charity walks, marches and demonstrations. Winter or summer we could always turn up and do something.

Although John Harold had now left the chorus our links with Manchester were still strong, and the gay village there had developed enormously. After a couple of years the original 'midnight vigil in the Sackville St. car park' event had grown into a Bank Holiday Saturday open-air garden party with health information stalls, a barbecue stand and a proper little stage. We would still go there to sing at the vigil but now had a special guest spot in the afternoon program as well.

In the beginning it had all been put together by a few guys from the local pub, but now there was a proper organising committee, and for our visits they would compile a list of people with spare bedrooms and sofa-beds who could put us up overnight. Eventually it came to be known as Mardi Gras weekend, and was always one of the highlights in our year.

By the time we got to the millennium, the local council had realised that it could be turned into a significant community event for the whole city, and gave permission for an annual Pride parade through the city centre.

There was a huge fun fair set up on the building site next door to the park, all the surrounding streets were closed to traffic, and two or three days of the wildest non-stop partying would happen. The midnight vigil for those affected by AIDS was moved to a separate site at Castlefields; it was still a significant part of the weekend, sometimes a crowd of a thousand would attend, but it was felt to be something different which didn't easily fit in to the mayhem of Mardi Gras.

Manchester City is a place that has grown to accept and even respect it's gay community, and for the past few years a formal 'Lavender Ball' has also been held in the Victorian-Gothic splendour of the Manchester Town Hall. A group of us would go by coach, stay in the university dormitories and do a concert for the ball, a spot on the open air stage next day, the open air vigil on the last night and a great deal of clubbing in between.

On one extraordinary Mardi Gras weekend the Friday night coach taking us there broke down on the M5 motorway at eleven-o-clock. There was an impromptu chorus party on the hard shoulder whilst we waited many hours for the coach-hire company to organise a convoy of emergency vans to collect us. The chorus eventually arrived in Manchester at 6am on Saturday morning, there was a sound check scheduled for 10am, and everybody had to get through the blur of the next seventy two hours on quick cat-naps, the adrenalin jags of stage-fright and very strong coffee.

Apart from our annual trip to Manchester, and an occasional day trip to Alton Towers, most of the chorus activities happened in and around London. During the nineteen nineties the public perception of gay culture was gradually changing, 'out' gay entertainers were appearing on TV, and although this was a novelty, it was not greeted as a scandalous shock. It was fortunate that we were based in London since attitudes there were possibly more enlightened than in many other places. There was only an occasional confrontation with some parish council official or other, who would tell us we were sinners, and had to hold our sordid event elsewhere. Most of the time we were tolerated, occasionally we would even be given some assistance. Islington Arts Council helped us to put on a concert called 'Light up the Night' at The Union Chapel one Christmas. Gay people qualified as a minority community, and along with the Diwali celebrations, the concert was publicised in all of the boroughs publications. Croydon Council let us put on several events in an old hall underneath their offices; and the people who ran the Hackney Empire were really helpful when the Sydney Lesbian and Gay Chorus came to visit, and we wanted to put on a big combined concert featuring them as our guests.

The chorus was now doing shows all over London; some of these events were absolutely huge, like the Royal Albert Hall concerts with major names that sold out immediately, or the Pride rallies that attracted crowds in the hundred thousand. Others were tiny and just marketed to a local audience. Several times each year we would put on one of our own shows in a better known venue, and we usually seemed to get a decent sized crowd.

Even though we were experiencing some success as an out and gay organization, it was obvious from the reactions we got and the messages of support we received, that this 'work' we were doing was more than just entertainment. Tolerance of us, our lives and our values was patchy, acceptance was often only superficial, genuine understanding rare. The time had come for us to make a CD and try to reach out to a wider national, and maybe even international, audience.

We drew up a list of songs that made a statement about the issues we considered to be important, songs concerned with a universal message of liberation, freedom and equality. We then included some that had an element of 'joie de vivre', glorious uplifting pieces that were a celebration of just being alive, and made sure that there were a couple that, in the context of a gay choir, became somewhat camp and slightly self-mocking, just to show that we weren't too earnest. It was an eclectic collection that was actually very specific to us and our agenda, no one else we could think of would have the motivation, or the cheek, to put these particular pieces together.

The professional recording studios that we found in the phone book all proved to be horrendously expensive. The chorus wasn't associated with any production company and we had to finance this whole project out of our own pockets. Some years earlier Paul, Dan, David and I had been very surprised and somewhat disappointed to discover that the glamorous sounding prospect of recording a CD with Lorraine Bowen, had actually been a few late-night sessions in a spare bedroom in Edmonton. Now we realised that this was the most realistic way to get things done, and called her engineer.

Wayne was used to working this way, and had all the reel to reel tape machines, editing desks, cables and microphones that were needed. The chorus was too big to fit into his spare bedroom, so he came over to visit one of our rehearsals in Voicespace, and thought that with a bit of luck we might be able to get something done there.

We rehearsed our collection of songs with special care, and a few weeks later booked an evening session for Wayne to come and set his equipment up in the basement hall.

It took far longer than we had anticipated to record a good take of each track. Sometimes it was our own singing that went wrong; all sorts of minor imperfections that were forgivable in live performance were not acceptable when making a permanent recording.

On other occasions we were doing a good job, but then heard a lone police-car siren howling in the distance and had to start again. Luck was not on our side that night; during the tea break Jeremy and Wayne had a listen on sensitive headphones and could then detect a persistent hum on every track. It turned out to be the fridge in the far corner. We unplugged it and redid everything from scratch. The session carried on till nearly midnight and people were anxious about getting the last tube home from Angel station, there were only four songs recorded by the time we had to finish.

When we had a chance to listen to the four finished

songs properly, we reluctantly had to admit that they sounded really dull, flat and lifeless. The ceiling height of the basement was only seven foot and there was no resonance or ring to the space. The recording demonstrated to us just how poor an acoustic our home space had, and there was nothing we could do about it.

Determined to carry on we found a church in Hampstead that we could use for free and booked Wayne for a whole day. We got there efficiently early and the chorus sounded wonderful in the lofty space, but it was so cold that our breaths hung with mist, and we had to wait half an hour for the tape machine to warm up enough to run smoothly. The recordings were timed so that we didn't pick up the bell in the church tower striking the hours, and at the end of the day we felt we had most of the CD recorded. We were booked to do a concert in Croydon a few weeks later, and decided to get Wayne and his gear there and risk doing the last few pieces 'live'.

Technically the sound quality of the live concert wasn't as good as that which we had achieved in the icily empty Hampstead church, but there was so much more energy and enthusiasm evident in the singing that we ended up using those live tapes for most of the CD. There was only one song we couldn't use. For Bali H'ai, our romantic South Pacific interlude, we had given out half a dozen palm fronds to members of the audience to wave atmospherically, and one of them could be heard brushing against a microphone all the way through.

Recording a CD meant that we had to begin thinking about marketing 'The London Gay Men's Chorus' as a product, and we felt it was time to redesign our logo. The original 'nine heads' image had been useful, but it didn't scale down well, and it was too complicated to be a really effective graphic. There was a members' competition and Andy Ford, who also worked for a top design company, came up with a simple circular rivet or stamp-like pattern for the text. I added a generic 'man' symbol to the middle of the disc, and it then satisfied all our needs. There was a slightly aggressive 'rough and ready' edge to it, and a vague whiff of graffiti and toilet doors that was confrontational rather than overly corporate.

We had striking new black and white t-shirts printed, and on the first available Saturday we all met up in central London to do some group photos for the CD sleeve. Like a hoard of Japanese tourists we wandered around for most of the day, posing in front of London landmarks. After visiting the Festival Hall, where we arranged ourselves in front of a Thames panorama, we went along to Trafalgar Square where we all mounted a lion. Westminster came next for a shot with Big Ben in the background, and then we came across an unusually large expanse of empty grass. I arranged the chorus members into groups and clusters receding into the distance so that we resembled a crowd scene from an old master painting. This was the image that was eventually used on the back cover, and it was only months later that I discovered the grass we had been trespassing on was the front lawn of the Ministry of Defence.

Our first CD was officially launched in November of 1998, with a big party at The Yard bar in Soho. Although we were pleased with the results of our efforts, there was a slightly uneasy undercurrent about the evening. This 'product' from the chorus was being released into a much wider world than we had ever reached out to before, and that world was not a very safe place for gay people.

In the summer of 1998 there was shocking news of a young African American, James Byrd Junior, who had been tied to a car and dragged to his death in the town of Jasper, Texas. His only 'transgression' was to have been noticeably gay, and only a few weeks before our press launch there had been another ghastly murder in Wyoming. On October 10th a young gay student, Matthew Shepard, had been attacked, tortured and left hanging on a barbed wire fence outside the city. When the body was found the police estimated that he had hung there for two days before he died. There was public outrage at the brutality of the crime but only a few days later, at the quiet family funeral, there were large contingents of aggressive evangelical Christians shouting quotations from the bible and waving banners saying 'God is Glad that Matthew's Dead', 'God Hates Fags' and 'Aids is God's Answer to Gays'. Such militant homophobia occurring in a supposedly enlightened western nation was hard to believe, but the images were on all our TV screens, and we knew that such intolerant beliefs were widespread in many other cultures and religions. The World Health Organisation declassified being gay as 'a mental disease' on 17th May 1990, but there remain many countries which continue to discriminate.

EIGHT
Admiral Duncan and the TV

Our ability to improvise and react to difficult circumstances proved to be vital when the Admiral Duncan bombing incident happened. The nail bomb had exploded at 6.37pm on 30th April 1999; it was a Friday evening in the middle of Old Compton St. Three people had been killed instantly; one of them a pregnant woman, and initial reports stated that at least seventy three others had been seriously injured. This estimate was subsequently doubled.

The newspapers next day carried appalling pictures of wounded people lying in the gutters, and accounts of emergency double amputations and carnage. It was the third, and by far the most serious, bomb attack in a fortnight; all of them very obviously targeted on minority communities.

The news spread fast. I had heard about it via a radio newsflash only twenty minutes after it happened, and that evening everyone in the chorus was frantically phoning around their friends trying to find out if they were all right. The initial and very individual fear and horror everyone was feeling very rapidly consolidated into a sense of shared communal outrage. Perhaps the other minority communities that had been attacked, Bangladeshi and African-Caribbean, did not have any obvious means to express their group solidarity. The gay community had several recognisable figureheads and spokespersons, and it also had us; we were a very visual manifestation of gay culture, and we were willing to stand up and be counted. There wasn't any question that we should, and could, do something.

Steve Bustin was our chairman at that time, and his 'day job' was Head of Outside Broadcasts for the BBC. Without much difficulty he was able to mobilise the chorus, and I think everyone felt it was a good idea to have some positive task to do. Although it was the start of a bank holiday weekend, websites, emails and mobile phones enabled us to organise ourselves. Anger was easy to access, but we wanted to provide the gay community with something more healing and positive. The vigil events we had experienced in Manchester and Trafalgar Square would be more appropriate, and Westminster Council granted us permission to use Soho Square on the Sunday. At incredibly short notice the Metropolitan Police gave us their full support, and assembled a squad of exclusively lesbian and gay officers who would assist on the day.

There are many gay shops, bars and clubs in and around Old Compton St, and at that point all of them had very good reason to not participate in any activities that would draw attention to themselves; but they all offered as much help as they could. Within hours we had managed to borrow a PA system and all the other props and equipment that would be needed. Hundreds of flyers were printed and distributed round all the local venues that afternoon and evening. Steve spent the Saturday going through his address book and assembled a list of politicians and significant media people who could make a statement, give a speech or offer support in some other way.

On the Sunday morning we took my home-made stage platforms over to Soho Square where the chorus had assembled. We were astonished to find that a crowd of about two and a half thousand had gathered, and the place was packed with international news reporters and camera crews. There was of course a planned running order already drawn up, a set of relevant songs interspersed with speeches or statements, but it had to be adapted as the event unfolded; so many people were coming forward at the last minute. The best friend of two of the people who had died approached Steve, and he had a poignant wedding day group photograph showing them all together. He showed the picture to the cameras and spoke movingly to the crowd of his personal loss. As the ceremony was drawing to a close a spokesman from the police came over to speak to Steve. He was bought to the microphone and informed the crowd that Old Compton Street was being re-opened that afternoon. He then announced to the assembled media that a 22 year old suspect had just been apprehended and charged with all three bomb attacks.

It had been the most extraordinarily intense ninety

minutes; our emotions had oscillated between feelings of extreme anger and unbearable loss. There were many cameras and reporters present, and we were aware that the entire event was being broadcast live by two national TV channels. We later learned that sections of it were even being picked up worldwide, but whilst the event was happening all their prowling and prying attention had felt irrelevant. People had come along to Soho Square to demonstrate their support for each other, and share in a common grieving.

It was less than forty eight hours since the incident had happened, and most of those who had been injured were still in intensive care units all over London. Someone in a medical team revealed a ghastly detail; the bomb had deliberately been packed with faeces as well as nails. All the injured were now desperately fighting severe blood poisoning as well as devastating shrapnel trauma.

Many wanted to speak, but we understood that music was also important for such an emotional gathering. There had been no rehearsal so we sang pieces that were already known. The old Shaker hymn 'Simple Gifts' came at the beginning, and between readings and speeches we fitted Sondheim's 'Not a Day Goes By', the gentle 'True Love' by Cole Porter and 'Donna Nobis' (give us peace). After 'Man Going Round Taking Names' Steve announced there was to be a brief period of silence, and for some participants that intangible and fragile moment seemed to be the most significant part of the whole occasion. That stillness spread about Soho Square like a great shining lake, holding the sky within its depth and uniting the crowd within its peace. Amen.

I remember the final song 'Something inside so Strong' seemed to have been written for the event, and was aware of a palpable tension throbbing in the air like ball-lightening. I wasn't conscious of any applause as we finished and stepped off the platform; the intensity of it all had been frightening and we instinctively reached out and held on to each other for comfort and reassurance. I glanced behind and saw just a few feet away a startling tableau of three uniformed policemen; as if in a renaissance altar-piece the one in the centre wept uncontrollably, and was comforted by the two companions.

We met some of those gay police officers again the following day. Steve had received a phone call requesting assistance in moving some of the floral tributes from outside the Admiral Duncan to Soho Square, where a temporary garden of remembrance was set up. At midnight on Monday seven chorus members, with helpers from the police and the London Lesbian and Gay Switchboard, began the task of reverentially moving many thousands of flags, candles, letters and flowers to where our vigil had taken place. They were laid out in blocks, with paths between so that mourners could walk amongst them and read the messages. There were so many tokens of respect that eventually two lorries were used, and the mission continued until dawn on Tuesday.

In the year 2000 David Copeland was found guilty of killing three people and injuring one hundred and thirty nine others; he received six life sentences.

After the Admiral Duncan bomb, life for the gay community of London would never be the same again.

The London Gay Men's Chorus was frequently encountering the voracious machinery of the mass media. When our CD had been released there had not been a great fanfare of publicity, but there was a favourable review in the Sunday Telegraph, and one or two tracks had been played on the radio. Chris Evans had come across one of the promotional copies we had sent out and played a track called 'Add a Riff' every morning for a week. The song didn't have any proper words, but started with the bass section going 'bom, bom, bom,' so he referred to it as 'the bum song'. Steve phoned him up and did a little interview live on air, and when Christmas approached Chris remembered us and asked if we could come in to the studio to do some carols.

Fourteen of us got to the BBC radio studio in Golden Square for six in the morning, and stood in their little kitchen drinking strong coffee. It all looked like complete pandemonium, but Chris Evans and his team were actually a tightly knit little unit who were able to improvise as they went along. We all grouped round the microphone and when the red light came on, did a minute long excerpt from a well-known carol. These festive interludes occurred every half hour or so, and we used the gaps in between to work out a routine and practise for the next spot.

When the show ended at 9am, Chris came over and chatted amiably. He had liked the way we were able to fit in and respond to his live and unscripted comments and questions, and asked if we would all like to spend the day recording with him and Danny Baker at the Riverside studios, and be on that evening's 'TFI Friday' TV show. It sounded like fun, and since it was the highest-rating entertainment show around at that time, was an amazing opportunity to plug our new CD. We spontaneously said yes and set off in a couple of taxis. Whilst some of us 'called in sick' to their various offices, the others phoned round other chorus members to see if we could get a bigger group together by the time it all started at midday. The TV show was much more complicated than the radio production, but only slightly more organised. There was an initial quick run through of the proceedings for the technicians to check sound levels, but nothing more could happen until all the other guests were there.

Robbie Williams arrived early, did a sound check and then amiably sat on a speaker cabinet, talking, eating sandwiches and waiting around with us and the rest of the studio crew. 'The Corrs', who had a hit single at the time, were the exact opposite. They swept in pompously surrounded by security guards, and then hid in their dressing rooms, not participating in the buzz of the studio or mixing with anyone else.

It was fun, but like all the time spent in TV and radio studios, a surreal mixture of high tension and interminable boredom, a sort of interlude in limbo, insulated from reality.

As well as our extraordinary day with Chris Evans, the chorus also did in quick succession an all-night Comic Relief Special with Princess Anne and S Club 7 at the White City studios, a couple of Graham Norton shows from the LWT studios, including a Christmas special where we sang with Latoya Jackson. There was also a 'Jerry Springer on Tour' show and a scary Ruby Wax Christmas special. Whilst we stood and sang carols she walked between the rows and pushed polystyrene snow into our faces; we couldn't tell if she was drunk that night or maybe she always behaved that badly.

Sometimes there was backstage hospitality or a 'green room' for guests, a case of beer was supplied and you got to meet some interesting people. The singer Meatloaf, his daughter and their backing band turned out to be very good company for an entire evening, and the actor Jack Black was really enthusiastic about the idea of singing in a chorus. We swapped stories and he told us he had spent a lot of his early years in a local church choir.

More often than not the apparent glamour of being involved in a TV programme was deceptive; the catering was a left-over box of doughnuts, the various celebrities nondescript, and the experience utterly indistinguishable from all the others.

You got to see people off their guard, and sometimes it was disappointing. Perhaps because of their undeniable good looks, the band East 17 were always admired by the gay press, but when we watched them rehearse at the Albert Hall it became painfully apparent to our trained ears that they couldn't play their instruments or sing well.

It was their unacknowledged backing musicians who had the talent and made the sound.

An unexpected spin off from doing TV appearances was that our membership was gradually rising. Every time we participated in a high profile event there were enquiries from people who wanted to join, and by 1999 there were often seventy or eighty people coming along to rehearsals in the Voicespace basement. It was to make a great difference to both our sound and our financial security, and eventually meant that we would have to find a new home.

NINE

The Dome and Jerusalem

One of our higher profile encounters with the media occurred when we were asked to be part of the massed choir that was to sing at the opening of the Millennium Dome. Apparently the invitation had come about because Howard Goodall, by then a recognised authority on choirs and music education, was asked to act as the consultant for the government's advisory team. He fondly remembered our participation in the Sainsbury's Choir of the Year Competitions from years before.

The Dome was a vast project that was dogged by controversy throughout its brief history. The original plan had been to stage a new version of the 1851 Crystal Palace 'great exhibition', and 'The Dome' was attempting to celebrate everything that was glorious about the twentieth century. Richard Rogers's extraordinary building was at the heart of the scheme, and it appeared to be spectacularly over budget, very behind schedule and the whole scheme inevitably turned into a political hot potato.

We were both honoured and astonished to be invited, and during the preceding two months we rehearsed our specially written pieces with enthusiasm and some trepidation. Since the Dome building straddled the Greenwich meridian, and was therefore the place where the new century would actually begin, the event was going to be televised globally on millennium eve. There were wild estimates of anything up to two and a half billion viewers. The opening night was being promoted as 'the biggest party of the twentieth century', and we were going to be right in the middle of it.

As well as rehearsing for the Dome we had our own Christmas show to produce, a memorably strange production called 'It's about Time'. The title was a pithy comment on the state of gay rights, as well as a description of the on-stage action. To celebrate the end of the twentieth century I devised a scenario which explored both the evolution of the human race and the art of making music. This ambitious folly happened in the Place Theatre, Euston, and began with a clock ticking in the darkness and a spot lit pastiche of the prehistoric ape/flying bone/obelisk sequence from the movie 2001. It then moved briskly through the eons to end two hours later with a futuristic roller-skating nun zooming across the stage wielding a ray gun.

As soon as our own show was finished in mid-December, the awesome prospect of 'doing the Dome' became inescapable.

Our first massed choir rehearsal at the Dome happened immediately after Christmas, and the affair was a knotted tangle of security checks, metal detectors, plastic passes and waiting. There was no dressing room, just a lounge area in the 'Skyscape' cinema building, with a hundred or so seats for three hundred very apprehensive performers. No food was supplied and very little information. When we eventually got on to the wobbly scaffolding stage in the central arena, we discovered a huge Perspex screen had been put up between ourselves and the audience. Paul Daniel, the E.N.O. conductor who was musical director for the show, explained that it was a makeshift sound baffle, and that it would be removed, or at least cut down, before the performance.

There seemed to be an awful lot of waiting around, and some of us drifted off to hunt for food and water. The choices were a not-really-open-yet McDonalds outside, or a couple of nearly empty vending machines on the other side of the arena. The glittering promises of the Dome's £738 million budget suddenly grew dim; it seemed that nobody had remembered the needs of the performers.

Eventually we got as far as a sound check, and each of the participating groups took a turn at singing through the National Anthem. The Welsh miners sounded powerful. The E.N.O. Chorus positioned to our left sounded shrill and pretentious. The children's choirs, on balconies above us, sounded hesitant and quiet. Paul Daniel gave an encouraging pep-talk as a haze of acrid diesel-smoke filled the great empty space. The central arena was still inhabited by lorries full of equipment, bulldozers and other heavy industrial machinery, and there were less than three days to go before the opening night show.

The next day's rehearsal was washed out by a bomb threat. As the main arena was repeatedly and exhaustively searched, we hung around in the waiting area. With nothing to do for more than six hours, impromptu singing groups evolved. We all joined in when we knew the song, or else just sat on the floor and wondered.

The catering had improved; there was now a tea urn, but with three hundred bored people it was only a couple of hours until all the supplies ran out. At six o'clock we were shepherded across the dark, muddy building site to a construction workers' canteen shed for an unidentifiable, brown-coloured, warm meal. By the time we left at 9pm we had managed an hour on stage and sung through our repertoire once. The day had been dismal, and yet the atmosphere still crackled with suppressed excitement. It was an exhausting combination that did nothing to inspire calm or composure.

The remaining rehearsals carried on in much the same way. Seemingly interminable blank gaps where we waited around with nothing to do were punctuated with periods of frustration and jags of panic when we were on stage without clear instructions. At one point we had just sung through 'A New Beginning' when a wild-eyed character, dressed in jumble sale cast-offs, approached the stage. It was the composer of the piece, Sir John Tavener. At that time I had heard the name before, but didn't realize quite what a musical mega-star the man was. When he was aged 24 an early work of his, 'The Whale' had been recorded and released on the Beatles 'Apple' label. In

1989 his piece 'The Protecting Veil' achieved international success, and in 1997 his 'Song for Athene' was used in the Lady Diana Spencer memorial as the cortege exited Westminster Abbey. As we rehearsed 'New Beginning' in the Dome he was apparently not happy at the way a section in the middle of the strange and dissonant song was going, and began to re-write it on the spot. The conductor stepped in and tactfully pointed out that about a third of the massed chorus comprised school children who didn't have sheet music, and that drastic last minute alterations would not be beneficial.

Another piece of music we had been practising, 'Siyahamba', had large chunks cut out of it on the last day; the performance had to coincide exactly with the chimes of Big Ben which would be transmitted live from Westminster, and the show was running too long.

On one magical afternoon the E.N.O. orchestra brought the Dome work to a standstill by playing through 'Jupiter' from Holst's 'The Planets'. The power and majesty of the music was stunning, and to be sitting on stage right next to the musicians as they played was, for me, the highlight of the whole Millennium Dome experience. Another memorable and utterly ridiculous incident happened one lunch-break. Amongst all the rubbish which still lay around the arena, somebody had come across a discarded architect's plan. We saw the location of the royal box marked on it, and went there to eat our sandwiches, taking it in turn to play the biggest queen of all.

During the four days we were at The Dome, we had all spent many hours wandering around the various exhibits.

Security had been as tight as a rock guitarist's leather trousers but, like us, the guards had been left totally without any information. Equipped with our special 'central arena performer' passes, we had been able to explore unhindered and free to wander into any of the special exhibits that looked interesting. There had been a press embargo, so we felt very privileged to have had a sneak preview of everything that was about to be unveiled.

By the time we arrived at the final blank gap, the two hours before the show, most of us seemed to have become 'Domed out'. We sat in the changing area feeling bored, wearing our uncomfortable and lurid nylon jerkins (courtesy of M&S), and ate an uninspiring airline-type meal of frozen pasta and a hard green apple.

A running order for the show we were about to perform in would have been appreciated, but nobody had thought to give us one. The organizers had their hands full with an audience of 10,000 people, many of whom would be left stranded in Stratford because of a train dispute. When the time finally arrived, and in spite of all the organizational difficulties, the show was magnificent. Willard White, the operatic bass, wowed the crowd with his singing. The Corrs drew a stampede of screaming teenagers to the front of the stage. Mick Hucknall got a standing ovation and a thousand flash-bulbs glittered like stars in the darkened velvet gulf of the vast arena.

After the assorted acts had done their separate sets, the main section of the show began with what was referred to as the 'kabuki drop'. A circular screen of suspended fabric panels, each one 120ft high, that had enclosed the central arena, dropped down in sequence to reveal the outer reaches of The Dome where all the 'experience zones' were located. As soon as the nearest panel to the stage fluttered down, seemingly in slow motion, there was an appalling stench of burning nylon; had the enormous sail snagged on a hot spotlight? Were we all about to be engulfed in flames? Images of the R101 airship ablaze in the night sky came to mind, and I imagined a panic-stricken scramble for the rickety staircase at the back of the stage. There had been no fire drill, and no emergency exits had been indicated. I waited for sirens and shouting to start, but somebody somewhere must have found a fire extinguisher, and the air-conditioning silently sucked away all the tell-tale fumes. We never found out what had occurred backstage, and the press and assembled audience never realized anything untoward had happened.

The show continued. The orchestra played and our songs were sung and transmitted live around the planet. As midnight approached the world's largest diamond, the flawless 'Millennium Star' was uncovered on its stand at the very centre of The Dome. An eerie green laser beam was projected along the axis of the great building, and shafts of emerald light were shot around the enormous space. Two child soloists sang the final bars of Taveners' 'A New Beginning' and then snuffed out the light to symbolize the end of the twentieth century. The amplified chimes of Big Ben struck midnight, the timing was precise.

'Auld Lang Syne' was practically overwhelmed by cheering, and then a magnificent carnival costume parade entered and wove around the circumference of the arena. The aerial ballet, two gymnasts suspended by wires from the central roof gantry, quieted the audience temporarily, but after we sang Jonathan Dove's strange 'New National Anthem' and the royal party departed, the real celebration began. It seemed to go on for hours, a jumble of bright lights and strange faces, old friends and endless free champagne; it was the start of the twenty-first century.

The Millennium Dome was an extraordinary project for everyone concerned. It was only ever designed to be a one year long enterprise, and when it's time was up, the government sold it. There was much media mockery about the folly of such a building, and after embarrassing delays it was eventually bought by an American led consortium called AEG, reputedly for a nominal sum of one pound! The place was renamed The 02 Arena, and over the next decade it developed into the world's most successful entertainment venue.

An unforeseen consequence of the publicity surrounding our participation at The Dome was that we had to move out of Voicespace sooner than we had anticipated. A TV crew had done a little news feature on the chorus and shown us rehearsing in the basement. Some officer from The Environmental Health Department at Islington Council saw it, recognized the location and said we were contravening the fire regulations; a couple of weeks before the end of 1999 we received an official letter informing us we would have to go.

We started a London-wide search to find a suitable home, and as the new-year began each rehearsal was held in a different location as a test run of the potential venue. Some had a suitable main space, but not the smaller rooms we needed for splitting into voice sections, others had no parking, or were too far from a tube station. It was proving difficult to find a space that would fulfil all our needs.

One of the central London possibilities was a Catholic Convent in Knightsbridge that had let out their main hall for choir rehearsals before. We had a satisfactory evening there, but didn't meet any nuns. A couple of days later we received a letter from the Mother Superior saying that they had not realized we were a gay men's choir, and we would have to state on the hire agreement that there would not be any lewd behaviour in the toilets. Our chairman Martin wrote back politely stating that if we decided to use their hall we could indeed comply with that requirement, and then asked whether they included that particular clause when dealing with other organizations such as the Young Conservatives.

We didn't miss a single week's rehearsal, and although the disruption was a nuisance it was an interesting experience to see all the different possibilities. Eventually we found Cecil Sharp House in Camden, a wonderfully eccentric and rambling Edwardian institution that is the headquarters of the English Folk Dance and Song Society.

It was frequently used by the English National Opera, and all sorts of other interesting and fringe musical activities happened there; the place even had a folksy little bar in the basement. After nine years spent underground in Islington we had found ourselves a new home.

Perhaps it was the process of moving, and certainly it was all the attention that had been focused on us because of the Dome, that caused a certain amount of introspection and re-evaluation. We could often perform wonderfully inspired concerts, but realized that they were transitory events which ceased to exist as soon as the curtain came down. The only permanent recording of our achievements was a solitary and somewhat primitive CD. The chorus needed to come up with something a bit more impressive.

Professional studios that were big enough for the whole chorus were really expensive. We could only afford to hire such a place for a day or two, and would have to be very well primed and efficient to record a whole CD in such a short time. For the next release we would have to do some serious preparation in our new rehearsal space. Some of the material was already prepared and could come from the most recent concert 'From the Ritz to the Anchor and Crown', and there were some other pieces from our recent past that we wanted to redo with additional backing arrangements.

We found The Henry Wood Studios in Southwark, which was often used by the London Symphony Orchestra, and booked a couple of Saturdays. The acoustic in the studio was similar to the big hall at Cecil Sharp

House, so we were able to explore the correct pace and dynamics of our pieces before we went in to do the recording.

A whole day spent in the studio with the chorus was an extraordinary experience. The hire fees together with the backing musicians and the engineer came to nearly two thousand pounds, so every minute counted and there was a lot of pressure to get everything absolutely perfect. We experienced all the anxiety of an important concert, but of course there was no audience present, and the recording session went on for six times as long. It's not until you are suspended in the middle of total silence that you realize how rare that state is, and when you hear a harp being played flawlessly, and a hundred well-rehearsed performers are able to sing in synch with it, the experience is truly spine-tingling.

Jeremy the conductor was inspiring. He had been practising this set of songs for months and was able to lead the four separate sections of the chorus, the two pianists and the backing musicians, and give instructions to the sound engineer via the video link simultaneously. It was like watching a jump-jet pilot flying through a dog-fight; any miscalculation would have caused a fatal collision, but every movement he made was executed calmly and with perfect skill.

To get the very best results a day spent with the singers in a studio has to be followed up by hours of concentration at a mixing desk. The various inputs have to be balanced and mixed together; and sometimes different sections of separate takes have to be cut out and joined seamlessly. Computers programs and digital mixers may be cleaner and quicker than old fashioned audio tape, but it's still human ears and aesthetic judgment that have to sort everything out. It was many months before the finished CD was ready for release, and in spite of the greater experience and digital manipulation that is now available, some of those recordings still stand as our best work.

Professional recording was a very glamorous luxury for us, and very shortly after we had moved to Camden an interesting request came through from a record producer. He wondered if we could do some backing singing for a band called Fat Les who planned to do a football song. 'Fat Les' turned out to be Keith Allen the actor, Damien Hirst the artist, Alex James the bass player from Blur, Michael Barrymore and a load of their celebrity friends. Even Colin Pillinger, the eccentric scientist who masterminded the unsuccessful 'Beagle 2' mission to land a probe on Mars was involved. The song they wanted to record was William Blake's Jerusalem, mainly because the lovely old hymn had been appropriated by far right political groups. It became the official Football Association song for the Euro 2000 competition.

They were offering to pay the official Equity rates, which for a choir of 60 volunteers turned out to be just over £5000, and it was scheduled to happen at short notice in George Martin's Air Studios in Hampstead. We jumped at the opportunity to get into the prestigious studio, and also earn the huge fee, and had a sing-through of the emotive and suddenly controversial song at our next scheduled rehearsal.

The Air Studios were every bit as impressive as we had hoped. The recording complex was in an old church building that was now acoustically insulated and equipped with massive mixing desks, separate sound booths and rooms full of equipment. The producer had booked us in for a full evening's work, but our prepared professionalism took him by surprise and after about fifty minutes we had it done. With over two hours left to play with we had a tea break and worked out some more elaborate harmonies. The second take was even better than the first, and apart from a boy treble who did the first line, the finished recording is all us; the assorted 'Fat Les' celebrities aren't really audible in the mix!

The single was released a few weeks later and we were delighted to find that an extra Pet Shop Boys dance remix of us had been included on the CD. A month or so later, when the England football team played Ukraine at Wembley stadium a group of us got to perform 'Jerusalem' live on the pitch before the game started. From where we were it sounded as if the wildly enthusiastic capacity crowd were all singing along.

The single started to go up the charts and we were then asked to perform it on Top of the Pops. We spent an afternoon and evening with Fat Les at the Elstree Studios, being repeatedly filmed miming to our own music along with several other pop groups who were fashionable that week. Nobody took it very seriously, Alex James asked to wear one of our black and white logo T-shirts for the session, and on the video appears to be a member of the chorus. Michael Barrymore was in the tabloids that week for dumping his wife and claiming to be bisexual; he got embarrassingly 'emotional' in the bar afterward. The jingoistic old hymn got to number seven in the charts before the England team was knocked out of the competition and then it dropped like a stone. Although a commercial pop single may seem like one of the most trivial things we have ever done, in some respects it signalled some very profound changes in British culture. An out gay chorus featuring on a prime-time, mainstream music programme, or being invited to Wembley, would not have happened ten years previously.

Because it had been a hit single, as well as a rather good story, we included the song in our next concert. Keith Allen came along to the Piccadilly Theatre to sing it with us, whilst we all waved red and white St George's flags.

Jerusalem is undeniably a very patriotic song, and although we had now performed it on Top of the Pops, a truly venerable cultural institution; we hardly felt ourselves to be the new ambassadors of British culture. We were very surprised when only a couple of months later that is exactly what we turned out to be.

TEN

All the way to San Jose

Although we were not aware of it when starting London Gay Men's Chorus, the idea of gay choirs was actually an American invention. The first one seems to have been formed in San Francisco at the end of November 1978 after the out gay mayor, Harvey Milk, was assassinated. The original idea has now grown into an international movement, and every four years the American Gay and Lesbian Association of Choirs (GALA) holds a big festival where all the relevant groups gather together to give a series of concerts. There was a festival happening that year in San Jose, California, and we decided to go along.

No Arts Council grant or external funding was available to us, so everyone involved had to pay their own air fares and accommodation; it would be a very exciting, but expensive summer holiday, and nearly sixty of us were able to participate.

Many British people thought of California as the birthplace of gay culture, and the chorus trip there was going to be a huge undertaking. In order to make the journey to the west coast a bit easier, and also to make the whole thing more worthwhile, we arranged for a stopover and concert with the Boston Gay Men's Chorus on the way. They would be able to host us for a few days and then we would travel on to the main festival in San Jose together.

All the planning and preparation for the American trip had been going on for so long that it was a shock to finally arrive at Heathrow airport and board a plane. Everyone had booked their own flights so we weren't sitting in one big group, which was probably just as well; spirits were so high that I can imagine a rowdy party would have ensued if we had been together. It wasn't until we landed at Logan airport in Boston that the chorus really assembled, and in the arrivals hall we were greeted by the welcoming committee from the Boston Chorus with a great big banner that simply said 'Hello'; it was the nicest welcome we could have had. We paired up with our hosts and set off to unpack and get ready for the joint concert on the following day.

In preparation for our debut before an international audience we had commissioned a new piece of music. The composer Morgan Hayes was a very avant-garde pianist, and he had set a poem written by one of our members, John Moysen, to some very discordant and atonal 'crashing' piano sounds. It was all about the gay obsession with gym culture and was called 'Citizen Vain'. We had tried out the weird piece of musical experimentation in one of our London shows at the Piccadilly Theatre, but the real premiere of it was going to be at the Boston concert.

The Blackman Auditorium at Boston University is a medium sized theatre, plain, utilitarian, and very satisfactory for our needs. Apart from some uncertainty as to where the huge grand piano would cause the least obstruction, the run through went smoothly enough. The Boston chorus had gathered for their rehearsal and a sound-check, so we did a swift 'Love Don't Need a Reason', planned as a joint encore, and left them to it.

We all went off to find local food and snacks, so it wasn't until the first half of the show itself that we heard what they sounded like. Their set started with a couple of show tunes, and then a camp anthem `Keep it Gay', before they launched into excerpts from 'Eos', a seriously 'big concept' CD length piece. It was all very polished and professional, and was well received by their regular local audience. I found it reassuring that a degree of mockery and camp was obviously an acceptable idea, but rather worrying that the standard was set so high. Were we going to be good enough? Everyone understands that joint concerts are not competitions, but comparisons are unavoidable.

Perhaps a little tension in the air is a good thing; maybe it makes you try a bit harder. Whatever the mysterious mechanics of good, or bad, performances are, that time it worked in our favour. I think it was probably the best show we put on in the whole of the U.S. tour. The full length and uncensored version of the trashy pop song `Barbie Girl', was undoubtedly one of the highlights. Robin played the part of Barbie, and even without his usual London helpers and dressers, still managed to give a turbo-powered performance that bought the house down. The next item was meant to be a formal statement from the British Consul, and the poor ambassadorial assistant who had to deliver it had a very difficult time maintaining his dignity. Very endearingly, he managed to accidentally 'out' himself in the process.

Before launching into the new 'Citizen Vain' song, Jeremy explained to the audience that we were going to try something a bit different. They listened to the piece, and applauded afterwards, but we wondered if it was just good manners. We also included two Robert Frost poems set to music by the American composer Randall Thompson. The first of these was bright, life-affirming and joyous, but the second piece, called 'Stopping by Woods' was slower, immensely quiet and spoke enigmatically of the many miles we would have to go before we slept. We could feel an intensity hanging in the air, and a gasp of admiration came from the audience when we finished that section of the show on a darkened stage with bowed heads and closed eyes.

There was a brief speech from our chairman Steve, and then another formal address from the assistant to the Mayor. He announced that we were considered to be cultural representatives of Great Britain, and the London Gay Men's Chorus had been awarded the freedom of the City of Boston. It had been a really good concert. As so often when on stage, one's perception of time passing was completely disrupted; suddenly we were doing the joint number with the host chorus and then the show was over.

Many of us stayed up late, celebrating and exploring the local gay scene, and at 6.45 the next morning the bedraggled bunch of singers that gathered in the airport fast-food cafe looked burned out and hung over. Whilst waiting to board the plane we compared notes and wondered what San Jose and the big festival was going to be like.

The plane was tiny, primitive looking, and packed full. We flew, hour after hour, across the entire width of the American continent and the huge landscape was magnificent. Cityscapes slipped rapidly away and dropped beyond the horizon; a perfect geometrical quilt of pastel-coloured agriculture extended in all directions. A plastic-wrapped budget breakfast of anonymous puffy carbohydrates was served, and hundreds of miles later the geographical jigsaw still spread with a trance-like repetition beneath the wings.

It changed, really abruptly, when we reached Colorado. A great divide had been crossed and the wild mountains now filled the moving map with a random tawny abstraction. At thirty thousand feet our own living reflections on the inside of the cabin window were being superimposed transparently on to the slowly shifting scenery beneath; like a mirage, the inside floated over the outside. I was lost in tiredness, introspection and wonder; this day was all so very strange, and this continent so vast. I looked at the profile of the clean-cut business man sitting next to me, and he never hesitated as he typed incessantly into his laptop. The smooth cocoon of the Great American Dream might have been an illusion; but for some of the time, for most of the people, it mostly worked just fine.

The great white drifts of Utah's salt lakes stretched

grandly beneath us. Any human being would have been less than microscopic in that stupendous and alien flatland. I could sense the emptiness of blue void surrounding the thin shell of our aeroplane.

As we were coming in to land at San Jose, the works of man became all too evident again. There was the biggest collection of private jets I have ever seen, lined up like basking beetles at the edge of the runways. This was the infamous Silicon Valley, and some people would think of it as the cutting edge of our entire evolutionary destiny. The airport buildings were low rise concrete slabs; palms swayed, the air was hot and drying.

It had been an internal flight, so there were no immigration or customs procedures, just straight off to 'baggage claim' and the exit. Some of us boarded the coach that was waiting and others had hire cars booked. We would not all meet again until the rehearsal at the city's Civic Auditorium. I got in a big white hire-car with Paul and Dan, and the three of us made our way to the University of Southern California student dorms to register for our accommodation. It was about a ten minute drive, and then a two and a half hour wait to get to the head of the huge queue at the dormitory office.

An understandably bored collection of blond, laid-back, low-rent Californian secretaries assigned us our rooms at random; the chorus was now dispersed all over the huge campus. Nobody knew where anyone else was staying; everyone felt like finding a bed and catching up on some sleep. What time zone were we in now?

Paul, Dan and I couldn't bear the thought of being so

close to San Francisco and not seeing it. We got in the car and drove off. With only a postcard sized map to guide us we were soon lost in the sweeping tangle of freeways. Driving, walking and exploring, we wondered at how all the filmic scenery looked so familiar and yet felt so alien. We missed the official Gala festival opening ceremony, but heard from others who made it that it was a predictably tedious presentation of worthy speeches.

The Gala festival was a huge event. With two large theatre spaces in the city centre running continuous shows simultaneously, sometimes from 9.45am to 11pm at night; it was not physically possible to see everything that was going on. The chorus would all assemble together for our own shows, (on the Tuesday afternoon and the Friday morning) but otherwise we mostly went round in twos or threes, bumping into other little groups of singers as we raced between hotel and theatre, snack bar or conference centre, swapping notes on the run. "You must see the Turtle Creek Choral," or "Have you caught the Rainbow Group from Delaware?" sometimes it was just "Where the hell's our next rehearsal?"

Apart from the amazing singing that was being presented, there were also small-scale workshops on all sorts of other choir related topics, anything from fund-raising and choral improvisation, to strategic planning and media skills. There was a market hall in the main Conference Centre where you could buy sparkly badges, macho watches, and of course a thousand gay CDs. In addition to this were film shows and meet-the-composer receptions and, of course, everywhere you went was thronging with eager gay men.

As if there wasn't already enough going on in the festival, several of the larger choirs were putting on their own exclusive events. San Francisco Gay Men's Chorus hired the ballroom of the Fairmont hotel and staged The `X' Party; loud disco, dance floor and laser light-show, fan-dancing muscle men, a budget of thousands. Boston held a much more select reception; the canapés included a four foot long silver gondola, overflowing with pacific prawns on ice. LGMC weren't one of the `big' groups, but for various reasons, we were a bit notorious. We hadn't planned to do a social event, but then thought we ought to, and spontaneously decided to stage an English afternoon tea party.

Andy Ford, Neil and I raced over to the internet cafe one lunch time and used their PC to put together an invitation, the 24 hour printer did two thousand copies for the next day, and the chorus spread them around. The catering corps (Tony Matuska, Tony Miller, Andre, Robin Thompson and Martin McGonnigle.) somehow managed to bake one and a half thousand scones in the dorm kitchens on the Thursday morning. Martin Brophy obtained an obscene amount of aerosol cream and twenty catering-size buckets of strawberry jam. Tea urns were supplied by a local company, Peet's Tea. Trestle tables came from a pushy lady who was something to do with the GALA organisation; she bullied the nearby hotel until they agreed to lend them to her.

We held our genteel afternoon tea party in a little landscaped park surrounded by traffic in the city centre, apparently without the correct official permission from the civic authorities. The cops turned up and demanded that we remove our string of Union Jack bunting, but perhaps remembering the Stonewall Riot fiasco, decided it was best to let the gay boys continue serving free cream-scones. The temperature must have been a hundred degrees, and it was wonderfully eccentric. Pinafore costumed members of the chorus paired up to distribute the scones, one serving, and the other squirting cream. We circulated with napkins and trays, and with style, snobbery and a fair amount of innuendo, served our guests. The crowd loved it. There were complaints later on that the concert audience from the nearby Civic Auditorium was severely depleted as most of them came out to join us. If it wasn't for the photos, it would be hard to believe it really happened. In the middle of California, it made us all feel very proud to be British.

Our more official performances on stage went down a storm, even our version of the song `Crying Game', which went so catastrophically flat that it actually sounded intentional and artistic. The premiere of our newly commissioned piece 'Citizen Vain', at the first show, was greeted with such a stunned silence that at the end Jeremy had to turn around and announce, "OK, that's it", before anyone realised it had finished and politely began to applaud.

There are a thousand strange memories from that week in San Jose, some were shared with others as part of an audience in one of the concert halls, and others were more solitary. I remember seeing the startling iridescence of tiny 'chin-strap' humming birds as they hovered and flashed in the warm dusk air, and the perfect poetry of a bare-chested and brown-skinned man, dancing with a sweeping rainbow flag beside a turquoise pool. A group of us sat with two thousand others and were so moved as we listened to the men's chorus from Seattle singing that we cried. I wept again for the Rainy City Chorus, but they were tears of laughter at the wit and invention of their genius choreographer.

If it wasn't for the huge choral festival in the place, the city of San Jose would have been very dull; nothing but shopping malls, freeways and tower blocks full of software corporations. The local business owners must have been very glad to have all the extra customers. One evening The Grand America amusement park, situated in the waste land beyond the town suburbs, bizarrely declared it to be 'gay night'. Many of the nearly six thousand excited gay singers boarded coaches from the city centre and had the wildest of late-night parties on their extravagantly over-sized roller coasters.

There were, naturally, catastrophes as well as highlights. For us, the biggest must have been when our conductor crashed. One day Jeremy just ground to a halt. With all the activities on offer I think most of us had been getting a bit run down and over-tired. Jeremy, however, managed to get genuinely and seriously ill with hepatitis. As the week went by he gradually became more and more exhausted. By the time of our final show in Grace Cathedral, San Francisco, he was unable to continue. Some of us felt it was the end of the line and that we would have to cancel. The chorus had an official 'assistant musical director', Roland, but he was three thousand miles away, preparing for a gig in Manchester with the chorus group who had stayed behind. Fortunately, the tour group was by then a well-oiled machine and we discovered that we had in our midst a secret weapon. Most of us realised that Chris Pethers was an accomplished musician, but at that time he had never actually conducted us. He was able to step forward and put on such a convincing show that a lot of us approximately followed his directions. There was only one song which didn't work, `Barbie Girl' came out so fast that it sounded like `Bubgl', but perhaps we shouldn't have been doing that in a cathedral anyway. The quiet confidence of Chris Pethers had saved the day for us, but after that extraordinary debut he unobtrusively resumed his regular singing part. It was many years later that he was to step forward again and become our assistant musical director and a corner-stone of the organisation.

Our final San Francisco concert was put on in conjunction with the local 'Golden Gate Chorus' and 'Melo Men', from Paris. After the show we all went out to an authentic, but actually rather messy, Chinese restaurant in the city, and yet another late night. It was the last event of our American tour. The next day we would all split up and have our own separate adventures; north, south and east, before meeting up again in London.

As the quintessentially Californian band Grateful Dead had sung so many years before, 'what a long strange trip it's been'.

ELEVEN
The Queen Mother and the Roundhouse

In the ten years since the chorus had started the cultural climate of the country had changed. In the beginning there was widespread homophobia and we were considered to be outcasts from the fabric of society, shunned, feared and legislated against. By the end of the decade the tide had turned and the chorus was able to appear on family TV shows, participate in national competitions, and raise funds for established charities. What part we played in that transformation we will never know, we may have ridden a swell that was already in motion, or we may have been part of initial irritation that started the inexorable rolling of that wave of change.

Our original participation in the Choir of the Year Competition in 1996 had been almost accidental; we had no expectations and were staggered when we were chosen as 'Choir of the day'. We continued to enter the competition every two years after, and in 2000 were again chosen as Choir of the day and went on to the semi-finals which were to be held in the esteemed Buxton Opera House.

We had always defied convention by introducing

contemporary pop music to this serious competition, and that year decided we could go one step further and include some light hearted choreography. Our version of Teddy Bears Picnic started off as a formal presentation, but towards the end of the song a small group of the 'heavier' chorus members appeared with clip-on furry ears and did a dancing teddy bears jig around the front of the stage. They cavorted, hid, played and hugged whilst the front row of singers did chorus-line high kicks behind them. It was an outrageously unpredictable thing to do, and the audience sprang to their feet with clapping, whooping and laughing.

We knew we were being unconventional, and weren't that surprised when the judging panel commented that we were being a bit too 'show business' for the context. The BBC was filming the whole thing, and when the programme was shown over Christmas, Howard Goodall said he had never seen anything like it happen in the Choir of the Year Competition before. Many years later there were TV programmes such as 'Musicality', 'Last Choir Standing' and 'Britain's Got Talent', where all sorts of groups got up to all sorts of games, but no choirs did it on TV till we showed them how.

Sometimes it was necessary for us to challenge the law because specific legislation was unjust, and sometimes we just wanted to bend the rules and have some fun. It wasn't often that some venerable institution could turn the tables and take us by surprise, but it happened shortly after the Buxton competition.

For the chorus to be considered as participants in any

recognisable establishment activity was still unexpected, and we were astonished to get a request from the BBC to take part in a programme that was being prepared as a memorial for the Queen Mother. She was then a hundred years old, and for all significant national figures, obituaries are discreetly and disconcertingly prepared in advance.

The producer of the TV programme had been a member of the chorus for a while, but before his time with us Kris had been a military footman on duty at Clarence House. The BBC obviously realised he had the proven patriotic credentials necessary to work on this important obituary project, and when some extra backing vocals were needed for a particular four-minute sequence, Kris suggested that The London Gay Men's Chorus could do it.

Being asked to sing for a person as significant as the Queen Mother was an awesome prospect; but we couldn't help but feel appalled with the macabre knowledge that our song was destined to be part of her memorial.

One Tuesday morning, a small team of us went to the Oasis TV studios in Soho, wondering what on earth we were getting involved in. As it turned out the actual music recording was a joyous and high-spirited affair, and the resultant section of the finished film a mixture of the poignant and triumphant that would have been difficult to achieve with spoken words alone; the right song can sometimes express feelings so much more effectively.

The section we were to participate in showed a Smithfield meat-market porter, telling the story of an official visit from the Queen Mother many years previously. As she had progressed around the market, a group of porters had gathered and sung her a song, "If you were the only girl on the world..." and presented her with an honorary membership of the union of meat-market porters, known somewhat unfortunately as 'bummerees'.

We were to sing the song for the soundtrack. We donned headphones and formed a tight half circle in the tiny sound-proofed booth.

Banks of slick black equipment glowed and the TV monitors flickered into life. The first run through was a bit tense; we came out sounding like opera singers, rather than market porters. The producer conferred with the engineer whilst we practised in the stifling studio. We had another go and added a cockney accent. "If you were..." became "if yew wos..." it sounded much more authentic and that was the recording which was chosen.

Allen was asked to whistle the tune for an earlier section of the film. The recording was then put through an echo chamber so that it seemed to float eerily across the great vaulted glass ceiling of the Smithfield market hall. The producer seemed pleased, and whilst the engineer did a bit more editing and splicing, we retired to 'the lounge' and devoured the large box of cream cakes that had appeared for us.

Half an hour later we all went back into the studio and watched the final edit.

As the sentimental little anecdote unfolded, the atmospheric soundtrack fitted in and flowed with the narrative, the song swelling into the foreground for the final images.

It was a perfect little exemplar of visual story-telling. On the 30th March 2002, when the Queen Mother died aged 101, the piece was televised nationally.

The original chorus group had developed out of social and political necessity. A profound love of music making was always part of the equation, but we had evolved from a gay social group, so initially there were no links or affiliations with any other musical organisations, it wasn't long before some formed. The 'Super-choir' that was put together for the first Royal Albert Hall event had demonstrated to us the value of some choral cross fertilisation, then the Choir of the Year Competitions showed us what was possible in group singing and how high the standards could become. We gradually came across all sorts of other choirs, gay, straight, mixed and multi-voiced, youth, senior, local or international, and realised that whether we had intended it or not, we had become part of a diverse and widespread musical community.

The richness and power of that community was brought to light when the Flemish theatre producer Alain Platel, came across the Last Night of the Proms on Belgian TV, and was amazed at how many people sing and the power this has. This unified and controlled exhalation of air seemed to have a primeval and universal magic. He contacted an unconventional choir leader named Orlando

Gough, and together they were inspired to use the investigation of groups who sing as the basis for an extraordinary cultural project called 'Because I Sing'.

They got financial support from Bloomberg Bank, advice and guidance from an artistic promotions company 'Artangel', and backing from Channel Four TV, then began to research the bewildering variety of multi-cultural groups and choirs that they knew they could find in cosmopolitan London.

I was first contacted by them in mid-1999, and after nearly two years of development, the project culminated in a concert performed four times at The Roundhouse in Camden during March and April of 2001.

The vague idea sketched out in their initial letter gradually developed into a tidal wave of emails as time passed and concepts expanded. Dozens of ideas were explored, meetings were arranged and visits made. By early 2000 a shortlist of choirs had been drawn up and days and dates for a huge collaborative performance were being discussed.

We were by far the largest single group involved, and comparatively well organized, but there were fifteen choirs altogether, and the logistics of staging such a large scale happening had to be confronted and explored with thought and care.

Once work started on the construction of twelve huge moveable staircases, we knew that a Rubicon had been crossed; this amazing event was really going to happen.

It was such a complicated exercise to bring all the participants together that only two rehearsals were possible before the first performance. On the opening night Will Morgan, an actor and singer with The Shout, stood prepared at the very edge of the upper balcony in the Roundhouse.

All around him the lights had dimmed down to darkness. The circular sea of upturned faces faded. He flexed his diaphragm, exhaled across a taught larynx, and sang.

Ancient Arabic words echoed across the dome of the old building. "Leh betghanni" (why do you sing?) From the outer dark all around, a reply came back from the massed choirs, "Ma baaref" (I don't know).

It was the beginning of a song cycle that carried on without interruption for the next one hour and forty minutes. A sweeping spectrum of sounds that seemed to arc across the whole of human experience; from deeply religious through classical to ethnic, folk, gospel, theatrical and political. Sometimes it was sombre and sublime, at others startling, convoluted and confrontational. Each of the choirs was positioned on its own moveable flight of steps, and sang its own choice of music. At various points the choirs, and the flights of steps, were all moved around and joined together, and we sang the unifying musical themes that connected the different sections into a single concept. During the final piece an enormously enlarged moving image of the human larynx in action was going to be projected on to a great circular screen, suspended like a giant Native-American dream-catcher above our heads.

Throughout the concert TV cameras were recording

their eerie electronic messages. Balancing and zooming from graceful telescopic booms; hunting, finding faces, transmitting coded data. Mixing-desk needles flickered, operators eyes edited, technician's ears were expectant; dreams were being captured. The mystery of why we sing was being explored.

This extraordinary concert was the culmination of a very long planning process, and whilst it was being developed a lot of other things had been going on. As soon as everybody returned from the American trip we began work on the second chorus CD. This continued until January, and then we unexpectedly got an offer of a 'short notice' cancellation booking for a potential concert at the Queen Elizabeth Hall.

Although the pressure of rehearsing and recording had been relentless for the last six months, we decided to accept the QEH offer. It was unfortunate that it was only three weeks before the start of the 'Because I Sing' event, but it was such a good opportunity to launch and promote our new CD.

For the majority of chorus members, their only awareness of the Because I Sing project had been limited to an occasional announcement, an odd fact about a strange idea, yet another film crew prowling around during the rehearsal. It only became a reality for the chorus when we were asked if we could change our choice of repertoire to make the overall mix of the Roundhouse programme 'a little lighter'.

Jeremy decided that we should put it to a vote; there were significant implications as to how we would appear in the spin-off 'Because I Sing' TV documentary that was being prepared by the film maker Sophie Fiennes.

The song 'Crying Game' was an early choice, but that had to be dropped because not enough of us knew it. 'Your Disco' was considered, but it wasn't very polished, and it was a shallow bit of fun, rather than a meaningful message. After an urgent last minute email vote, 'Keep your Lamps' was chosen, along with 'Keep it Gay', as our main contribution, it was on the last day before the programmes printing deadline. 'Teddy Bears Picnic' was thrown in as an afterthought, to be used during a strange ambient-noise interlude that provided cover for the moments when all the huge staircases were moved into position and the choirs gathered together for the finale.

Alain and Orlando had devised the programme of music to run seamlessly straight through, and had requested that the audience refrain from applauding until the end. It was a nice idea, but we couldn't help but feel secretly delighted when the crowd broke the rules and let out a huge cheer and clapped loudly after they watched us doing 'Keep it Gay' with choreography for the first time.

The atmosphere was extraordinary. The separate components of the evening were sewn together by a recurring chanted refrain, written by Orlando and Richard Chew. This was sometimes performed by their group, 'The Shout', and sometimes by different combinations of the other choirs. We felt that we were all participating in the same grand concept, and even though none of us had met before, a network of enduring collaboration and communication between the different choirs rapidly developed during the communal rehearsal breaks.

A sense of fellowship and solidarity established itself among the diverse performers. Only one group, The Congolese Christian Choir, seemed unable to relax their cultural barriers. After the first joint rehearsal their spokesperson complained that they didn't want their changing area to be anywhere near the gay men; they felt that 'gays' were diseased and dirty. The project director reassured them that they wouldn't catch anything, pointed out that there was limited space available in the Roundhouse, and told them to get over it.

We didn't hear any more officially about that clash of cultures, but if the Congolese group decided that their beliefs were not being respected, and they would have to take their own measures, it could perhaps have been connected to a disturbing incident that occurred during the final performance.

The sweeping flights of steps on which each choir was performing were in fact just light wooden shells sitting on top of cross-braced structures of scaffolding poles. Each unit was on wheels so that the separate pieces could be moved around into different configurations, and because we were such a large group, we had been allocated two of the highest and widest platforms bolted together.

We were in the middle of our set during the final show, when there was suddenly a loud and persistent metallic hammering sound from underneath one end of the platform, and the steps started to vibrate alarmingly.

Several of the stage hands who were positioned nearby whilst waiting for the next scene change raced forward and dived beneath our platform. There were muffled shouting and scuffling sounds, and from the corner of my eye I glimpsed a couple of dark figures running through the shadows beneath our flight of steps and disappearing through the fire-exit doors.

We hadn't stopped singing, and in fact many other people in the chorus didn't even realise what had been happening. I still suspect that sabotage had been attempted, not least because when I was eventually able to speak to the stage-hands after the show, they had already spoken to the director and I was met with a tight lipped, shifty-eyed and evasive silence. We were never able to find out anything more; nobody had been caught, questions remained frustratingly unanswered, and none of us actually knew what had really been going on.

The original inspiration of 'Because I Sing' had been a simple question, but after two years of project development it had turned into a gargantuan undertaking. During the performances, seven separate camera crews roamed the arena, all connected to an enormous outside broadcast unit in the car park. Hordes of lighting and sound technicians swarmed amongst the singers. Stage managers and a team of choir co-ordinators managed to keep everything running smoothly. Yet the elaborate arrangements were still flexible enough to allow for opportunities to fine-tune and alter the running order over the three evenings of public performance.

On the Thursday night the combination of Women's

Institute and Gay Men's chorus, known unofficially as 'the battle of the queens', worked particularly well, and was captured on film. On Saturday the Jewish Choir's slot had to be rearranged because they couldn't begin travelling until after sunset and the end of the Sabbath. For the final Sunday show I suggested to Alain Platel that we could do it differently yet again, and this time finish with a last round of the refrain and then a synchronised bow, to signal to the audience that this really was the end; my suggestions were incorporated and the show was concluded.

What an amazing week it had been, and what a lot of combined choral celebrations there were in the pubs of Camden after the last performance.

The event received huge press coverage. All the major national newspapers ran a feature on it, and when, some months later, Sophie's documentary was shown on Channel Four, it got impressive ratings and was again favourably reviewed. At the end of that year, when the newspapers ran their reviews of the previous twelve months, the music critic of the Times named the 'Because I Sing' meeting between The Women's Institute and The London Gay Men's Chorus as his musical highlight of the year.

The original question "Why do you sing?" was deliberately left unresolved. Our irrefutable and enigmatic conclusion was provided by the lyrics in one of our final shared pieces. The statement was simply, "I sing because I sing".

TWELVE
Planet Upside Down Under

Jeremy had been with the chorus for nearly six years, and Because I Sing was supposed to have been his final concert. He had just given up his teaching post and was working for the newly formed internet project 'Queercompany' with Steve and a few other chorus members. Although he had devoted all his spare time to the chorus he had never been paid any wages, and his relentless personal sacrifice of time and money had just become too great. There was no escaping the fact that his departure would be a devastating loss to the chorus, in both emotional and musical terms, but it had to be faced.

Roland had been acting as Assistant Musical Director, and assisted by Chris, they tried to fill the gap. We all knew and accepted that it would never be the same, but were nevertheless surprised at quite how quickly it became apparent that it wasn't going to work. It certainly wasn't due to any lack of musical expertise, and both had been part of the chorus for several years, so there was no 'culture shock' factor. It was some intangible chemistry that didn't produce the right results and rehearsals were no longer enjoyable. Jeremy had been a populist educator, no one was ever left out or overlooked during his rehearsals. Roland didn't seem to have as much patience; many of us felt he went too fast and skimmed over the details. The non-music readers in the chorus rapidly became disenfranchised. The solid cohesion of the assembly broke down and the music just didn't happen. We continued to go through the motions, but it felt as if the poetry had no power inside it.

We had known that Chris was temporary and would have to stand down because of work commitments. The expectation was always that Roland would lead in the long term, but then suddenly Roland's loyalties were split in two. He and three other members had formed the group 'Four Poofs and a Piano' just before the LGMC were hired to do a pilot for the new Jonathan Ross Show. There were intimations that this show could turn into a regular booking for us, so we were keen to get involved. It wasn't a difficult requirement, a group of us would just have to sing excerpts from a couple of vaguely topical songs each week, and we made a good job of the pilot try-out. As we were leaving the studio Roland privately mentioned to the producer that 'Four Poofs' could do it, and would charge less. A few weeks later we heard that they had undercut the fee the chorus had quoted, and had landed a contract to be the regular resident house-band.

At an emergency Steering Committee meeting Roland was asked to resign as Musical Director. Unsurprisingly, he decided to leave the chorus altogether and 'Four Poofs' went on to achieve fame and fortune. Jeremy was asked to come back temporarily so that we could continue work on the show we had planned for the end of that year.

It was 2001, the tenth anniversary of the chorus. We wanted to do something a bit higher profile than usual, and had been discussing a combined Christmas concert and Birthday celebration. I had successfully applied for a £5000 lottery grant, and for the first time ever we had some external funding and could stage a bigger and more ambitious production. In spite of the uncertainties of our own internal rearrangements, we were all optimistic that we could make this concert an extra special event.

We were all hugely relieved that Jeremy had been temporarily reclaimed, and the chorus held its first rehearsal of the new season at the beginning of September. It was then that the events now remembered as '9/11' happened.

Two planes flew into the twin towers in New York, and for a while it seemed as if the whole world held its breath and waited.

After only a few hours we heard from our friends in the New York Gay Men's Chorus that several of their members had been in the towers and were now listed as missing. In London we were all horribly aware that we too lived in a great city that was acknowledged to be a terrorist target.

There was a widespread expectation that there would be American retaliation and global war was inevitable. Transatlantic air travel was instantly suspended and the appalling images of carnage and ruin were replayed endlessly on the news; any thoughts of recreational tourism ceased. As the weeks passed the imminent threat of total war receded, but it would be a very long time before any travellers or city dwellers could ever disregard those nightmare images.

During the preceding summer break a small group of five from the chorus had been rehearsing with a dozen singers from other London choirs. The project was an ecologically themed song-cycle for the Thames Festival called 'Ballads for a Living Planet'. The performance was due to take place on Saturday 15th September, on the embankment promenade adjacent to The Festival Hall, and we wondered if the entire event would be cancelled. It might have seemed foolhardy, but somehow we felt that regardless of whatever the official policy might be, we should carry on.

It was a complex and intricate hour-long piece that involved costumed actors, poets and a small brass band, so on the appointed day we met up early for a final rehearsal. The centre of London was eerily silent and empty, and we imagined we would be left standing on the riverbank alone, performing the 'Living Planet' songs for ourselves and a few seagulls.

It was the right decision to carry on, and by lunchtime there seemed to be many other members of the public who felt the same way. It was poignant and apt that our Ballads dealt with pessimism, death and the end of civilisation. People wandered along the embankment walkway and stopped to listen to us. There was both horror and hope; we looked each other in the eye, and then beyond to the great buildings of the city centre.

Music and song is intangible, nothing more than a

vibration passing through the air. The feelings that are generated are transitory and unquantifiable, and we have little idea why it seems to be necessary, but at the right time and in the right place, it is.

It's said that the psyche of the American people changed for ever on the day of the twin towers tragedy, not just in what they did or where, but in the way that they thought about themselves. There were certainly long-term repercussions all over the world, and one of the unexpected consequences was that in the ensuing months many of the theatres in the West End of London had to shut down.

With few tourists in the city and an apprehensive resident population, audiences dwindled and one production after another closed its doors. There were exhortations from the mayor that it was our patriotic duty to go out and support the cultural industries, special-price ticket offers appeared in all the newspapers, but one by one the theatres went under.

We were trying to find a venue for our Christmas show and the prospects looked bleak. No one could be confident that they would still be open in December, and we began to look around for alternatives. I remembered seeing something about The Barge House, a derelict warehouse space behind Oxo wharf, and went along to have a look. It really was an empty shell; if we tried to put on a show there we would have no electricity, no stage, amplified sound or lighting, no chairs or heating. The chorus as well as the audience would have to wear coats and carry torches, and I felt it should be our grim task to articulate all the fears that were being experienced. I began to devise an apocalyptic 'end of the world' concert. There would be drifting smoke, barking dogs and howling sirens, uniformed figures would stand in silence; menacing black-robed wraiths on stilts would stride around in the gloom with hand held spotlights. The chorus would sing lamentation, sorrow and anger, and then walk away to some other icy upper floor, the audience would have to follow or else be left alone in the shadowy nightmare.

I shared this dark scenario with Jeremy, but even if he understood the exorcism I was proposing, he didn't want to go there, and so we waited.

A month before the show we heard that the production of 'Rent', then running at the Prince of Wales Theatre just behind Piccadilly Circus, was planning to ride out the storm and try to stay open. They were running at a loss and desperate for any extra income; we hurriedly signed a contract to hire the place for one night and with crossed fingers printed our tickets. The set was an uncannily accurate reconstruction of a wretched New York alleyway, and although we didn't sing all the apocalyptic songs of my fantasy, it did feel like an environment that was gritty and harsh enough to accommodate some pertinent social statement.

The tenth anniversary concert wasn't much like the show that we had been envisaging for the previous twelve months, but miraculously we managed to sell all the tickets and it was successful. The throwaway encore was an extravagantly over-the-top rendition of Copacabana, and that laughable song was the last instance of Jeremy conducting the London Gay Men's chorus as our Musical Director.

In January 2002 we hurriedly put out adverts in the national press and music trade papers for a new Musical Director. Martin Brophy was now our chorus chairman, he was very clued up about the proper way to run a business and keep track of income and expenditure. We had at last been accepted as an officially registered charity, had drawn up budget forecasts and for the first time were now offering to pay a realistic wage to any potential new conductor; the chorus was growing up.

Formal interviews were held and a short list of potential candidates drawn up. Paper qualifications were only part of the picture, the real acid test was finding out if the person had the charisma to empower the chorus, and whether the membership would respect the authority of the conductor, so each candidate had the daunting ordeal of an audition rehearsal with the whole chorus.

At the last moment Charlie Beale turned up out of the blue. He had not seen any of the adverts but had heard about the post from another choir. As well as teaching at the Royal College of Music he led a jazz big-band, so passed his 'baptism by fire' chorus audition with flying colours; we were confident we had found our Mr Right.

There were occasional moments of tension and flashes of uncertainty as new patterns were established, but we felt that a crisis had been passed, rehearsals were relaxed and enjoyable again and preparations for the next show got under way. It was the early summer of Golden Jubilee year, and we had a run of small informal performances booked at the plethora of charity lunches and street parties. This would give us all the opportunity to get to know each other without the pressure of any major events.

The Heartland Gay Men's Chorus from Kansas were touring Europe that summer, and we put on a little show with them in a Highgate pub. It was a chance for us to run some of the pieces that would feature in our main Queen Elizabeth Hall Jubilee concert a month later. We couldn't resist calling the QEH show 'The London Gay Men's Chorus celebrates a Golden Reign' and half hoped that there would be tabloid outrage at the disrespectful double meaning of the title; but perhaps luckily, nobody outside the gay community picked up on the very unsavoury 'golden rain' joke.

Apart from the fact that we had Melo Men, a gay choir from Paris, and Surrey Harmony, a women's barber shop chorus, joining us on the two successive nights of the Queen Elizabeth Hall concerts; it was more or less the standard chorus production of a very mixed classical and pop repertoire incorporating a couple of comedy moments. Alisdair gave the audience a wickedly accurate 'queen's speech' and there was a glitter bomb for the finale. Our newly found director Charlie was waiting to see what we could do before he introduced us to any of his own ideas.

In November 2002 the chorus went down under. The 'Gay Games', a sort of alternative Olympics, were being held in Sydney, Australia, and as well as all the sporting events taking place there was going to be a great cultural festival. Choirs and choruses from all over the world were invited to participate, and the culmination was to be a concert in the awesome Sydney Opera House.

At the previous American GALA festival held in San Jose, the choral performances had all been in the formal settings of two big theatres, it was very much an event by, for and about gay culture; the general population didn't get much involved. In the Sydney Gay Games celebration, the performances were spread out in all sorts of unlikely venues throughout the city, audiences were the general public, and the whole populace seemed to be invited and involved in the festivities.

During the two weeks of the cultural festival, the fifty of us who went to Australia had only two days when we weren't performing somewhere. Locations ranged from a grand room full of formal portraits in the Art Gallery of New South Wales to the commercial bustle of a mid-town Victorian shopping mall; from an open-air stage in the Sydney central park to the echoing emptiness of an industrial warehouse at Darling Harbour where a section of the AIDS memorial quilt was on show. The original memorial quilt had been started in America around the mid-1980s, and the Australian extension to it was begun in September 1988. Each embroidered panel measured 180 x 90 cm, and since this display incorporated both native and imported panels it was a huge and heartrending presentation of bereavement. The chorus stood at one end and sang as people wandered thoughtfully along the footpaths laid out between the panels, and for once were glad that the atmosphere wasn't interrupted by applause.

Since all the events we were performing at were of differing character, our repertoire had to be flexible. To make sure we were 'tuned in' to what was required, rehearsals were arranged before each one. It was rare to be able to hold a rehearsal in the proper venue, so we got to travel everywhere in the city, gathering in scruffy colleges and church halls in the suburbs as well as in the regular tourist sites of the centre.

One of the strangest events took place on a blazing hot afternoon at the Olympic swimming pool, and was part of the presentation from the British 'Out to Swim' competitors. The Olympic pools complex had been built right on the edge of the city, and the journey there started with a long train ride through the suburbs. Each station seemed to have a familiar name, Orpington, Oxford, Twickenham, Enfield, Bromley, but to our London eyes they were all in a surreal wrong order.

When we arrived at the sports centre the chorus assembled on the tiled walkway between two huge swimming pools. We played the part of a plane-full of stuffy business men in plastic novelty bowler hats and pin-stripe suits we had brought all the way from London. At the end of the song, 'There Ain't nothing Like the Games', we all stripped off in front of the audience of a thousand buffed up swimmers and dived into the water.

With over nine thousand participants in the main gay sporting events, and lots of supporters and cultural visitors as well, the city was overwhelmed with parties and gay celebration. The scale of the proceedings was apparent when we sang at the official opening ceremony, held in the vast Aussie Stadium. The capacity crowd of twenty thousand heard an empowering opening address from Chief Justice Michael Kirby, and was then entertained by an amazing display of laser lights and pyrotechnics. We got to sing with a bare-footed k.d. lang, and also heard from Jimmy Somerville and the local opera diva Debra Cheetham during the course of the evening. From our prime front-row seats we watched a presentation of choreographed Aboriginal ritual using 6-metre high puppets, a spectacular carnival costume parade and an extraordinary motorbike ballet put on by the local dykes.

Everything about the Australian trip seemed to be excessive: the magnificent beaches at the end of every bus route; the space-age architecture of the city itself; watching fruit bats circling the skyscrapers at midnight; the open-air all-night parties and the macho muscle men in the gay bars on Oxford Street. Some of these tourist attractions were predictable and deliberately sought out, but on other occasions one could be startled by something unannounced and everyday; the alien strangeness of the 'strangler-fig' trees in the parks or the weirdly sculptured sandstone cliffs at Bondi Beach; the enormous snake I saw one afternoon in the car park at Botany Bay, or the chance discovery of a lively Chinese market at the bottom of George Street. To those of us who were used to organising and stage-managing our own chorus activities, it was inspiring to understand the metropolitan wide planning holding the massive 'Gay Games' together; a project on this scale was only possible through cooperation between civic authority and gay community.

On one of our free days we hired a couple of bush-whacker buses and drove out to see the epic grandeur of the Blue Mountains national park. In the southern-hemisphere summer of 2002, the area was being devastated by huge fires sweeping through the eucalyptus forests, and we could see great columns of smoke spiralling into the sky in the hazy distance. We were taken to see a colony of wild kangaroos in a shady valley with a cool stream, and then stopped for lunch in the forest at a lodge built from logs. During the afternoon our bronzed and burly bush-guide took us to some extraordinary natural limestone caverns. Created by some ancient waterfall, they were now suspended half way up a sheer cliff face. The rocks were banded with rusty ochre and streaked through with cream and rose. We walked in single-file along a narrow path as it wound through sculpted caves, and where it approached the edge huge mouth-like windows opened to reveal panoramic mountain scenery and a giddy azure sky.

Everyone must hold their own particular archive of treasured memories, but one experience we all shared was the concert in the landmark Sydney Opera House.

The pine-clad interior of the great building was

strangely reminiscent of an overgrown Viking long ship, and because the great arched roof canopies are all built on different levels, the backstage areas are a mass of cantilevered ramps and sweeping staircases. It looked modern from the outside, but the inside felt like a medieval cathedral.

It was somewhat cheeky of us to include a pop song from a home-grown Australian icon, but our version of Kylie Minogue's 'Can't get you out of my Head', with white gloves and clever choreography, was one of the highlights of the show. The insistent rhythm and bass notes of the catchy melody seemed to make the great sculpted ribs of the roof throb, and you could hear members of the audience still singing snatches of it on the Opera House terrace hours afterwards.

The next day there was a formal closing ceremony with solemn songs and sincere speeches, followed immediately by one last enormous party at the Fox Studios. Five thousand of the games' participants drank and danced in a laser-lit temporary village of marquees and tents. By the time the party was over the unfamiliar stars of the southern constellations had swept right round the sky and a new dawn was rising.

The Games were over and we split up to take our various routes back to the London winter. A little group of chorus members used the opportunity to fly north to Queensland where the great Captain Cook highway sweeps majestically around the glorious coastline, and tropical rain-forests fringe the coral-sand beaches. We spent some time recuperating in the spacey peace of the

Great Barrier Reef, and whilst reminiscing during a shared dinner at a beach café one evening, realised with some awe, that this amazing journey we were on had actually started long ago and far away, back in 1991 at the Angel tube station.

THIRTEEN

Christmas Unbroken on the Farm

The timing of our trip to Sydney meant that we more-or-less missed Christmas in 2002.

It was a season we usually enjoyed. As well as our own end-of-the-year shows there were so many other things going on. We sometimes got invitations to sing at exclusive private parties in Chelsea penthouses or Kensington mansions. One such event was for Charles Hart, who wrote the libretto for Phantom of the Opera. I was shocked to recognise an original Picasso in the hall, and there were Dali drawings going up the stairs, hordes of celebrities and costumed footmen at the front door. Once we got booked to do two spots every night for a week at the vegetarian restaurant in the ICA, and on the Saturday there was an outstanding 'Fire Ball' party event with Andrew Logan, Eartha Kitt and the people who put on the Alternative Miss World contest. It's not always glamourous, some years we don't get anything more exotic than carols under the Christmas tree in Covent Garden of Trafalgar Square.

Various charities would ask us to do carols and a collection, and these informal performances often took place in the rush hour amidst the grime and distraction of a main-line railway station; London Bridge, Euston and Kings Cross were all regular spots. It was always a challenge to try and compete with all the hustle and noise, but we could never say no to a worthy cause.

One of our favourite bookings was with the Vauxhall City Farm. It was a real community event, and because the local children were actively involved it had a very strong seasonal flavour. None of the other Christmas parties had anything like the same atmosphere, and our first year there was particularly memorable.

It was the 14th of December, and a cold, dull drizzle had been falling for most of the day, but as night fell, the sky cleared and a pale moon shone through a haze of mist.

I was supposed to be coordinating this event so had planned to arrive early, but got lost instead. I looked at the map, and tried to work out where a 'city farm' could possibly be hidden amongst such unremitting urban desolation.

In the distance, the incessant rage of rush-hour traffic roared around the complex of junctions and roundabouts at Vauxhall station. The pavements seemed deserted, and a quilting of dust and lead vapour had rendered everything into shades of dull grey

Tyers Street was a dark turning at the back of a deserted church. A hundred yards down it there was straw trodden into the road, and a ripe smell of turned earth and animals hung in the damp air. Through a brick arch was a muddy yard and a ramshackle cluster of little buildings with a row of stables and a tiny paddock. Bare bulbs glared overhead, and notices announcing 'The five rights of animals' were pinned on to doorposts.

A group of local carol singers had gathered in the meeting room. Candle light, steamy mulled wine and hot mince pies helped to kindle an air of expectation.

As we waited an odd assortment of people gradually filtered in. Ben, the farm manager, showed us around his little kingdom. Two big bristly pigs grunted and shuffled in their straw-filled sty. In the wooden stall next door a curly-coated mohair goat and an inquisitive and affectionate little sheep nuzzled and huffed. Jacko, the dear old donkey, stood patiently while his muzzle was stroked and fat flanks patted. There was a little brown cow, and a tiny bull calf named 'Red', a tall horse and a pair of sleek ferrets, one of them a pink eyed albino; chickens, ducks and a family of foxes that had taken up residence in an abandoned house two doors down.

It was all such an odd little oasis, a Noah's ark of logic, labour and caring amidst the urban predictability; a farm, in the city.

Back in the communal room, a dozen excited children bounced about and prepared tissue-paper lanterns. Twisted tinsel and a glaze of glitter were being added to painted faces and animal masks. We could hear that some players from a brass band had arrived and were practising in the yard outside. 'Santa Claus', in full festive rig, came out of the kitchen. We tucked our scarves into our coats and got ready to set off.

There must have been about forty in the party; a dozen

or so from the chorus, friends of the farm and family types with pushchairs, the trumpet and horns, Santa and Jacko the donkey. Sprigs of holly and song sheets were shared around, the night was now clearer and colder, stars glittered overhead, bells tinkled.

We ambled, a bit disruptively, down the little back streets. Shouts of laughter and snatches of carols disturbed the quiet of the evening. We soon discovered that a few of the girls in the party were part of a local women's performance group, and had excellent singing voices. This was suddenly turning into an amazing event, a proper little choir, live music on the move, striking visuals and improvised performance.

Santa, and a gaggle of children, stopped at a lamppost. The horns played a few notes and we all launched into 'Hark the Herald Angels'. Curtains were drawn back and silhouette figures waved. Front doors opened and the donkey leaned over a garden gate to investigate an outstretched hand.

The party moved on, singing boldly now, deeper into the maze of old Vauxhall.

We turned a corner and it was as if we had entered a different world. This little close of houses was cut off from the traffic outside. The residents had built extra garden beds on the pavement out of breeze blocks. Ivy climbed the telegraph poles and scrambled across the wires overhead, hanging shaggily on the gutters. Lamp posts twinkled behind screens of leaves and a spiky Chusan palm stood tall and exotic in one corner.

Children came out of the houses to witness the strange

and exciting things that were going on in the night air. The spirit of Christmas had arrived. The horns played 'Once in Royal David's City' and strangers joined in the singing. A small boy, his eyes wide with wonder, called out to the crimson-coated myth from an upstairs window. An old woman, pulling on her thick coat, came across the road to join us.

The party moved on.

Glad voices, singing the old music, echoed around the houses until we turned into a larger main road. The two horses stood, their breath steaming, in a perfectly posed cameo picture, framed by the glow of a suitably decorated Dickensian bay window. The traffic stopped and we crossed over the road to a brightly-lit pub.

The people inside peered through the plate glass to see the startling arrival of the spirit of Christmas on the pavement outside. "Show them the donkey", chanted the children with painted faces, as if to prove that we were more than just real, we were magical. The donkey ambled forward and lifted his great shaggy head into the pool of light; his gentle liquid eyes reflected a soft golden glow. And we were magical; suddenly alive, and unannounced, and walking through the night in the middle of Vauxhall. One middle-aged man seemed to be so startled and moved by the image of a collective folk memory suddenly appearing before him, that he impulsively ran after us and stuffed a folded ten pound note into the collecting box.

We moved on, magic doesn't tarry. There were songs to sing and other places to visit; we left a frosted sparkle of enchantment wherever we went.

The party wound across the front of Tesco, paused to sing 'Deck the Halls', and turned off towards a gentrified square of Georgian houses.

I had the strangest feeling that things were being changed. The heaps of builder's sand by the pavement seemed to transform into deep drifts of soft white snow. The skip full of discarded bathroom fittings took on the look of a great sleigh, laden with gifts and free for everyone. The lacquered paper lanterns glowed and swayed, wreaths of laurel and bright red berries hung upon the old lamp posts and the horns played 'Good King Wenceslas'. Harmonies hung in the air and a young mother listened from the shelter of an open front door, her baby bundled up and held close.

The icy night seemed to tingle with expectation. One of the local feral foxes paused to look at the scene from the top of a garden wall and then, like a wind-blown candle, evaporated silently away.

I caught a brief glimpse of a small dark figure I hadn't noticed before, was it a child? It stood beneath a tree at the edge of the party and sported stag's antlers. The hairs on the back of my neck prickled, this suddenly felt like more than folk-myth and children's make believe, it was strange and disquieting, as if the old magic was becoming manifest; strong, wild, pagan stuff was tangible and animate in the air.

Every Christmas that I had ever wanted, and knew could never be real, was happening all around. Stars glittered up above and spirits flickered and flew as the fairy tale extended. A cold wind did blow, but it felt as though a soft blanket of peace and warmth enfolded us all. Christmas was alive, and magic is afoot.

From somewhere a hip flask of brandy was passed around, and one of the home owners came out from a glowing doorway with a handful of forks and an oven-tray loaded with sizzling hot sausages.

We eventually arrived back at the city farm in Tyers Street, and the party slowly dispersed. What work we had done that night, weaving spells, walking the ancient paths and leaving behind us rich memories that might last for a lifetime. We carried echoes from the past, and we flung them forward into the future so that other children might remember.

The ageless songs had been sung.

The circle remains unbroken.

Robert and Louis, 1992, unknown photographer.

Chorus in Voicespace, 1994, unknown photographer.

Before the Toyah appearance at Pride, 1997, photo Robert Offord.

Choir of the Year competition,1996, photographer unknown.

Highgate Woods, 1998, photo Jo Marcou.

Michael and Pietre,
Down in the Woods, photo Jo Marcou.

The Launch of Pride and Live 8, 2005, photo Robert Offord.

Anti-gay protest at Warsaw Pride, 2010, photo Robert Offord.

No to Hate, Trafalgar Square, 2009, photo Nic Chinardet.

On the 'Sno Graham Norton' set, 1998, photo Michael Cheetham.

Blue Mountains Trip, Sydney, 2002, photo Michael Cheetham.

Recording studio with band, photo Robert Offord.

Andrea conducts,
*   photo Robert Offord.*

*   Simon in the*
*   studio,*
*   photo Robert*
*   Offord.*

Rainbow Road, photo Robert Offord.

Palau de Musica Catalana, Barcelona, 2008, photo Michael Cheetham.

FOURTEEN

Touring and Troubles

Travelling to exotic locations and meeting other groups and communities had been an amazing adventure, but there were many places in middle England that we had never visited; the time had come to do a British Isles tour.

To attract an audience to some out-of-the-way venue, we would need a theme that had some universal relevance. A hot political issue that was being debated at that time, and we thought would engage most audiences both gay and straight, was partnership and marriage. In 2003 gay people were not allowed to be either married or engage in civil partnerships, and we had something to say about it. The music committee compiled lists of relevant music that ranged from sentimental love songs to deeply cynical pieces that explored disillusionment and divorce. Most of the repertoire came from shows and musicals, so although the collection was initially called 'Tying the Knot', by the end of the tour it became known simply as 'Showtime'.

The tour programme evolved as it went along, we would do a concert in one location and then have a gap of a couple of months when we could fit in a few new pieces, drop the less successful ones and then present an updated show in a different place.

The first performance was at The Stables in Milton Keynes, a lovely little theatre owned and run by Cleo Laine and Johnny Dankworth. We had met them on several occasions before, had shared a concert with them at the Royal Albert Hall and also a big millennium retrospective with Michael Parkinson and lots of celebrity guests at the Royal Festival Hall.

The show went well, but in spite of distributing flyers to the few nearby pubs on the previous weekend, not many local people turned up to see it, and we wondered if this touring idea was going to get us into financial trouble. It was very practical for us to have a set of songs we could use for several shows, but it would be expensive to hire coaches to take us around and visit different audiences.

The next location we were due to visit was Dublin, and to make the long journey more worthwhile, Martin Brophy organised a whole weekend of events based at the City University; we could do workshops with various other choirs and the culmination would be our main show in the prestigious National Concert Hall. It was like a junior version of the big American GALA festival where everyone got to hear other groups and experience different techniques and ideas. Gloria, the lesbian and gay choir based in Dublin, hosted an Irish ceilidh for all the participants on the Saturday evening and the whole city felt like a very friendly and lively place to visit.

By the time we did our concert on Sunday evening we had had an entire weekend immersed in collective creativity, and that performance was blessed by all the angels and muses of singing. It was astonishing to stand on stage and feel as if the chorus was somehow communally levitating to a higher level of consciousness. The atmosphere seemed to transport over to the audience and an intense poise seemed to be present in the hall. Our inklings that a special experience was being shared were confirmed at the end when the entire audience leapt to their feet with enthusiasm. The theatre manager told us that in the twenty years he had been at the venue he had never seen such a standing ovation before.

As well as being known as a capital for the arts, Dublin is a city notorious for its pub culture, and after such a successful show the chorus was on adrenalin high. Everyone stayed up late to experience the city, celebrate the concert and prolong the experience.

Next morning very few of us managed to get to the university canteen for breakfast, and the double-decker bus taking us on to Belfast had to wait as bleary stragglers staggered from dormitory blocks to the main gate with their hastily packed luggage. The motorway miles rolled past and thankfully it was a quiet journey, the concert was that evening and people with thumping hangovers wanted to catch up with a few hours' sleep before doing a sound-check and run-through in the theatre.

Belfast is a city of contrasts. We recognised the grim, troubled housing estates that were so often seen on the news, but there is also a spacious and prosperous Victorian city-centre, and by the docks the Waterfront Arts Complex where we were due to perform looked like a high-tech flying saucer flown in from the future.

I had never been to Belfast before, so as soon as I

dropped my bags in the hostel I went out to explore a few art galleries. The first one I went into had a poster on a board by the door advertising our concert that night. I explained to the receptionist that I was with the chorus, hadn't seen that picture before, and asked if maybe I could have it for the chorus scrap book? She said I could and that they were "very pleased to have us come and visit, the gay community in Belfast often had to deal with prejudice, and it felt like significant public support to have such visitors."

As I went back to the notice board I heard her pick up the phone and start saying excitedly to someone on the other end "They're here, they're here and I've met one".

I realised that this concert was indeed going to be special.

The sound check and run-through in the theatre did not go particularly well; many of us were sounding rough and Simon the pianist seemed to be groggy. We promised ourselves that we would do better that night and went off to find strong coffee and something to eat.

Everywhere we went in Belfast it was apparent that this was a troubled area. Road blocks, uniformed men and guns were part of everyday life and plainly visible in the city centre. Security at the theatre had been tight; we were very clearly a British group and would have been an obvious terrorist target.

When we got back to the Waterfront complex there was a demonstration happening outside, but it was 'gay' that was the issue, more than nationality. A group of about 40 middle-aged Presbyterian men in suits and anoraks were carrying placards and marching slowly round in a circle. One of the signs read 'Sodomites go home', and a huge banner had the words 'Except a man be born again he cannot see the kingdom of God' written on it. There was also a counter-demonstration led by a glamorous local drag queen known as Baroness Titti von Tramp, (referred to as 'a transvestite' on the front page of the paper next day) and it occurred to me that of all the people there, it was ironically 'she' who probably had the most right to claim the title 'a man born again'. The combination of the two opposing groups looked utterly ridiculous, but there was an undercurrent of confrontational fanaticism about it and it did not feel at all funny. No one could say how far these people would go, or who else was lurking silently on the side-lines waiting for an opportunity to cause significant damage.

The demonstrators stayed there to threaten the audience as it arrived, and apparently sang a few hymns outside as we sang our songs inside, but there was no serious trouble and they had all gone home by the time we finished. The hung-over chorus managed to put on a passable show, but it was nothing like the sublime performance that had materialised from the ether in Dublin the night before.

Afterwards we all went to one of the very few, and always well concealed, gay bars, and although it was crowded there was a distinctly besieged feeling to it. The statements of support and gratitude for our visit were frequently repeated to us by the local Pride organisers. The impression we received from the gay community of

Belfast, that there was a general lack of acceptance towards gay people, was given some statistical credence in early 2007, a couple of years after our visit. The University of Ulster released the results of a 'Human Beliefs and Values Survey' which found that the province of Ulster had the most bigoted population in the whole of the western world, apparently 36% of the respondents said they would object to having gay neighbours, and analysis of the figures revealed that there was greater intolerance of the presence of gay people than there was towards any religious or racial difference.

Late that night I walked back alone to my hostel which was on the other side of the city. Compared to Dublin the streets were eerily deserted, and somebody later told me that it might not have been a safe thing to do; there are many conflicting opinions about life in Belfast.

Next day the flight back wasn't until the evening, so I had an opportunity to walk around both the Falls Road and the Shankill Road, looking at all the folk-art and political murals painted on the flanks of the houses. Sometimes such acts of communal creativity can be signals from the front line; these paintings weren't decorative, they were a call to arms.

A painted mural, a religious tract on a banner, or a performance of songs, is an idea that's been turned into an action, and in the entire history of the world ideas have never been laid low by guns or bombs, only by other ideas. Weaponry can certainly cause instant and appalling damage, but in the longer term, it's ideas that are the more powerful force.

We presented the 'Tying the Knot' show again at the end of that month in the Queen Elizabeth Hall back in London, then recorded it as a live CD during a wild bank-holiday weekend in the Manchester Library Theatre, and it had a final outing in Brighton at the end of the year. Each time there was a completely different mood and meaning to the set of songs. No matter gay or straight, the underlying theme of relationships has always been an unpredictable battlefield.

We tried to incorporate some of the advantages of a touring show in our next production. It was called 'Eclecsis', an evocative word I made up that seemed to suggest a varied collection of different songs, styles and techniques. Charlie, our new musical director, was introducing some ideas from jazz into our repertoire.

We first performed this show in Birmingham with the local gay chorus 'Rainbow Voices' as our guests, and then presented it in London with 'Carnival Collective', an extraordinarily loud samba-style marching band from Brighton. There were a couple of preparatory workshops when we got together with two rainbow haired leaders from the collective, and they taught chorus members how to use their various percussion instruments. In the concert they joined us on stage and we all let rip with the Brazilian piece 'Mais Qui Nada', and then proceeded to turn the old Donna Summer song 'State of Independence', into a deafening cataclysm of cross-rhythms.

There was more experimentation and improvisation when the spiritual 'You gotta Move' was performed as a plantation-slave style 'ring shout'. The chorus suddenly ceased to be a coherent group and became a collection of individuals; all the lights went out and each person randomly sang different bits of song whilst walking round the circumference of the auditorium. Fifty years before George Gershwin had used a similar trick for the prayer sequence in Porgy and Bess.

It was a weird and wonderful concert, not like anything we had ever done before, and the audience must have been both fascinated and bewildered by what was going on.

The strangest piece of all was 'The Singing Apes of Khao Yai'. This was an avant-garde sound-scape from the iconoclastic Swedish composer Jan Sandstrom. Patches of it were written in sixteen part harmony, and the singers had to imitate the howling and whooping calls of the white throated gibbon. Even though we had been practising it methodically for the previous fourteen weeks, it was still very easy for groups of singers to lose their place in the cyclically repeated patterns, and for once we decided to have the sheet music on stage with us during the performance. It was a necessity for us, and it also signalled to the audience that unlike the previous improvisation, this piece had a seriously complex and tightly composed structure.

Someone at the BBC had read in a press release that a gay choir was undertaking the British premiere of an interesting new piece, and thought it might make a novelty news item. A reporter came along to a rehearsal, and Charlie recorded an interview. The eccentric little story turned into a four minute feature on the radio 4

Today programme, and that evening it was chosen to be Pick of the Day and broadcast again. At the end of the week listeners voted it to be a Pick of the Week, and it was once again repeated. The London Gay Men's Chorus was often newsworthy, but this time we were pleased that it was because of the interesting music we made, rather than our gender preferences.

Later that summer we took some of the more accessible Eclecsis repertoire on tour. The first stop was Washington DC, where we did a concert with the Gay Men's Chorus of Washington DC at the university auditorium. We had first come across them in San Jose, and knew that they were a very different choir from us; they always wore dress-suits on stage and usually used sheet music. In some subtle and unspoken way they seemed to mirror and carry with them the elite status of their home city, the imposing capital of an immense nation. Although there was some extreme poverty in the housing projects of the Washington suburbs, the central area round the White House was all grand avenues and neo-classical pomp and circumstance. To some of us 'outside observers' the architecture and ambience of the city-centre felt vaguely threatening, like a formidable cross-fertilisation between ancient Rome and Nazi Nuremburg.

During the week that we stayed there Paul Tame was celebrating his birthday, and that was a good excuse for us to have a themed party. A set of three stretch Limos were hired. We stocked them up with Champagne, exaggerated our English accents and set off for a night-time cruise around the city. The party moved round all the monuments, memorials and tourist sites in style, stopping for photo opportunities at each one, partly mocking the vulgarity, and privately marvelling at the scale and grandeur of everything.

An important institution in Washington is the Kennedy Centre for the Performing Arts, a vast, pillared, Parthenon-style block next door to the notorious Watergate Hotel on an escarpment overlooking the Potomac River. We did a free afternoon concert at the Kennedy Centre which not only attracted a large and very mixed crowd but was simultaneously web-cast live around the world. It was weird to know that friends back in London could see each move as we made it. As soon as we came off stage some of us started getting text messages from the UK saying it had sounded great. Unusually the Kennedy Centre kept our performance available on their web-archive for several years.

Four years had passed since our visit to the previous Gala Choirs festival in San Jose, and the ultimate purpose of this trip was for us to attend the current festival which was to be held in Montreal. After a week of performing and sightseeing in Washington, the chorus made the short jump across the Canadian border and abruptly experienced a completely different culture.

With nearly 6000 participants Gala was the largest gathering of singers there had ever been, and was potentially a most extraordinary opportunity for us to see and hear alternative ideas. Montreal was the ideal host city since it was used to holding music events, conferences, competitions and gatherings of every description. At the same time as we were there, the anarchic comedy festival 'Just for Laughs' was happening in the streets and clubs, and every night there was an International Fireworks competition lighting up the eastern sky. There seemed to be an endless round of extraordinary things to see, hear and do.

If Washington had an air of establishment authority about it, Montreal almost seemed to personify its opposite; it was like a randomly put together collaged scrapbook of multi-cultural possibilities. I wondered if the richness of this diverse ambience was also enhanced by the extreme variations in the Canadian climate. I was told the mood went from reserved, solitary and academic in the long sub-zero winters, to gregarious, open-minded and casual during the blazing hot summer months. Fashionable boutiques with the latest high-tech gadgets and sports equipment sat alongside antique shops stuffed with books and old agricultural tools. We sometimes saw apparently homeless street-people hanging about, but they were just as likely to be poets or painters as much as junkies and pickpockets; there was very little crime. A huge and obviously prosperous gay village had developed at the edge of the city, and it didn't feel as if there was any intolerance towards minority communities. Canadian identity seemed to encompass everything from American, French and English to Norwegian, Chinese and German. Towards the end of our visit I discovered that as well as an impressive collection of world class museums there were also dozens of little contemporary art galleries and design studios scattered around the side streets. Several of us observed that the small and self-contained city of Montreal seemed to fulfil all our needs; it felt like a good place to live.

As in San Jose, the Gala festival was a nonstop roller-coaster of different events and activities. Within such a packed timetable we were lucky to have been granted two performance slots during the week, one on the main stage in the Theatre Maisonneuf, and another on a large temporary stage set up in a spectacular semi-subterranean shopping mall with a sub-tropical jungle and fountains in its huge atrium.

For various reasons that none of us fully understood, the London Gay Men's Chorus had acquired a reputation and wherever we performed there was always a crowd. There were many good choirs visiting Montreal, some of them much more polished than we were, but the LGMC was always considered to be something special; to have some extra and indefinable quality of integrity. It must have been a hangover from San Jose and was a mystery to us, but we tried to live up to expectations.

One of the things that made our performances different was that we always had a sign-language interpreter on stage with us. It may seem odd, that an art form as essentially auditory as singing should concern itself with those least able to appreciate that sense, but that was partly the point. Why should those with a hearing impairment be excluded? Many people with a degree of hearing-loss could still catch some of the sound, and in our shows there was always much to look at as well as listen to.

We had first come across Russ our sign language interpreter, years before at a Stonewall concert. He had been in the RAF, but changed direction and retrained when he realised he had a genuine vocation for interpreting. As soon as we saw his work we realised that he could add an extra dimension to our performances, and invited him to come along and see what we were doing. He moved in such a graceful and expressive way when he signed that as well as providing a service for deaf people, he was visually interesting for the entire audience. He became a regular fixture at all our London concerts, and accompanied us on tour whenever his other work permitted. It wouldn't have been the same without him standing to one side of the stage.

Russ had been with us in California, and although we rarely ever paid him for his interpreting skills we gladly paid his fare so that he could come to Washington and Montreal. America and Canada each use a slightly different signing system, and although we weren't sure how much of the English signing was getting through, we knew that like a solo dancer, his expressive movement was being noticed and understood. Wherever we went, audience members often commented on his contribution to our shows.

The schedule in Montreal was busy, and in the rare gaps when one wasn't sightseeing around the city, watching a performance or rehearsing, the coffee-shops, restaurants and malls constantly swarmed with Gala participants. The crowds were often people on their way to, or just coming from, one of the concert halls and other singers could easily be identified by their chorus-branded T-shirts, or the plastic security pass hung around their necks. It was delightfully easy to meet and talk with strangers; you knew that there was such a strong common culture of music, singing, and of course gayness!

It was a social as well as a musical event, and at the closing ceremony when everyone gathered in the biggest of the theatres, we felt that a real camaraderie had developed. This was an international movement, with obvious political aims and common objectives, and for some of the smaller choirs not associated with a big sophisticated metropolis, the festival was a rare chance to celebrate group solidarity. An intense week of communal gay choir-culture had been a really special experience, not often available to even the most seasoned of city dwellers, and the final closing ceremony was a poignant occasion.

There is a common perception that a gay sensibility can be sarcastic or world-weary and cynical, but the underlying warmth, sentimentality and even vulnerability of those same gay people becomes apparent when 6000 of them come together to express an emotional and heartfelt gratitude to each other, before parting and returning to their separate lives. We were enriched by it all, and events such as Gala Festivals happen because the participants feel a need for them. Gay culture has to shape its own reality, and we are especially privileged when we can manage to create for ourselves a mutually empowering experience such as a gay choral festival.

FIFTEEN
Bright Lights and Dark Shadows

Chorus activities were sometimes rushed affairs, sketchily planned and semi-improvised whilst they were actually happening, and all the more exciting and genuine for being so spontaneous. Some of us found it an exhilarating and creative way to work, but others were more cautious and didn't welcome the extra stress that inevitably came with 'making it up as you go along'. The safer scenario would have been a predictable event which had been slowly and methodically constructed on solid foundations carefully prepared a year or more in advance.

Our Washington and Montreal trip had been long anticipated, and similarly the 2004 Christmas concert had first been dreamed up on the train coming back from Manchester, fourteen months previously. All the necessary steps for us to get to these significant milestones in an efficient way had been well timetabled. Our meticulous strategies suddenly became more complicated when another event was slotted in at short notice.

'For the Public Good' was a centenary celebration for the London Coliseum. It was being organised by a team from English National Opera, and was originally supposed to have happened in January 2004. Building work at the Coliseum hadn't been finished on time and their whole concert schedule had crashed. Even august institutions were subject to an occasional derailment, and the celebration was now going to happen in October. This was an obviously prestigious project and we were keen to be involved, but the new date was in the middle of our Christmas run up. Because of the trip to Canada, our 'For the Public Good' rehearsals couldn't start until the month before the event was due to happen.

Luckily, just before the Tying the Knot tour we had recruited a very competent new Assistant Musical Director, Olly Medlicott. Whilst Charlie and the main chorus started doing the Christmas show on Monday nights, another smaller group of us were also meeting up on Wednesdays with Olly to do the 'Public Good' project. The music had all been specially composed by our old friend Orlando Gough, and although we had an excellent rehearsal CD to work from, the score was seventy pages long, and some of it looked worryingly complicated.

The theme of 'For the Public Good' was a variety show woven around excerpts from all the extraordinary acts that had performed at the London Coliseum during its 100 year history. Everything from romantic Eastern mystics to madly eccentric Italian futurists were thrown in and stirred up together. For the anniversary event some impressive contemporary opera 'names' were included as soloists, and there were six other small groups from established choirs to boost the sound. We had our own little cameo moment which was a piece about Vesta Tilley, who used to appear on stage dressed as a soldier, recruiting young men to sign up for active service in the Great War. It was deliciously ironic to choose a gay chorus to sing this part; at the start of the twentieth century no 'out' gay men would have been allowed to enlist.

There were only three occasions when all the various participants were able to rehearse together before the big day, and during those sessions we got to work with Mary King, the remarkable voice coach for the ENO, and Matthew Morley their Musical Director. They took us through the long piece section by section until most of the problems were ironed out, but there was still an element of "do your best and let's see what happens". It might have sounded OK on the surface, but in reality we weren't at all secure.

The chorus contingent dressed up in their best Edwardian evening attire, acquired from charity shops or borrowed from the wardrobes of ancient uncles, and 'For the Public Good' with the ENO was performed three times in quick succession on one extraordinary afternoon. By the third repetition it began to feel like a weird 'groundhog-day' dream to us, but the audience wouldn't know which bits were intentionally chaotic and which were going off the rails, so a certain degree of musical anarchy was permissible.

It had been a huge amount of fast work at an inconvenient time, but the result was favourably reviewed in several newspapers, so in the end we were all rather pleased to have been associated with such an adventurous and well publicised project.

Our reputation as a 'proper' choir with serious musical ambitions had been established quite early on in 1996, when we were involved in the BBC Choir of the Year competition. Now that we were regularly appearing on big London stages, and getting mentioned in reviews, we found we were able to attract high calibre singers and musicians. People were interested in joining or working with us not because we were a gay novelty act, or a worthwhile cause, but because we made good music.

While our full schedule of events was pleasing, it meant there was a constant pressure of events one after another; there was no space for us to relax and explore performance possibilities. We always tried to tackle interesting and alternative music as a regular part of our shows, but were also aware that there was more we would enjoy. Both the professional musicians we employed and our membership had hidden depths and unfulfilled ambitions.

To find some free space for ourselves we often had an annual retreat, a weekend when we could go away together and research and experiment with some different ideas. There had been a couple based at the music department of the University of East Anglia in Norwich, and another at York University; un-pressured time in the country when we felt we could stretch our lungs and open up our minds.

After the Washington and Montreal trip we arranged a long weekend at the Benslow Music Trust in Hertfordshire. It's an inspired combination of a rambling old country house and purpose-built new facilities all set in gorgeous gardens just to the north of London. The chorus took over the whole complex and we were able to set up a range of different activities and workshops.

The timetable included Stuart Burrows our choreographer doing 'Advanced Movement'; Angela, a freelance voice coach, who did 'Voice fitness'; Olly did 'Barbershop' and a startling exploration of 'Minimalist Singing', Charlie tried some different warm ups', Gerry explained diaphragm anatomy; John demonstrated the possibilities of the computer Sibelius programme and use of the internet; Chris facilitated 'production techniques' and Martin considered potential futures. There was even a workshop on the last day when Simon and Leslie played hilarious Eurotrash games.

The Benslow retreat took place in October 2004, when we were in the middle of the Christmas season, but there was an agreement that 'the festivities' would not be mentioned. This was playtime, and for just one weekend 'Christmas' was one of the pressures we were able to leave behind.

The festivities were likely to be especially significant this time around. At the beginning of the year we had been approached by Raymond Gubbay, a music business entrepreneur and big-time concert promoter. His research had revealed that when we did the Golden Reign production the Queen Elizabeth Hall had sold out on both nights. He was interested in expanding into an alternative market and offered us the chance to do a Christmas show at the 2000 seat Barbican Concert Hall. Their organisation would look after all the promotion and publicity, always a difficult and expensive problem for us, and we would get a guaranteed fee regardless of how many seats were sold.

It was an attractive proposition since it was always difficult for us to find a suitable venue in December. The smaller theatres often had a pantomime or 'family show' season, and the big venues were block booked by promoters such as Gubbay for carol concerts. We could certainly have earned more income by doing our own independent show, but we would never have obtained a space like the Barbican, and it would be a real luxury to leave all the work of promoting the show and selling the tickets to someone else.

The first of the chorus Christmas show meetings had happened in January. Different ideas were discussed, a few of the key songs were chosen and a team volunteered to develop the proposals. We thought that an inventive way of tying the songs together and developing a narrative flow would be to have a group of three characters appearing at intervals throughout the show to tell a Christmas story. They could be called the 'three wise men', or since this was a show by a gay chorus, 'three old queens'.

For publicity and profile purposes the Gubbay Organisation wanted us to have a celebrity guest; we imagined our three characters would be able to interact with the guest to help the story along. No celebrity had been booked at that time, so we kept the script a bit vague and started to suggest people who we thought it would be fun to work with. Everyone from Liza Minelli to Sir Ian McKellen was mentioned, and the Gubbay Organisation began making phone calls to find out who was available and if their fee demands were realistic.

Our artistic development team carried on with their regular meetings. The show proposals had to take into account our cut-down profit margin, and some of the wilder ideas of giant masks and pantomime donkeys were jettisoned. The major chorus preoccupation that summer was the imminent GALA tour, and as the long, light evenings grew warmer it required great dedication for that little group of us to meet up regularly in a stuffy office with scripts, scores, charts and stage plans to discuss a distant Christmas.

We suggested to the promoter that they contact the actor Simon Callow to be our celebrity guest. He had been to a previous show of ours and even mentioned the chorus in a press interview, so we hoped he would be keen to do it. A positive answer came back from the agent, but because of his filming commitments there was a proviso that a final contract wouldn't be signed until November.

Time passed, the tour happened, and in September the chorus started to rehearse the Christmas repertoire. It was a tight schedule to get about twenty songs practised and polished in only about fourteen weeks, and it would help that some of them were relatively well-known carols.

There were constant distractions. Some of us were also involved in the ENO project, and another group were planning and preparing the workshops for the Benslow retreat. Then in the early hours of October 30th the whole country was shocked by the news of a callous gay murder. David Morley, also affectionately known as 'Sinders', was attacked by a gang of teenagers as he and a friend sat on a bench by the Festival Hall on the South Bank. He died from his injuries. The police concluded that the only motive for the attack appeared to be the fact that the two victims were gay.

The story hit the headlines and the gay community was outraged; it was discovered there had been two other assaults in that vicinity by the same gang on that night. Indeed, one of our own members was involved and had been injured. He appeared at the next rehearsal three days later with a bandaged face and severe bruising. It was widely reported that Sinders had been a survivor of the Admiral Duncan bombing in Old Compton St, and many people were reminded of the indiscriminate horror of that incident some five years before. This casual murder could have happened to any of us at any time; it felt as if we were all being attacked.

We decided that there should be some sort of public ceremony or vigil in memory of Sinders, and that no matter how busy we were, the chorus could do it; Martin and Phil contacted St Anne's Church in Soho. A date was fixed for the next weekend and we got on with sorting out the myriad details at very short notice. Our final arrangements were widely publicised by the media, and on the evening of November 5th several thousand people turned up for the memorial event. The churchyard was packed full and all the local streets blocked solid with people who felt a need to demonstrate their defiance of such acts of homophobia.

It was a salutary reminder to us all, in the middle of our preparations for Christmas, that regardless of big-time concert promoters, 'income' and 'entertainment' were not the primary motivation for a gay chorus to perform a high-profile concert at a major London venue. Prejudice, ignorance and hatred were still present in some sections of our society.

At the beginning of November the various entertainment agencies and promoters had ensured that all the correct contracts for the Christmas show had been signed, so Paul and I, who were the most active and experienced in the artistic development team, arranged a meeting with Simon Callow.

His choice of venue was the Claridge's Hotel, and on the chosen day Paul and I met up half an hour early to run through our plans for the concert. We waited slightly nervously in the foyer, and only a few minutes after the appointed time Simon Callow swept in dramatically wearing a long black cloak. Paul and I introduced ourselves and we all moved towards the little hotel coffee shop, it was crowded with guests and visitors, so was the restaurant, and so was the bar. We needed to find a table so that we could sit down, talk and spread out a few papers, and stood in the foyer feeling a bit nonplussed. Even when he wasn't doing anything dramatic Simon could have a commanding presence, and I was uncomfortably aware that the group of us were being scrutinised. When the face is a well-known one, sometimes even the polite clientele of Claridge's can stare rudely. He seized the moment and as if orating Shakespeare to an enraptured audience announced loudly, "Oh fuck it, we're going to Starbucks".

The second we were outside in the street the magnetic thespian aura was switched off. We walked along unnoticed, found a table in the corner of the café and sat down to talk.

It turned out he had a busy schedule and was going to be in Switzerland till the evening before the concert. This meeting, and an exchange of emails, were the only opportunities to coordinate his guest appearance.

Since he had been to one of our concerts before he understood our style, and was happy to go along with the idea of starting off on a traditional, serious and slightly mystical theme, before developing into comic, high-spirited and decidedly gay areas with the appearance of three queens in the second half. We all realised he was likely to improvise along the way, but nevertheless he asked me to write him a proper script that Paul could email to Switzerland. We discussed what it would be suitable for him to wear, said our goodbyes and didn't meet him again till four hours before the show.

His performance was masterful, smooth, relaxed and apparently spontaneous. He wore an understated black Armani suit and delivered both eloquent drama and crude farce in the right measure and at all the right moments. Simon Callow, the three Queens and the chorus seemed to be playing a game of tag throughout the evening as each in turn tried to 'steal the show' from their predecessor. The audience were encouraged to join in towards the end with a competitive and riotous rendition of 'The Twelve Days of Christmas', and by the time we reached the finale I think the general consensus was that everybody had had a good time. Every single seat in the Barbican Concert Hall had been sold out a couple of nights beforehand, and later on we were amazed to learn that it had been one of the fastest selling shows their box office had ever handled.

After the big concert at The Barbican there was still a week left before Christmas which we spent carol singing at Selfridges. We did four half-hour spots per day, for five days, and the amount of money they paid us made up for all the losses that we had incurred by accepting the Raymond Gubbay deal. It was hard work. There had been about 140 singers on stage for the show, and we were now reduced to a group of between 12 and 20.

Leslie, who was then a headmaster at a primary school, had volunteered to organise it for us, and on his clipboard was a complex roster of people who were able to take a day off work to help raise the much needed funds. Some of us were able to commit to the entire booking; others were only able to take a long lunch hour, so there was an ever changing group of people performing. Some knew all the words of the carols and others didn't; we had to have a quick run through in our changing room before most sets. Luncheon vouchers for the steamy staff-canteen had been negotiated into our fee, and it was an odd experience to go behind the scenes in the vast department store and see all the slick sales staff off duty. Public school accents and impeccable manners were turned off and the more genuine council-estate roots were sometimes revealed. The security guards, so impressive in their smart uniforms, mostly turned out to be eastern European immigrants doing temporary part-time jobs, and parts of the great Art Deco building were startlingly tatty when one left the shop floor and saw behind the scenes.

Our singing was broadcast live throughout the store, and both the shopping public and the Selfridges staff seemed to responded warmly to having carol singers at the bottom of the escalators. Perhaps because a live performance was unexpected and out of context we found we had to be really 'full-on' and extrovert when we sang. We were 'acting' just as hard as the shop staff were, and winning the attention of a casual passer-by, as opposed to the already captive audience we got in a theatre, was like busking in a tube station; by the end of the fifth day everyone was exhausted.

The relentless frenzy of West End Christmas consumerism from early in the morning to late at night, every day for a working week, was both grotesque and awesome. On Christmas Eve, as we packed away the last shreds of tinsel and left the store, the staff were all busily preparing for the onslaught of 'the sales' that would begin on Boxing Day.

SIXTEEN
Paris and the Police

The first Barbican concert had been a well-prepared and polished affair, and we all felt it would be worthwhile to preserve some of that achievement on a Christmas CD. There hadn't been any time to do it during the run up, so in the New Year we started a punishing two and a half months recreating Christmas in various different recording venues.

The first session wasn't too difficult. We were all glad to be back together and singing again after the two week break but, perhaps inevitably, precision had slipped and it took a couple of rehearsal sessions to get the first batch of songs up to recording standard.

At the end of January we hired an echoing empty church in Hampstead Garden Suburb, and spent a chilly Saturday singing and then repeating the same four or five songs until we had them sounding as good as we possibly could.

There were three separate recording days, each one preceded by a couple of preparatory rehearsals, and the process became noticeably more tedious as we got further away from Christmas. By the last one, the days were getting noticeably longer and the first hints of spring were in the air; songs about blazing Yule logs and angels in the snow felt very unreal, and only about sixty singers turned up for the last recording session. We had been doing Christmas songs since the previous September and were now eager to move on.

The coincidence of two other events conspired to make that January and February particularly depressing. The first was the funeral of one of our oldest members.

Philip Dewdney had been with the chorus since the late nineties and had been an enthusiastic participant in all our activities. He never missed Monday rehearsals and frequently came to committee meetings on Tuesday nights as well. In the 'From the Ritz to the Anchor and Crown' show and CD there had been an item about London during the war, and in the concert he delivered an evocative speech about his memories of the blitz with bombs falling all around. After the war Philip had been in the merchant Navy, and he had even been married for a while. In later life he suffered from diabetes, and after the millennium his health deteriorated and he had to have a leg amputated. His courage and determination not to be defeated were inspiring and he continued to come along to rehearsals and perform in concerts. Every week his battered wheel chair was hauled up and down the steps at Cecil Sharp House by whoever happened to be nearest, and he thought nothing of travelling across London on the buses without any assistance if he wanted to get to a committee meeting.

Even when he had to move to sheltered accommodation he rarely complained about his circumstances, and I was surprised when he rang me one day at the beginning of December to say he felt weak and thought he might miss the next rehearsal. A few days later we heard that he had died of heart failure.

The funeral was on a bitterly cold Wednesday in January, and Martin organised a small group of people to go to Bromley and sing. We did the old Bob Dylan song 'He was a Friend of Mine' at the beginning of the service, and 'Seasons of Love' at the end. When the Christmas CD eventually came out in November of that year it carried a dedication, 'To Philip Dewdney, who showed us how to live a full life'.

The other very sobering event that coincided with the CD recording was singing at the Holocaust Memorial Day Ceremony at the London Assembly's City Hall. It showed how far we had come in terms of social acceptance; when our organisation had formed at the beginning of the nineties there may have been a few people in power who realised that we might have had a valid reason to participate in such a ceremony, but no one would have dared to voice it. Now we were invited by the Mayor himself, and although there were very probably still several traditionalists who might have thought it improper to invite a gay chorus, no one had the nerve to challenge it publicly.

The newly opened City Hall building is extraordinary, a great lop-sided, glass walled hemisphere situated next to Tower Bridge. A spiral ramp winds round the inside from top to bottom and the main council chamber where we sang, occupies the hollow core. The Mayor, Ken

Livingstone, gave a reading. He was followed by Trude Levi, an Auschwitz survivor, and Rosemary Museminali, the Rwandan ambassador, who told of the rebuilding of her country after the inter-tribal genocide.

The speakers gave factual information and lent gravitas and authenticity to the event, and although at one point a symbolic memorial candle was lit; it was only our singing that appeared to introduce the very real and necessary emotional component.

At the end of the ceremony, as a last few guests stayed behind to sign a book of commitment, our pianist Simon Sharp felt moved to spontaneously improvise. The music that he played was a swirling rush of melancholy and desperation. Wild yearning and impulsive renewal seemed to sweep like a torrent around the spiralling spaces of the great building. Sometimes the urgency of music can be more expressive and honest than any spoken words.

Our preparations for 2005 got off to a very late start because of the time we spent on the Christmas CD. We were due to go over to Paris in early May to participate in a 'Various Voices' festival of European Lesbian and Gay Choirs. It was a smaller version of the American Gala festival idea, but perhaps because of the multiplicity of languages involved, it felt far less unified and organised. There were about eighty different choirs participating, mostly tiny amateur groups from obscure towns with no more than a dozen or so members. We were noticeably the largest group there, and seemed to have a much more professional approach than anybody else.

Paris is a marvellous city to visit, renowned the world over for its art, architecture and culture, so it's very odd that it doesn't seem to have anything equivalent to New York's 'Broadway' or London's 'West End'. There is no obvious theatre district where big commercial shows and musicals have long runs, just a scatter of venues that put on fringe plays to local audiences. The festival had taken over two of these, La Cigale and Le Trianon, for concerts on three evenings, and in addition there was an interesting assortment of workshops that were supposed to happen in a couple of other locations.

The initial 'festival registration' arrangements seemed to be enormously and unnecessarily complicated; each participant had to get themselves to an out-of-the-way Various Voices office in a little back street, and then wait in a series of separate queues to collect their theatre tickets, tourist information, travel cards and security passes. Everyone involved in the festival had to undergo this process, so each queue was long and slow-moving; the multi-lingual personnel tried to be efficient but were overwhelmed. This bureaucratic procedure was merely a foretaste of everything that was to follow.

The opening ceremony was dire; it was in a theatre called the Palais de la Mutualité, and it started late. The Rainbow Symphony Orchestra were supposed to open, but for some unexplained reason couldn't manage to get themselves on stage and in tune at the right time. Once they had, they slowly murdered Prokofiev's Romeo and

Juliet.

There were a couple of other musical items, but lengthy technical problems seemed to be delaying everything. For most of the time we had to listen to interminable worthy speeches, some of which were laboriously translated into three languages. At one point the programme was supposed to be lightened by a drag compere who told Parisian 'in-jokes' in un-translated 17th century French dialect.

As the evening wore on there was some intermittent jeering from the balcony, but luckily there was a bar in the foyer so a lot of the bored audience just wandered off to get bottles of beer and socialise on the pavement outside. By the interval it was nearly time for the metro to close down so I don't think many people could have stayed for the second half even if they had wanted to.

The next morning we discovered that most of the workshops we had signed up for on the previous day had been called off because the group leaders had cancelled. It was disappointing. There were several musically relevant ones that I had been interested in, and I had been eagerly anticipating the life-drawing sessions with other gay men and a professional tutor, but at least there were now several unexpectedly spare mornings and a wonderfully eclectic city to explore.

Paris is an amazing place to wander through. Some undeveloped areas still remain as a labyrinth of tiny medieval alleyways and passages, quiet courtyards paved with worn cobbles, the heavy air seemingly sepia-tinted with so many layers of history. Walk for another few meters, turn a corner and you suddenly find the area is bisected by a great boulevard filled with grand buildings and busy with human traffic. A shabby little old shop like a Walt Disney dolls' house can easily sit amongst the smart designer boutiques, and everywhere you go there are street markets, pavement cafes and bars.

Any major city is going to be somewhat multicultural, and Paris has been recognised as a last haven for immigrants for hundreds of years. The intellectual, the desperate and the just plain eccentric have all settled there; diverse cultures now sit side by side with roots that have become tangled and dense. This complex amalgam of human possibilities is not always peaceful. For days, or even decades, there is no indication of pressure, but then some tiny trigger can spark an incident of intolerance. The Parisian population may appear to be multi-cultural, but it can also be disturbingly nationalistic. French bookshops arrange their shelves first by nationality rather than by genre, all writers born in France are displayed together, those from elsewhere are separated. In 1994 a new restriction, known as the 'Toubon Law' was imposed on radio stations that played pop music. It states that forty percent of their output has to be sung in the French language. The dominance of English and American pop is now repressed. The roots of patriotism can run from the shallow and trivial to a profound depth.

It's not difficult to find poverty in Paris, and even occasionally sense danger in certain neighbourhoods at the dog-end of a day. In 2002 there was a shocking incident concerning an out gay man, Francoise Chenu, who had been callously murdered in a suburban park by a group of right-wing skinheads out for kicks. The crime had been recorded as a racial, rather than a homophobic attack, and that did nothing to reassure gay people.

By day it feels safe. In the city-centre the tourists get everywhere, and the palaces and museums are magnificent; jam-packed with the fruits of their own home-grown talent displayed alongside the legacy of looted booty from the days of French empire.

The contemporary music scene in Paris seems to have been particularly enriched by the cross-cultural fertilisation, and there are obvious Arabic and eastern influences not often found in London. For a brief time the Various Voices festival introduced German, Scandinavian and other European traditions into the rich mixture, and after one of our concerts it was possible to go from theatre to nightclub, and then wander on to the local bar, and feel as if you had sampled sounds from the whole world.

One of the very pleasing things about our large chorus is just how many different age groups and cultures it encompasses; you often share activities and cross paths with people and interests you might not otherwise meet. One long-term member, Martin Kaufman, has an interest in history; particularly the chance meetings and passing moments that seem to become the turning points of destiny. He'd volunteered to lead a walking group around the more interesting areas of the city and tell some of the stories. Perhaps because of the lack of other organised workshops the idea proved very popular, and early one morning a big group met up at Place Bastille and set off for a walk. Along the way we heard the many tales of mobs and revolutions, madness and murders.

It was amazingly evocative to hear the history of the place in the actual location, and since we were a group of singers, we couldn't resist the opportunity of letting rip with a couple of pieces from Les Miserables at relevant moments. Other passing tourists stared in amazement, but we were used to performing in public and just carried on with a brazen confidence.

At the end of the Various Voices week the chorus gathered for our last official open-air concert on a quaint old bandstand in the small Place du Temple park, and even though it drizzled with rain, a crowd materialized to listen and applaud.

The final party to mark the end of the festival took place in a gay nightclub next to the Arc de Triomphe. I was expecting something along the lines of our big central London venues, maybe even something a bit more stylish given the French reputation for fashion and glamour, but I was disappointed. It was a very ordinary and basic affair, the sort of 'gay night out' you could have found in an outer London suburb about a decade ago. Perhaps it's something analogous to the cultural difference I had noticed about theatres. There seems to be a preference for smaller and more intimate venues; one day it might make an interesting thesis subject for some dedicated social anthropologist.

The Various Voices festival had been a wonderful week

for everyone in the chorus because of the richness of the environment where it had been held, rather than the erratically planned event itself. Subsequently we heard that huge debts had been incurred by the organisers; many bills were left unpaid and the reputation of those involved seriously compromised. If we ever aspired to hold a festival of choirs in London this would be yet another valuable experience. Choir competitions, charity fundraisers, pop festivals or week-long conventions all involved multiple participants and posed complex logistical problems; there was much to learn.

The chorus's schedule in London was always hectic. Immediately after we got back from Paris I received an invitation from Westminster City Council for us to participate in a free event called 'West End Live' that was being planned for Leicester Square. There was going to be a big temporary stage constructed for three days, and the intention was to promote all the theatre shows and events occurring in the West End that summer. Several of the big musical productions were going to put on half-hour excerpts for the public, Mamma Mia, Mary Poppins and Chicago were involved, and Ronnie Scott's, The Borderline, The London Jazz Orchestra and The Baroque Choir were also going to perform.

I was very flattered that we were being included with such illustrious names, and also thought it would be a good opportunity for us to promote ourselves to a different audience. The quick turnaround of acts on the stage meant all would have to be kept simple and efficient, and since the chorus often had to improvise under difficult circumstances, I was confident we could cope.

The organisers had not set themselves an easy task. During the course of the first day several of the acts overran, the timetable slipped, and there were frequent technical problems with microphones, but the weather was wonderful, and the public loved it. There was an estimated audience of 50,000 during the weekend, and many people who would not normally have dreamed of attending a concert by a gay chorus, realised that actually we weren't that frightening after all. The idea of free showcase weekends had already proved a popular attraction in some American cities, and after the success of 'West End Live' in 2005, the idea became a regular London event.

Only a week after singing in Leicester Square we had a spot on the stage set up in Trafalgar Square for the Pride celebrations. The London Pride march was now an established annual occasion, but it had not always been so. The early years in particular had been a real battle. The first somewhat militant marches happened in the early nineteen seventies, when a small group of defiant activists had walked through the streets from Islington to Hyde Park for a picnic. The authorities and the police had not been able to arrest any members of the Gay Liberation Front, which formed in 1971, but they were very reluctant to allow any more public gatherings to happen. No doubt they were aware of the events which had occurred in New York in 1969, when a group of gay men, lesbians and drag queens decided they could no longer tolerate the repeated and brutal police raids on the Stonewall bar in Christopher St. On June 27th, the day of Judy Garland's funeral, a two day riot against the New York authorities began. At one point the bemused cops found themselves confronted by an angry chorus-line of high-kicking transvestites singing 'We are the Stonewall girls'. The events of 1969 proved to be a watershed, and many consider them to be the birth of the modern gay rights movement.

In commemoration of the Stonewall riots In New York, the London Pride gathering was always scheduled for the first weekend in July. It remained a relatively small and unofficial event until the middle of the nineteen eighties. By then more and more people were beginning to participate and the march was allocated a recognised route through Piccadilly. 'Pride Day' always ended with a free party for everyone and, as numbers grew, it moved from the Embankment Gardens to Victoria Park in Hackney or sometimes to Brockwell or Finsbury Park. The role of the police had also changed. At first they were there threatening to arrest people; later on they had to switch sides and protect the marchers from hostile homophobes and eventually, as the prospect of a public gay parade became more acceptable, they simply acted as stewards who could control the traffic and crowds of spectators.

The idea that there might be gay policemen had always titillated the tabloids, and in 1990, just when the chorus was getting started, a Gay Police Association (GPA) was formed. The press had a field day. By the end of the 1990s a few brave members of the GPA were openly participating in the Pride march and for their 15th anniversary in 2005, they planned to hold a European conference and have a significantly larger contingent demonstrate their solidarity with gay culture and join the parade.

The chorus was invited to perform at the end of their two day conference at a formal dinner dance in the art-deco ballroom of the Hilton Hotel in Piccadilly. Although it meant a disruptively late night just before the Pride march, we simply couldn't say no.

The prospect of a party with all those intercontinental policemen, and women, proved to be an irresistible lure to the chorus members. When I sent out an email request for volunteers more than eighty people signed up for it.

We all crammed on to the tiny stage and sang our songs. Peter Tatchell was an honoured guest at the event and was presented with a lifetime achievement award. In his good-humoured acceptance speech he told an ironic story of being arrested by the police for his gay activism some years before.

Greg Battle, our new chairman, made a short speech which mentioned that one of our members, Gerry, had been thrown out of the police force in the 1980s for being gay. It all felt rather emotional, and our old warhorse of an anthem, 'Something Inside So Strong' got a huge response. That immaculate art-deco ballroom must have seen many interesting happenings, but the Gay Police conference must have been one of the most unlikely.

A lot of champagne was drunk that night, and both

guests and hosts must have been feeling a bit groggy for the important march next morning.

The day was likely to be chaotic; the Pride celebrations clashed with 'Live 8', a series of massive charity concerts being held simultaneously all over the western world, with a central hub in Hyde Park. The organisers of the Live 8 event wanted to draw attention to third world poverty, and although some criticised them for being naïve and idealistic, the original Live Aid event in July 1985 had raised over sixty million pounds and radically altered western perceptions of third world issues. Twenty years later there was a whole new generation to inform, and once again there would be a global TV audience of countless millions. As the chorus assembled with all the other marchers in Park Lane, we could clearly hear the sound-check happening on the main stage. A hundred yards away Paul McCartney was singing through Sgt Pepper with U2 as the backing band.

A flat-bed truck stopped next to where we were standing. It was packed with celebrities and being closely tailed by the media. Bob Geldof and Ian McKellen faced the cameras and gave their introductory sound bite to launch both events. This was 'cultural activism' in action and it felt as if what we were seeing and hearing was world news; history was happening here.

Traffic in central London ground to a halt, and all forms of public transport were overloaded with people going to the concert or joining the march. We didn't get to our own performance in an overcrowded Trafalgar Square until 5pm, and the big Hyde Park concert carried on until after midnight.

That day it seemed as if the power of music to generate emotion and effect genuine global change was unstoppable. Shortly after the event the political leaders of the western world announced that they would be calling on the World Bank to cancel all the crippling and untenable third world debts.

SEVENTEEN
Space and Time

In July 2005 the chorus planned to do a concert that we hoped might paradoxically become both a new departure for us, and also something of a return to our own roots. It was called 'You'll Do For Now'; the clever and cruelly cynical title had come from a t-shirt Charlie had noticed in a Sydney gay bar.

The seeds of the scheme came from Ping-Kern Ng, an independently wealthy young architect of Malaysian extraction who joined the chorus in 2001. His inspirations for the project were manifold and included the musical Follies, the idea behind the TV series 'Sex in the City', an admiration for the work of Stephen Sondheim, and also reading an early draft of this manuscript about the chorus story.

He drew up a list of relevant songs and devised an extraordinarily complicated story concerning three different characters, each represented by two actors playing different ages, whose paths crossed in London's gay scene during the era between 1950 and 2000. In simple terms it told the story of how the current gay scene developed, and it felt like 'our story' to many in the chorus.

Until recent times gay culture and history had been shrouded in shame and kept secret. Because of its illegal status it was deliberately kept concealed by the participants, rarely written about by outsiders and certainly not thought worthy of any social study. Most literate people would be aware of Oscar Wilde, his plays and his ultimate persecution. Perhaps a few would have heard of Quentin Crisp or Joe Orton, but even in the gay community there is an assumption that the current scene sprang out of nothing in a puff of pink smoke sometime around the early nineteen eighties. Even within the chorus itself, many members don't know our own history or understand the idealistic motivation and political principles that led to the organization being formed.

Right from the start it was obvious that 'You'll Do For Now' was an interesting idea, but it was also fraught with problems. The ethos of the plot was fundamentally gay, and although we had remained an unmistakeably gay organization, our audience was now largely mixed. Would enough people be interested in this story? Most of the music proposed came from the Sondheim back catalogue, and it was known that he wasn't enthusiastic about his works being used out of their original context; we were unlikely to get copyright permission from the publishers. Ping's extremely complicated scenario of multiple characters shifting back and forth through time and encountering previous reincarnations was impossible to present. It would need a lot of rewriting before it could begin to make any sense on stage. Most ironically of all, many chorus members who were unaware of all our own early shows said that we couldn't possibly tackle anything which involved a narrative theme and character-driven dialogue.

The chorus was now using big theatres and, with a membership of around 130 people to organise, the business of putting on a show was becoming increasingly complex and expensive. This show in particular looked as though it could well become an elaborate production, so the steering committee was reluctant to embark on it until a more realistic proposal had been prepared. The steering committee asked Ping to do a bit more development, and granted him a budget of £400 to pay for workshops.

He didn't seem able to understand any of the very real practical problems, and came back four months later with a presentation of five or six of the more obvious songs. He had used the money to commission musical arrangements, and a group of a dozen friends had been persuaded to rehearse them. The impossible script remained virtually unaltered, and it then came to light that Ping had also used a thousand pounds of his own money to pay for further arrangements. He wanted the project to happen, and his motives might well have been honourable, but it looked horribly like a bribe or a way of retaining a stranglehold on an impractical and unsound concept. It was becoming apparent that the originator of a wonderful idea was now the stumbling block preventing it from becoming a reality.

One Monday evening during a rehearsal the workshop presentation was made to the whole chorus. Predictably, the songs were good and the staging of them went down well. The steering committee was now in the difficult position that to a lot of people it seemed a most attractive proposition, but those of us who had looked at it in greater depth knew that it was still deeply flawed. The chorus was nearly split in two and there was heated debate about a separate group being formed to do 'You'll do for Now' independently. The solution came in the form of our choreographer, Stuart Burrows. He helped to run a stage school and had been working with the chorus for several years. He knew all our strengths and weaknesses, and was hugely experienced in every aspect of theatre production. If anyone could knock this into shape, he could. Stuart was appointed as Artistic Director and Ping was asked to withdraw from the project.

The original list of music was completely revised and much of the copyright-restricted Sondheim repertoire was dropped. A series of narrators would tell the stories of what it was like being gay in the nineteen fifties and sixties, and all the unnecessary complication about some of them being older materialisations of former selves was gently swept into the background.

Marsh and Mallone, the design consultants who were sponsoring the chorus that year and producing most of our visual material, came up with some very provocative and professional looking posters and flyers. There had been endless discussion about possible images, and Mike Thorn had drawn up a lovely set of graphic 'You'll Do For Now' tattoo designs for us, but eventually it was decided we should go with a photo-shoot of two semi-naked male figures in an atmospherically shadowy embrace. It was a sexy, and unambiguously gay, image; our audience was about to be reminded that although we were a registered charity, attended international festivals and even sometimes sang in front of the Queen, we were still an essentially gay organisation.

Stuart convened a group of seven dancers who could appear at various points throughout the programme, and there was now an outrageous song from 'Jerry Springer, The Opera' included. 'I Just Wanna Fucking Dance' was going to be set in a gay nightclub. Paul Tame could sing the solo and Charlie could do us a big production backing track on his computer. It would give us the chance to play with some adventurous light effects, the dancers could show off at the front, and the whole chorus would get the chance to improvise their own personal choice of bad behaviour live on stage. Predictably enough some chose to mime sex, a few went for drugs and others just did the rock and roll. We felt it would be tactful to add a small note to the bottom of the flyer announcing that 'this show contains adult material'.

Separate rehearsal schedules were drawn up for the dancers, the soloists, the small group and the main chorus, so that each piece of music had its own development timeline and the whole thing would synchronise at the right moment. Our ideal date would have been early August, but since the South Bank complex was being refurbished the Queen Elizabeth Hall wasn't an option. With all the regular South Bank clients competing for the remaining London venues, there were very few theatres available.

We found a newly-opened performance space, just off Sloane Square, that had been chosen as a new home by the London Philharmonic Orchestra. They had dates available at the end of July, and although the Cadogan Hall was very obviously a converted church and somewhat formal and conservative for this rather radical show, we decided to book it. Phil Hewson was our Production Manager, his proper full-time job was in TV and he had done many of our shows before, so we knew he would be able to handle any of the problems which would inevitably crop up in a new venue with an ambitious and complicated production such as this.

Initially everything seemed to be running smoothly, but the closer we got to the show the more the problems escalated. The lighting designer insisted that he needed more equipment, and that meant taking out a block of balcony seats to provide the space for another gantry. More room was needed for the dancers at the front, so we had to install an additional apron on stage and lose another block of front row seats. The chorus wouldn't all fit on the raised rostra, so we had to hire extra. The music team decided that since we wouldn't have our usual backing band they ought to have an extra grand piano to bulk up the sound.

The Cadogan Hall box office was also selling 'Proms' tickets for their other events, and when the public rang up to buy our tickets they were told they couldn't. The alternative online booking facility kept on crashing. Half way through the run up to the concert, and long after we had done our sums and drawn up budget forecasts, they decided they needed to change the seating allocations. What had been sold as top price seats suddenly became second rank. Because of some esoteric legal complication, Cadogan Hall had refused to sign a contract with us, and they suddenly decided to change the verbal agreement and not pay for any of the advertising that we had expected.

It had all turned into an absolute nightmare for Phil our producer and Chris Denning, the stage manager. There were only four weeks left before the show and our carefully prepared budget wasn't worth the paper it was written on.

We decided to add an extra matinee performance and attempt to sell the additional tickets at short notice. At every available opportunity groups of chorus members would set off for the gay pubs and clubs in greater London with handfuls of flyers, and try to encourage people to come along.

As the weekend of the shows approached, ticket sales increased and it began to look as though we might manage to break even, but our troubles weren't over. On the day of the technical rehearsal in Cadogan Hall, the extra grand piano got stuck half-way up the backstage staircase. It was jammed on its side at one of the hairpin corners and wouldn't seem to go any further. The legs were unscrewed and the lid taken off the piano, then the handrail was taken off the wall. In the restricted space there was no possibility of using a winch or hoist; it all had to be done with manpower and muscles. Eventually a deep groove was left behind in the plaster of Cadogan Hall's brand new ceiling, and ninety thousand pounds worth of stubborn Steinway was shoved protesting round the bend.

With such a complicated production the technical rehearsal wasn't straightforward, and tempers were noticeably frayed. There were still things going wrong on the opening night; the ever-present human error of words being forgotten and cues being missed, but we got through it. Both the audience and many in the chorus were impressed by the ambition of the plot and the sophistication of the production, and many seemed moved by the raw emotion captured in the historical sweep of the story. It was a memorable show, and a great achievement to have pulled it off, but it was not quite as special as we had hoped it was going to be. It had more-or-less fulfilled the prophesy contained in its title, You'll Do For Now.

It had all cost just over £31,000 to put on, and in spite of all our last minute efforts we didn't quite manage to break even; the final figures showed a £2000 loss.

The show hadn't actually been any more complex than the run of extraordinary 'performance-art' productions we had tackled in Voicespace during our early years, but with our hugely increased numbers everything about the chorus was scaled up; anything unconventional or adventurous became much more difficult.

That show was a stimulus for some of us to look back at our own history and consider our development. It felt as if the chorus that had started out as a ram-shackle life-raft, built from flotsam and jetsam and adrift on the open ocean, had managed to remake itself into a sleek racing yacht for a while. We had sailed far and that yacht was now transformed again, this time into a lumbering great liner. In some ways the enlarged chorus was quite magnificent, but our course was more predictable and our destinations fixed. It took a lot of work by a load of navvies to get it moving, and changing direction had become a problem. Life on board this great ocean liner was generally safer and certainly more stable, but without quite realising it, we had paid a high price for the ticket; perhaps the time had come to rethink our long term strategy.

When we first went to an American choral festival we noticed that several of the biggest organisations there also had smaller spin-off groups present. The original parent choir had grown so large that it was no longer logistically feasible for them to consider doing smaller events. They couldn't all physically fit on the stage together, transporting everyone around was a major undertaking, and rehearsing new repertoire took months instead of weeks. If an offshoot small group was formed a lot of these problems could be solved and the whole organisation would become more flexible and responsive.

We had always had solos, duets and smaller groups performing in our chorus concerts, but they were just self-selected temporary arrangements which assembled for one production and split up afterwards. Since our size was likely to remain a permanent problem, we thought the time had come for us also to have an enduring small group.

They could have their own name and identity, and would be able to perform independently from the main chorus. Since all the members would still be part of the parent chorus, they could sing the entire main group's repertoire, but would also have their own dedicated rehearsals and eventually develop their own set of songs as well. We frequently got requests to do things in small TV and radio studios at short notice, and either had to turn them down, or else struggle to find a balanced group of three or four singers from each voice part who could respond with only one hasty extra rehearsal. The small group could become our multi-purpose rapid response unit.

Although it would cost the chorus considerably more to fund the additional set of rehearsals every week, we were confident that the small group would generate extra income from their actions, and if they got involved in any lucrative corporate events, might even create surplus funds and enable us to subsidise more main-chorus events and social activities.

There were many obvious advantages for the proposal, but it still proved a controversial idea. Some thought the small group would monopolise all the most interesting events and that those in the main chorus would only ever get the chance to participate in a couple of big concerts every year. Since at that time there were so many invitations being turned down and opportunities being missed, this was unlikely. There would still be plenty of chances for people to get involved in all sorts of extraordinary activities. Having a smaller group available would open up new possibilities for us, not deprive the majority of any of the strange adventures that regularly seemed to come our way.

A more serious objection was that one of the chorus's core principles, written in to our very first constitution, was that we would be an open access organisation; anyone should be able to join. To be effective this new group would have to remain small, would have to comprise balanced voice parts, and to be of the necessary outstanding quality the participants should be auditioned. Many chorus members would therefore be excluded.

The result of our philosophical debate was a decision that anyone was now free to form their own sub-group within the chorus. For the moment there would be one official small group subsidised from chorus funds, but if other people wanted to start up a Gregorian plainsong, jazz, barbershop, folk, minimal or anything-else group they would be encouraged and supported. The lumbering great ocean liner would be able to become a flotilla of smaller craft at will. We were about to rediscover our life-raft roots.

It would have been pretentious for anyone to have actually said "this chorus is about more than just singing, it's a utopian republic", but that ideal had always hung unspoken in the air about us. We had to exist in a realistic commercial context, but somehow we always managed to preserve our original and idealistic principles. With all the financial planning, budgets, audits and accounts we had to deal with, it sometimes felt as if we were just running a business, but in fact this enterprise remained at its heart a socio-political and artistic experiment. Plato would have been proud.

The steering group announced its decision about the small group proposal to the main chorus, and all the cautious, the worriers and the just plain argumentative were more or less mollified. Auditions were held and the small group was formed.

It had been decided that sixteen was the ideal number of performers, so eighteen were recruited to allow for drop-outs. Members would have to commit to at least one extra rehearsal each week, and when they got busy with performing there were inevitably going to be all sorts of extra evening and weekend demands. Singers would have to be both dedicated and available to be a part of the new small group.

Their first performance was at the Victoria and Albert Museum, only a couple of months after the group started rehearsing together. The chorus had various ambitious development plans that couldn't be implemented without some additional funding, and we were attempting to gain some corporate sponsorship, or financial backing from any businesses that might gain from the publicity of being associated with us. Marsh and Mallone, our design consultants, had some previous links with the V & A and arranged for the free use of one of their prestigious private suites for an evening. The main chorus simply wouldn't physically fit in this venue, so the small group could now act as our representatives.

Everyone got together and brainstormed a huge list of contacts that might possibly be of some use to us. An impressively professional looking document that detailed our plans and needs was drawn up and printed. Gold blocked invitations were sent out, crates of champagne ordered and an up-market catering company booked.

We had never done anything quite like this before, so had no idea what sort of response to expect. I borrowed a 52 inch plasma screen TV and John Moysen compiled an amazing DVD presentation of significant chorus achievements and images that would be shown to our captive audience.

The important evening arrived, and various members of the steering committee wore their smartest suits to greet our invited guests. Some of the people who turned up were instantly recognisable celebrities and media figures, but others were more anonymous, and possibly more significant, business entrepreneurs.

Our chorus development plans were a well-mixed bag of the obviously practical and the inspired and visionary. We wanted to do some outreach projects which involved a group of singers going out to a school, delivering an empowering message and doing a short demonstration of harmony and solo singing. Young people, and their educators, needed to hear that being gay was not a problem and nothing to be ashamed of. Maybe we could even start up a Youth Chorus? We wanted to buy our own recording equipment which could then be made available to all sorts of other minority groups that needed to find a more public voice. If we had an efficient office, and could pay wages to a full time manager, we would be able to set up all sorts of cross cultural connections and events. We needed another member in our music team; we wanted to provide travel bursaries so that everyone could participate in the tours. How about a spin-off Lesbian Chorus? Or a gay arts and media lab?

The team had all been well-briefed with the messages we needed to get across, and we worked our way smoothly around the invited crowd. This sort of high-power networking might have been new to most of us, but I got the distinct impression that most of our visitors had experienced a lot of this sort of thing, many times before. The new small group came on and gave an excellent little show of likeable songs; the audience listened, canapés circulated, corks popped and our glossy literature was distributed.

I couldn't help but feel a personal wave of nostalgia as I watched the small group perform. Although the sophisticated ambience of a champagne-fuelled reception at the V&A was radically different from anything the original founder members had ever experienced, there were unmistakeable echoes. A small group of singers, each one privately feeling a little insecure and under-rehearsed, had all united for a greater purpose and were putting on a convincing show. Our own history had shown us that vision, determination, and courage enough to try, could make things happen.

At the end of the evening we all heaved a huge collective sigh of relief. Fundraising was stressful and expensive work. The chorus had invested about six thousand pounds of our precious funds on printing costs and bite-sized morsels on skewers, and it was difficult to measure how successful it had been. There were no big cheques flying around, but maybe relationships had been established that might bear fruit in the future?

When you cast your coins into a pond, and wished for a dream, you never knew how far the ripples might reach.

EIGHTEEN
Walking in the Air

The London Gay Men's Chorus was supposed to be an amateur organisation, a recreational hobby run by and for a group of volunteers. Only three professionals in the music team and Michael, our part-time manager, earned any wages from it, and they all had to have other jobs to supplement their income from the chorus. In reality it all proved to be such an astonishingly exciting adventure that it simply took over and became the major activity and raison d'être for many of us. If you were not vigilant and self-disciplined, proper jobs, other friends and a social life were relegated to second place by the never-ending rush of planning and preparation, rehearsing and performing.

At the beginning of the year Olly, our deputy musical director, had decided that he really should devote more attention to his future career and qualifications; he handed in his notice and left. We had struggled on through the 'You'll Do For Now' production with only Charlie and Simon, but it was obvious they were getting overloaded and we had to appoint a replacement.

The post was advertised in The Stage, Time Out and a few of the more enlightened national dailies, and over twenty serious applications came in. A little team of experienced committee members was put together to sort through them all, and we were amazed at the quality of candidates; we had received replies from some really hard-core music business professionals.

It was difficult to determine who might have all the right qualities from mere written CVs, but eventually we reduced it to a list of nine who were asked to come in for face to face interviews.

Charlie, Greg and I spent a gruelling day in a borrowed office grilling the candidates. It became apparent that some who had appeared distinct possibilities on paper were very obviously not right. One talented and well qualified young woman shut her eyes, screwed up her face and seemed to sink into an alarmingly somnambulist trance when she was asked a difficult question; she would not thrive in the chorus context. Another appeared too shy; one was just too young and inexperienced, he would do a great job but not just yet. One man that we all liked did the entertaining on cruise ships, had worked all over Europe and wanted to get involved in the West End. He was extrovert, gay, and we all thought he would do a great job, we also thought we wouldn't be able to keep him.

One candidate really shone. Andrea Brown taught in schools and at the Guildhall, and had a specialization in early music. She ticked all the right boxes, and when she left the room there was a slight feeling that she had been subtly interviewing us, rather than the other way round.

We thought we might have found the right person, but there was still one final test. Andrea and two other finalists came to Cecil Sharp House one Monday evening and had a go at working with the whole chorus. Each was given a twenty minute session and then the members filled in voting slips. As was expected they were all good, but Andrea was the best and was duly appointed.

In addition to her obvious musical skills, I thought it would be really helpful to have a measure of female influence amongst all the swirling and sometimes rampant testosterone of the chorus. There were only half a dozen people left from 1996 who remembered our previous female conductor, and no matter how unlikely it might sound, we knew that the non-competitive gender chemistry could work really well.

Immediately after the summer break finished, Andrea started working with the chorus and we began to prepare for the Christmas season.

After our first Barbican concert with the Raymond Gubbay Organisation had been such a sell-out success, they were understandably very keen to expand the partnership. For Christmas 2005 they proposed to put us on for two nights at the Barbican, and also organise two additional concerts at the Symphony Hall in Birmingham, and the Dome Theatre in Brighton. It seemed like a good idea. An amazing amount of rehearsal and preparation went in to doing a single concert, and if we could present the repertoire four times over we should be able to reap a much greater reward, both aesthetically and financially. The only extra effort needed would be the evenings spent on stage and a couple of coach trips getting to and from the different venues.

To boost ticket sales the Gubbay Organisation were always keen to include a celebrity guest, and after much thought and negotiation they came up with Rula Lenska. The previous year's guest had been our contact, Simon Callow, and although Rula wasn't quite such a respected theatrical 'big gun' as he, she was well liked and we were pleased that she had a training in musical theatre and would be able to offer us the possibility of playing along with some interesting song and dance material.

We had a meeting with her and explained the sort of thing we might do. It was immediately obvious that she was a very good sport, and happy to go along with whatever we could come up with. Stuart, our choreographer, devised a clever 'Let it Snow' dance break for her and Paul Tame to do, and they started practising. Paul had won various awards for ballroom dance; she had boundless energy and turned out to be great fun to work with. The pairing worked well and the only problem was that the extra rehearsals, and her necessarily glamorous ball-gown, made an unanticipated dent in our fee.

The repertoire for the show was 95% new material, but since one of the really successful items from the previous year had been the song Walking in the Air, we decided to repeat it. The whole chorus had sung it last time, but of course the well-known 'Snowman' version had featured the boy soprano Aled Jones, and we felt it would be more authentic if this time a few solo lines at the beginning and the end were performed by an angelic child.

One of our members gave private singing lessons, and

he knew just the right child student who could do it for us. The boy's parents were thrilled at the prospect of their offspring getting a solo spot in the Barbican Concert Hall with the chorus, and were eager to sign the necessary parental consent form.

Then there was an odd coincidence; the mother happened to know somebody in the Gubbay office, and one day she proudly mentioned the planned solo idea. Gubbay, the promoters of the concerts, were horrified. They imagined all sorts of lurid negative publicity in the tabloids, and angry demonstrations about little boys being encouraged to play with evil paedophiles on stage, and I got a phone call saying we were not going to be allowed to do it.

It was then my turn to be horrified. What did they think we were doing? Were they really making allegations that all gay men were paedophiles? Didn't they understand that this was just the sort of insane bigotry the chorus had been set up to fight? The blistering issue was batted back and forth for an hour or more. I was trying to be reassuring and reasonable; they were just getting more and more panic-stricken and entrenched. I was quite dogmatic that we could not back down, and so were they. The conversation ended with me saying that it was obvious we weren't going to reach any agreement about this, and I would have to pass the matter on to our steering committee, but pointed out that it would be just like poking an angry hornet's nest with a sharp stick.

I took a deep breath and sent an email around the steering committee. The instantaneous reaction was exactly as I had expected. "How dare they imply such things" and "we must cancel the contract and call everything off". Greg Battle, our chairman, was as convinced as everyone else that this was a non-negotiable issue, but offered to step in and try to find some sort of resolution. Gubbay had assured everyone that this was not their opinion; they were just worried about what 'others' might say.

It looked, for a very worrying week, as though our set of four Christmas concerts were going to be cancelled, but eventually Greg managed to negotiate a satisfactory but slightly peculiar compromise arrangement.

Andrea, our deputy musical director and a bona fide soprano in her own right, was going to sing the 'boy' part in Birmingham and Brighton, and the boy was going to be allowed to sing it in the two London dates, but not as the first item on the programme. It would have to be moved to halfway through the first act.

Quite what this implied about prejudice in Birmingham and Brighton (or indeed London) we couldn't decide, and although it would have made a good opener, the position of the piece in the concert wasn't ultimately that significant. We felt we had more or less won, agreed to the slightly ridiculous conditions, and the steering committee never told the rest of the chorus, or the boy's parents, exactly what had been going on.

The diverse programme we had devised for the show was really satisfying. Much like the institution of 'Christmas' itself there was an unlikely blend of the commercial and the sincere, the sentimental and the profound. Although I had written a script for Rula to work from, she herself came up with a very funny sequence of letters by John Julius Norwich about the 'Twelve Days of Christmas'. We redid the running order at the last moment so that it would fit in, and her contribution eased us smoothly through an awkward transition from formal to comic. For a segment of high culture there was also a magnificent modern/classical oratorio from Gerald Finzi, which mentioned distant church bells and angels aloft in the frosty air. We borrowed a spectacular four metre high winged white angel costume from our art director Nic Boisselle's carnival hire company, and had it mysteriously and silently materialise above the chorus for each of the four concerts. Alan, the long-suffering second tenor who volunteered to wear the costume, later commented that to him it felt like a public crucifixion, but the visual effect was startlingly beautiful.

Our final show on December 22nd 2005 was an historic date for the whole gay community; it was when civil partnership ceremonies were at last legally recognised in England and Wales. Nearly seven hundred 'gay marriages' had taken place that very day. Greg, the chorus chairman, used his speech to congratulate all those couples and to thank the many groups and individuals who had campaigned so fiercely to bring about a change in the law. Whether the promoter approved or not, we never missed an opportunity to make a political point, especially in the most populist of our performances.

The two nights in the big Barbican Concert Hall had drawn in an enormous audience, and as far as we could tell, there hadn't been the slightest raised eyebrow or murmur of impropriety when our boy soprano sang his 'controversial' solo with the chorus.

Somehow the reputation of the chorus hadn't travelled with us to Birmingham, and the attendance there was poor. Ironically all the risky logistics of arriving at an untried venue at lunchtime, setting up, and doing the concert on that same evening, had run as smoothly as clockwork. The hall's technical crew later said that we had been one of the best organised groups they had ever come across, and we could return the same compliment to them. The concert sounded wonderful in the beautiful Symphony Hall, and it was a great shame that not many local people saw it.

Most of the chorus had travelled there in the two coaches that Gubbay had booked, but those of us who had needed to be there earlier in the day had gone in their own cars. Very late that night Charlie was giving Roberto the tenor, and Nic the art director, a lift back to London when half way down the M5 trouble caught up with them. His trusty old BMW suddenly started sounding dreadful and showers of sparks were shooting out the back. The silencer box had half come adrift and was dragging along the road. Neither Charlie nor Roberto had much idea what to do, but Nic, the most unlikely of butch mechanics, solved the problem by whipping out his emergency sewing kit, crawling under the car and cutting through the rubber strapping with his dainty scissors. They were then able to bang slowly but safely all the way back home.

The chorus attracted a bigger audience to the Brighton

Dome, but the theatre staff there were hopelessly disorganised, and that show was blighted by their inattentive sound engineer who kept missing his cues. In the dressing room afterwards Chris our stage-manager, who is normally so even tempered and unflappable, was still so annoyed at the way their engineer had damaged our performance that he said he felt like taking him out into the car-park and giving him a good kicking. No matter how carefully one tries to prepare, the fates can intervene.

As well as the big theatre shows, several groups of our singers had been doing carols four times a day in Selfridges, and there was also a final rather rowdy but festive candle-lit session by the tree in Trafalgar Square to raise funds for the RNIB.

That season had been an exhausting and sometimes challenging experience for us, and we all hoped the next show that we were busily preparing for our fifteenth anniversary year was going to be an easier journey.

NINETEEN
The Fifteenth Anniversary

The first chorus performance in our anniversary year was appropriate, relevant and meaningful. It was an event in early February called 'Queer is Here' at the Museum of London, and it marked the start of the very first national Lesbian, Gay, Bisexual and Transgender History Month.

The occasion caused us to reflect on just how much cultural attitudes had changed during our fifteen years of existence. The idea of a significant institution curating an exhibition which celebrated gay history, achievements and pride would have been inconceivable when we first began. As well as collecting sound recordings that illustrated the lives of gay and lesbian Londoners, the museum was now gradually building up a collection of relevant objects and ephemera, and I decided that I would like to donate our first chorus banner to them. It had become redundant when we redesigned our logo at the end of the nineteen nineties, and ever since then it had remained folded up and forgotten in a box of sheet music. I could clearly remember making it during the week before the Pride march in 1993, buying the big rectangle of canvas in Enfield market, and then sitting on the floor for hours carefully painting the design. It had been carried on many marches, and hung on many stages, and for all our early years it was the symbol that proudly announced our existence and united our membership.

The banner was hung in the foyer at the Museum of London's main entrance, alongside an exhibition of photographs from Pride marches. The chorus gathered to sing their songs, and both Peter Tatchell and I delivered brief speeches about the importance of preserving and celebrating our history. One of the evocative pieces sung that day was 'Our Time' written by Stephen Sondheim for the musical 'Merrily We Roll Along'. The lyrics spoke of the possibilities of the present; of being poised and shivering on the brink of the future. Somehow it seemed to capture all the fragile feelings of shared optimism and hope that had always been so essential to the chorus.

Although Martin Brophy had retired from his role as chorus chairman, he didn't stop devising plans and projects that would develop our future. Various Voices, the pan-European event that we had contributed to in Paris was part of an on-going cooperation between the larger choirs; every four years a joint festival of singing was held in a different city. Martin thought it could be held in London in 2009, our steering committee agreed, and he set about formulating a bid that we could present to the Various Voices board.

A team of helpers was gathered together. Martin was the coordinator and the participants were ourselves together with representatives from 'Diversity' and 'The Pink Singers', two of the other LGBT choirs in the UK. They put some of their grand plans down on paper, added in some hypothetical figures, and then made approaches to key contacts we had already come across. Since the chorus had by then acquired a broad experience of participating in multi-cultural and international events, the plans were well devised; everyone contacted was enthusiastic about the idea of staging something ambitious in London.

The Mayor of London, at that time Ken Livingstone, responded that cultural activities such as this could make a major contribution to life in the city; he was committed to the fight for Lesbian and Gay equality and strongly supported our bid. The mayor's office controls the events that happened in Trafalgar Square, and they said we should consider using it as one of the open air venues for the festival.

The idea that the festival might well attract 4 or 5 thousand visitors to the capital galvanised the tourist board 'Visit London'. They immediately replied saying they offered their fullest support; London was one of the few places that could be called a world city, and they hoped it would be chosen as the site for our proposed festival.

One of the most promising responses came from Jude Kelly, the Artistic Director of the South Bank Centre, who said that the proposals were very much in line with their vision for the future of the South Bank. She hoped that we might become a companion organisation and help to develop a greater audience for singing events. An exploratory 'visioning' exercise was held in one of their boardrooms, and whilst our planning group spoke of why we had formed and where we hoped to go, a team of graffiti-style graphic artists produced a spectacular chart 5 metres long which illustrated the potential of these visionary ideas. The South Bank suggested that they might programme a major orchestral work of their own and include participation from the Various Voices festival. The Royal Festival Hall, The Queen Elizabeth Hall, The Purcell Room and the newly created terraces and balconies were reserved exclusively for our use between the 1st and the 4th of May 2009.

Our proposals had received a startlingly positive response. The development team began the work of putting together a document to present to Legato, the parent organisation of the festival; they were due to meet in London at the end of May, on the same day of our fifteenth anniversary concert.

The task of inventing an exciting future proved to be more straightforward than that of sorting out the imminent season. There had been the usual problem of finding an available theatre with a stage large enough to hold the chorus. I had rung around all the agents and promoters who controlled the London venues and, armed with tape measures and check lists, Chris, Steve and I had been to visit a couple of the possibilities. Over the phone it sounded as though The Queen's theatre was just about big enough, but when we saw the size of the huge Les Miserables set that we would have to work round, and were told that we couldn't use their sound system, we had to strike it off the list.

The Prince Edward in Old Compton Street looked promising. They were showing Mary Poppins and all of the set was hung in the fly-tower or stored in the wings, but with a basic hire price of £12,000 we soon realised it was too expensive.

The Piccadilly Theatre was the only one that was a vaguely realistic proposition. They had the Guys and Dolls company in residence, and we would have to hire the upstairs space in a neighbouring pub to use as our dressing room, but it was possible. Since the theatre owners were uncertain how long their current production would run, they wouldn't sign a contract six months ahead, and we had to hold off from advertising our own show and keep our fingers crossed. It didn't feel like a very comfortable position, but insecurity is one of the inescapable characteristics of show business.

Whilst all this was going on a possible trip to Italy at the end of the summer was also being arranged. Andrea De Tomas was a keen chorus member who had originally been a native of Turin but was now based in London. He always kept in touch with the cultural scene of his home city and at the end of 2005, when he heard that the Vienna Boys' Choir had pulled out from the annual Turin music festival, he wondered if we might be able to fill the gap.

At that time I was the chairman of the chorus Music and Performance committee, and when Andrea told me of the possibility of singing in Italy, I felt we could adapt our plans for the next year and immediately drafted an application letter to the organisers. A lot of it was lifted from the work that Martin and his team had put in to the Various Voices bid; we were an adventurous multi-cultural chorus who had experience of touring to foreign cities, we sang a diverse repertoire with mass appeal, and most of all, we were accomplished musical ambassadors for a significant minority group who were not represented within their society (there was not a single gay choir in Italy)

The 'Settembre Musica' festival organisers were very interested in our proposition, and Andrea continued to negotiate details with them. Not only were they willing to pay our air fares, they were also able to offer us free accommodation. The city would be hosting the winter Olympics that spring, and in September we could stay in the athletes' empty 'hotel style' apartment block. With such generous financial incentives we would be able to take the whole chorus including all our regular stage-crew, and still earn an additional small fee. In the overstretched and poorly-subsidised performing arts scene of the UK we had never come across anything like this before; Italy is obviously a society that takes its culture seriously.

Every single year in The London Gay Men's Chorus had been an extraordinary experience; there was no such thing as average. The fifteenth anniversary was typical, an unpredictable voyage into uncharted waters. Gubbay, the promoters of our Christmas shows were now negotiating with a German agent and talking about putting us on in the huge Cologne sports stadium that December. As well as the main London and Turin shows, we were going to visit St David's Hall in Cardiff, do another West End Live show in Leicester Square, have a guest spot at the Royal Albert Hall, stage a joint concert with other choirs in the Queen Elizabeth Hall, and participate in an extraordinary event to mark the 150th anniversary of the National Portrait Gallery.

The previous October I had been though all my old concert programmes and sent out to our membership an email catalogue of every song the chorus had ever sung. The plan was to celebrate the birthday with a 'greatest hits' concert and I wanted to compile a top-ten list. As replies came back it became apparent just how few of the current members had been around during the nineteen nineties. About three quarters of the chorus had joined since the millennium, and they voted for all the more recent songs that were their own personal favourites.

The top six songs from the membership ballot were eventually included in the anniversary concert, but the music team had to step in and select the remainder to make it into a more historically accurate and balanced programme. Since we were going to perform in Italy I found an Italian folk song, 'La Montanara' that we had sung years before, and to make it more interesting for everyone two brand new pieces from Rufus Wainwright were added.

As the year began the chorus began the exacting and enjoyable process of learning the songs and rehearsing the music.

We were still anticipating that our London concert was going to be at the Piccadilly Theatre, but every time I rang up to ask when we could finalise the details and sign a contract I was given a different excuse; first the stage manager was away, then they were rehearsing a new cast and everyone was too busy. We were having a hectic time also, it was going to be an eventful year and there were a thousand details to organise, but we were pleased to hear that the run of Guys and Dolls was obviously going to continue, and so time slipped inexorably by.

It must have been about ten weeks before our proposed date when eventually I had to insist on a written contract and went to visit the theatre manager. They were still keen to have us, the hire fee would have boosted their annual income and such things were significant in such an unpredictable business. Unfortunately the resident Guys and Dolls company had absolutely nothing to gain from our presence, didn't want any potential disruption and started being difficult. They insisted that we install a temporary stage covering to protect their set, said that we couldn't have either rostra or piano on stage, and that the orchestra pit couldn't be used either. They wanted to charge us a huge amount for use of their light-rig, and told us we would have to hire their technician and pay him double-rate overtime. We already knew there was no dressing room space, but now they wouldn't even let us have a store cupboard to use as the production office.

It was the last straw. Even without the new restrictions the Piccadilly Theatre would have been a difficult proposition; now it looked completely untenable and we would have to find somewhere else. A few people blamed me for all the problems, but those who had been following what was going on realised it was just one of those frustrating situations that can occur. We rang around all our contacts once more and decided that our best option was to try the Cadogan Hall again. It had been a brand new enterprise when we first went there, and after the organisational problems encountered during our visit, the management assured us that they had redesigned all their procedures to make things run more efficiently. This time we were able to draw up a binding contract, and could at last begin to advertise our show.

We knew that with a promoter doing a lot of high power advertising we could fill 4000 seats at the Barbican, but on our own we couldn't afford to buy big adverts in the press and had to rely on flyers and word of mouth. Although the standard of our singing and quality of presentation had grown immeasurably during the last fifteen years, our means of promotion had remained pretty much the same as at the beginning.

The chorus now paid professionals to help us with learning and musical development, choreography, lighting and sound, but public relations rarely figured in the budget. We paid for and overworked the part-time office manager, Michael, but everything else in our administration was accomplished by individuals who volunteered for free. Our stage managers, concert producers, art directors, web designers, committee chairmen, tour managers, CD sellers, graphic artists, costume makers, accountants, music copyists, secretaries and assistants were all ordinary members who sacrificed their spare time. To an uninitiated outsider the chorus must have resembled a well-run business, but in reality the chorus was powered by altruism, philanthropy and selflessness; it was an implausible way to organise such an ambitious venture. In spite of this we had achieved an extraordinary degree of success, and our fifteenth anniversary should have been an opportunity for us to celebrate.

Up until the day of the concert, we were all too busy to notice.

That morning the international delegates from the Legato festival were having their decisive meeting. With help from the Visit London tourist board Martin and his team had organised a splendid presentation. Most of the representatives from other European choirs had flown in on the previous day; early in the morning we met up with them by the big wheel on the South Bank. A trip on The London Eye was an ideal introduction to some of the attractions of the city.

There were about thirty people altogether, and amidst the clamour and activity of traffic and tourists, circling slowly through the air, high above the city, suddenly felt like a precious and silent meditation.

Calmed but elated, we disembarked from the aerial capsules and boarded a high speed catamaran to go down the river to the futuristic City Hall building, home of the Greater London Authority and where our meeting was to be held.

Martin and his team handed out slick presentation folders to all the delegates, and then confidently talked through our comprehensive plans for holding the 2009 festival in London. It was an unassailable bid and, although most of us didn't know it, the battle had already been won even before that day began. Other Legato representatives had heard rumour of our plans, and all the competing bids from alternative European cities had been withdrawn.

After the meeting was concluded everyone was invited to the panoramic top floor of the City Hall building for a complimentary lunch. Despite the technical rehearsal for that night's show having already started at Cadogan Hall, we had arranged for the chorus small group to be there, and they sang beautifully with the spectacular backdrop of the city spread behind them.

I think it was only then that some of us had time to reflect on how much had been achieved, our plans for the future, and what an extraordinary organisation the chorus was.

That nostalgic reverie didn't last long as all the chorus members had to get across to Sloane Square and prepare for the show. We had worked hard to get last minute sales, and although a lot of the audience seemed to be composed of friends, relatives, and ex-members, nearly all the seats were filled.

The concert just had to start with our old anthem written by Labi Siffre, 'Something Inside so Strong'. This song had stayed with us throughout our entire history. Ever more complex arrangements of it had been performed countless times in many different contexts. Sometimes it had been an angry tirade, at others it was an exultant celebration. This time it was split into three sections, and in between each Martin Kaufman stepped up to the microphone and interposed a high-speed rap of highlights from our story. It was an occasion when we felt it relevant to tell our own members, as well as the audience, where we had come from and why we had started. To turn the whole evening into a chorus history lesson would have seemed pompous and indulgent, so most of the show was simply a succession of wonderful songs from different eras; the real message was in the music, as it had always been.

The fifteenth anniversary show was a very enjoyable experience, but somehow much less grand and spectacular than I had anticipated. It felt more like a comfortable and informal party with a group of old friends rather than the triumphant and public retrospective I had imagined. Upon reflection that casual lack of splendour now seems exactly right, we weren't commemorating the conclusion of anything, the anniversary was merely a brief pause in an on-going process.

After the concert at Cadogan Hall a whole avalanche of events happened one on top of another. The chorus stage-managed an interesting show at the Queen Elizabeth Hall where six gay choirs all presented an evening of different styles and approaches. With pop, classical, spiritual, folk, comedy and tragedy, it was almost a trial run of the sort of event we were planning for the big 2009 European festival. The logistics of getting all the various groups in and out of their dressing rooms and on and off the stage was convoluted, but on the night it all went smoothly enough. It satisfactorily demonstrated that with a lot of preparation by the production manager, a well organised stage-manager a degree of cooperation from the participants and a bit of luck, it was possible to execute all sorts of complex theatrical manoeuvres.

Dealing with large groups of energized performers was always going to be difficult, and there was one unfortunate mistake. I managed to lock one of the baritones in our dressing room for the whole of the second half. Although I had announced a five minute call for everyone to get ready, and then spent an extra few minutes getting them all into their correct lines so they would go on stage in the right order, one person managed to stay out of earshot in the toilets. I was profusely apologetic when I discovered him waiting for us after the show, but for months afterwards he was the unfortunate butt for jokes about 'staying in the closet for too long'.

The next weekend we did another of the West End Live showcase events in Leicester Square, and the weekend after that we took an extraordinary motorised float on the Pride March all the way along Oxford Street to Waterloo Bridge. For once we tried to discourage the chorus from singing themselves hoarse on the parade by playing a rather startling dance remix CD of our greatest hits from the back of the lorry. We had to sing at the Royal Albert Hall the next day, and needed to hold back so that we could put on a professional show.

When we had received the Albert Hall invitation several months earlier, the producer Mig Kimpton had asked us if there were any other guest acts we would also like to sing with. Various names had been suggested and they were then approached to check availability. Heather Small was keen to do it, and had a terrific song, 'Proud', with a chorus part that would be just right for us.

It wasn't until a couple of days beforehand that Elton John was confirmed as the big finale act, and the addition of such a significant celebrity was felt to be a real triumph. Unfortunately on the night the planning wasn't quite tight enough and the show ran really late. The audience listened respectfully, but by the time Elton came on it was after midnight, the temperature inside the hall was in the forties and there were problems with his sound system; it was Heather Small and her band who really stole the show. The audience were literally dancing in the aisles, and 'Proud' with chorus backing, felt like the real highlight of the evening.

Although it had already been a ridiculously busy summer there was still one more important performance for us to do before we could take a break.

Many people still think of Wales as the ultimate home of the finest male-voice choirs, and Saint David's Hall in Cardiff had invited us to do a show for them.

When we had to do an 'away from London' performance we always tried to get some involvement from a local choir. The event was more likely to be covered by the local media, and the guest performers sometimes brought their own loyal audience with them and bumped up the ticket sales. The choirs in Dublin, Birmingham and Brighton had always looked on a visit from us as an opportunity to do a big concert in a prestigious venue and had been very keen to cooperate.

A couple of years previously we had done some workshops with the Welsh National Opera when they came to visit Saddlers Wells, but although they were based in Cardiff their agent seem distinctly frosty and said no one would be available. Perhaps they felt we weren't quite serious enough. The manager of St David's had agreed with us that some home-grown involvement was a good idea and recommended a local group called 'Only Men Aloud'. There were only eight of them and we felt that the contrast of size and style would make for a more interesting evening, so I arranged for them to do a ten minute spot in the second half.

It was a long trip, and as our two coaches swept across the Severn Bridge the landscape seemed to be satisfyingly exotic and unfamiliar. Only three people from the production team had been to visit the venue beforehand, and when we arrived I was delighted to discover that St David's was a beautiful auditorium. As the whole chorus did a sound check it almost seemed as if the place had been especially designed to flatter choral singing. The resonance was ravishing; even the gentlest of notes seemed to circle out from the stage and then hang in the air like an ethereal spirit.

In spite of all the advance publicity we had tried to do from London, ticket sales were still poor, and after our rehearsal we used the brief gap at the end of the afternoon to blitz the people in the shopping arcade and high street with leaflets. It was then that we discovered that there was a free concert that evening in the Cardiff Castle Park, only five minutes away from the theatre.

A mere 180 people turned up to the concert, and it was one of the most sublime we had done for a long time. The repertoire was more or less what we had done for the anniversary show, but since this wasn't a 'home' audience, we had taken out most of the spoken history anecdotes and just sang the songs. Our guest group performed their chosen pieces wonderfully, and provided the variation and change of pace that we had anticipated. Our programme included a strange and mystical Welsh song called David of the White Rock; it was about the power of great music being passed down through the generations, and the chorus delivered it as though it were a sacred bequest enshrined in a cathedral.

Although we didn't quite cover all the expense of going there, the Cardiff concert felt like a tremendous success. Generating profits had never been the main incentive for our activities and no matter how cautious we tried to be, it had to be accepted that sometimes it just didn't happen.

The chorus was often riotously high-spirited on the journey back from a gig, but for some reason this time the group seemed to be swaddled in a cloak of quiet content and calmness. As the coaches sped back along the M4 a vast, amber, harvest-moon hung low in the eastern sky ahead, and the deep night seemed filled with solemn peace.

Some weeks after the show I was able to send our

guest group 'Only Men Aloud' a live recording of their performance in our concert, and since they had no other, they used that recording as their audition sample for the TV show 'Last Choir Standing'. After weeks of stiff competition they won the hearts of both judges and viewers and were declared to be the winners. Only Men Aloud are now a professional group with a huge following, and it's very satisfying that the LGMC played a tiny part in their much deserved success.

TWENTY
An Italian Job

Although being on tour with the chorus usually entailed a lot of hard work, most of us thought of it as an amazing adventure holiday with a big group of friends. Many members used their annual leave and expanded the tour activity into their main vacation, and some of us who were self-employed and less encumbered used it as an opportunity to do some more extensive travelling.

On the way to Sydney I had an extraordinary week in Tokyo, and then visited The Great Barrier Reef and Hawaii on the way back. When we did Boston and San Jose, I also stayed in LA and went all the way down the west coast to Mexico, and on the way back from Washington and Montreal I had a week in Toronto and saw the Niagara Falls.

On the Turin trip a group of us spent some time in Milan first. It was only an hour away on the train, and the city is a great place for cultural sightseeing. Once the whole chorus had assembled in Turin for the concert there was a strict schedule, so I was glad that several of us were able to experience Milan without any pressure.

For the duration of our four day Turin visit more or less everything was being paid for by the Settembre

Musica festival organisers, so nearly everyone in the chorus had been able to come along. We were split into two groups, and the majority were in the ex-Winter Olympics accommodation, modern apartment blocks set in the midst of an ugly suburban sprawl. Turin is a big industrial city, and our flats were right next to a main railway line. As Mussolini had promised, the trains ran on time, and they started early. No matter what time you got to sleep, you were invariably woken up by the hammering of a goods train going through at 7am.

With a whole city to explore, and a big group of people to do it with, lots of us were choosing to stay up late. Whenever you went past the little sun-terrace at the back of the communal apartments it was occupied by a motley collection of singers, some nursing hangovers, others planning outings, and some just wondering where they could get a breakfast, or who had done what with whom last night.

We had a timetable with some compulsory rehearsal and sound check appointments marked in red, but most mornings were free time. One evening the city had laid on a civic reception for us; assorted dignitaries were going to be there and we were urged to dress more formally and arrive on time. It felt strange to be treated as an honoured guest of the city, but the novelty soon wore off, and after an hour of bilingual speeches most of us were impatient to investigate the medieval maze of little bars and cafes that lay nearby in the old city-centre.

There was a small but thriving gay scene in the city, and the Turin Pride association had arranged for an outing to a newly-opened gay bar. Many of the local people there seemed to have come specifically to meet the London mob, and it was already quite crowded. When two coach loads of chorus turned up it felt positively packed, but luckily there was a big palm-fringed patio outside, and it was fascinating to sit there in the warm midnight air and watch the social scene circulate.

A group outing that sounded like a nice idea, but wasn't quite so successful, was to a trendy show-biz themed pizza restaurant. We were all jammed on to tiny tables, and the staff couldn't cope with so many orders simultaneously. We couldn't move around to talk with our friends and had to wait at least an hour for each course to arrive. To add insult to injury it was outrageously expensive, and I've had a better pizza in Palmers Green. It felt as though the size of the group was now starting to inhibit shared activities as well as make many performance options impractical.

There was the opportunity for some cultural exploration as well, and several small groups led by Turin Pride volunteers went off for walking tours around the centre. In the 16th century the city had been laid out on a formal grid plan reminiscent of Paris, and there was a brief period in the 1860s when Turin had actually been the capital city of Italy. There is a fine legacy of grand architecture, dating from Roman times to the profligacy of the Mussolini era, and the current inhabitants take great satisfaction in displaying their history.

The venue for our concert was a masterpiece of art deco industrial architecture. It is known as the Lingotto and was built as a Fiat car factory in the 1920s. It was the first vertical assembly construction line, where cars were started deep below ground level, completed as they gradually moved upwards and finally tested on the steeply banked, oval race track that still runs around the roof. Fiat moved out to more modern premises years ago, and during the decades the building was an empty and elegant white elephant it was occasionally used as a film location. It played a starring role in the Michael Caine movie 'The Italian Job' when a trio of matching Mini Coopers zoomed around the roof-top track and ran riot through the Turin rush-hour. The iconic building was recently converted by the architect Renzo Piano into a smart commercial and cultural centre. There are now several floors of shops and restaurants, a large art gallery and the Giovanni Agnelli Auditorium where we were to perform.

The last time we had presented this programme had been in Cardiff just before the summer break, and when we got on stage at the Agnelli it seemed as if this acoustic was going to be similarly pleasing. There was some concern that singers' memories might have gone rusty during the seven week gap, so we had arranged for a run-through before we left London, and had also managed a makeshift rehearsal in a different Turin theatre the day before. Somehow the summer break seemed to have matured the repertoire, rather than left it stale, and we were all reassured to discover that the chorus now sounded really polished.

Nearly all the events in the festival had been presented

for free; we were one of the very few where the audience would have to pay for a ticket, and were pleased to learn that the box office had completely sold out five weeks previously. Such high expectations caused some trepidation, but both the organisers and the audience were showing such confidence in us that the supportive aura was almost self-fulfilling. They really wanted to have us there, the auditorium looked wonderful, the whole Lingotto complex was amazing, and we couldn't help but feel this was going to be a good concert.

After we had done our sound check, the lighting had been lined up and we had practised our entrances and exits, there was time for a meal break. I wandered off and found a copy of that days' La Stampa newspaper which had carried a piece about us, "La prima volta del gay chorus" it said, and I sat at a café table and slowly tried to translate it. The concerts started late here so there was still an hour left before we had to get ready. I had noticed a deserted goods lift backstage, the top button on the control panel seemed to indicate 'roof', so looking for an adventure, I tried it.

There is now a futuristic helicopter landing pad in the centre of the oval roof, but the old buildings original aerial race-track was still there; half a mile long, entirely empty and utterly exhilarating. It was as if an environmental artist had attempted to sculpt some extravagant emotion, made a feeling manifest in three dimensional spaces out of smooth tarmac and dusty concrete. A great swathe of magenta and mauve cloud swept high across the sun-setting sky. The first glittering of city lights spread away on one side; the massive silvery ramparts of the Alps rose up on the other.

It could have been a film set for an intense magic-realist Pasolini movie.

I might easily have been trapped there for hours, all alone in a trance on a rooftop, but as I looked over the barrier wall I could see a scattered procession of ant-people coming slowly towards the great doors far below. There was music to be made that evening.

Considering it was such an important event there seemed to be a surprising lack of nerves evident in the dressing room. An air of quiet assurance and expectation prevailed; it felt as if we were completely confident about what was about to happen.

The opening piece was Verdi's 'Va Pensiero'. This was almost an alternative national anthem for the Italians, and whilst it was dangerous to do something so well known, we felt it showed a degree of respect for the culture we were visiting. We had included two other Italian language pieces in the programme, and half way through the first half the beginning of the old folk song 'La Montanara', was drowned out by applause.

Singing was endemic in this culture; every village had its own competent choir and everyone from shop assistants to policemen sang easily and without inhibition as they went about their daily business. What they didn't have anywhere was a gay choir. Now that we had shown the audience we could sing properly, we could start to have some fun.

Incorporating pop songs, edgy modernism and hits

from the musicals into a serious music festival must have seemed an extraordinary thing to do, and judging from the audience reaction they certainly weren't expecting us to whip out red feather fans from our back pockets and start doing choreography either, but we are a gay choir, and that was the way we did it.

The ending of the concert and the encore must have seemed unconventional also. It was a variation on the 'ring shout' idea we had tried in Birmingham years before; a richly arranged spiritual gradually dissolved into harmonic white noise as groups of people began to sing different lines and casually wandered off the stage, it must have looked as though we had suddenly been distracted, or thought of something else to do, so like a gay man cruising in a crowd of strangers, we just moved on.

The audience wouldn't stop clapping, so we had to go back on and do a repeat of Va Pensiero to signal that we really had finished; the show was over, the coaches were waiting in the car park and it was time for us to go.

An extraordinary degree of approval and acceptance had been demonstrated towards us as a coherent group on stage, but as soon as the performance finished the chorus transmuted seamlessly back into a group of individuals. When that inevitable transformation took place there was an unspoken recognition amongst us that public tolerance and our personal safety were no longer guaranteed; we became separate strangers in a strange land. Some of us might get on the coach and go to explore the nightlife offered by the city's clubs and bars; others might get a late bus back to where they were staying, or risk walking through the empty and unfamiliar streets alone. We knew that most of the time gay was only acceptable when it stayed behind the glare of the footlights; there was still real danger for us if we lingered too long in the darkness.

Only later did it occur to me that the Turin concert in mid-September 2006 could well have been fifteen years to the week that John, Louis and I sat together in the coffee bar at London Friend and first thought of forming a gay choir. My diaries and calendars from that date are long-since discarded, taking with them the exact logistical details of how the chorus began. It is all lost beneath the accumulated weight of event and adventure; at that time none of us understood that history was happening. Initially our motives had been to improve our immediate circumstances, and it was only in retrospect that any wider historical significance was discernible; who could know that the first rehearsal of the London Gay men's Chorus set the fuse on a ticking culture-bomb?

Fifteen years later we were invited to participate in a series of events at London's South Bank entitled '100 Ideas That Changed the World'.

The huge task of restoring and updating the South Bank arts complex had been underway for several years. Towards the end of 2006 The Royal Festival Hall was nearing completion, and some of the other elements in the project were already finished and standing idle. The Hayward Gallery was empty, and with six months to fill before the next exhibition was due it was decided the space should be used. The '100 Ideas That Changed the World' events were put together at short-notice and on a small budget. A variety of significant and visionary individuals were invited to deliver evening lectures and presentations about their work. Theodore Zeldin, an Oxford historian and thinker was one of the first, and Claire Short the politician and social reformer came soon after. Tracy Emin the artist and Alain de Botton, philosopher and TV personality were also included.

We had performed at the South Bank before, and I remembered the stage-crew as particularly efficient and easy-going. I rang up Eddie, the senior technician and asked if he could move a piano and a couple of stage platforms into the Hayward. I also suggested that on such a blank canvas at the gallery then was, he might try out some of his newly acquired lighting gadgets. To further help the ambience a temporary wine bar was installed in the foyer, it could secure some income and ease the strain on the over-stretched redevelopment budget.

Our evening scheduled for March 2007 was being co-ordinated by Mary King; she had been voice-coach with The English National Opera for many years, but had recently moved to the South Bank and was full of radical new ideas. We were mid-way through preparations for our summer concert and had a rag-bag of previously performed and half-rehearsed new repertoire. Mary proposed the first part of the evening could be a few songs by Hans Eisler based on Brecht poems, and sections from a very strange 'sound-environment' called 'The Great Learning' by Cornelius Cardew; it was reassuring to know that the Cardew piece was meant to be semi-improvised. Due to the impromptu nature of this project there was only time for a couple of rehearsals and 'make-it-up-as-you-go' was exactly what the composer intended.

For our '100 Ideas' event, banks of portable state-of-the-art lights were hidden behind each pillar, and whilst we sang the strangest choral music, colours washed and swept, span and speared the enormous womb of white gallery space. The effect was of a clique of avant-garde intellectuals channelled from another dimension into a New York nightclub; the audience were treated to a remarkable experience of radical singing.

Perhaps ideas and actions improvised spontaneously and out of necessity, have a more urgent certainty of purpose that renders them powerful.

TWENTY ONE
The Show Goes On

For 2007 I devised a show entitled 'Bad Boys', which addressed some of the lessons we could learn from the more regrettable aspects of male behaviour. Villains and the various ways we can all go off the rails have given rise to some of the best songs since storytelling began. The show was popular with the membership and well received by our growing audiences; we presented it a couple of times in London, and later that summer took it to the Usher Hall in Edinburgh and the Royal Concert Hall in Glasgow.

It was after the Glasgow show that some regrettable bad behaviour took place off-stage and within our own ranks. There had been a well lubricated 'end of tour' party after the final show, and the coach to our accommodation in Edinburgh was late. When we finally arrived back well after midnight, some of us went off in search of yet more celebration whilst others took to their bunks in our communal dormitory. There had been some misgivings about roughing it in a cheap hostel, and some had chosen a budget hotel, but most had joked about the prospects of a late night orgy, and thought there was nothing wrong with a dormitory as long as everyone was considerate.

Unfortunately the message didn't register with everybody. One of the very late revellers had to get an early flight back to London, and set his alarm for four in the morning. It went off at 4am, but instead of turning it off and going to the airport, he switched it to 'doze' and went back to sleep. The alarm call repeated five minutes later, everyone groaned, but the traveller still didn't think he needed to get up or even turn the devilish device off. At 4.25, after the fifth time the entire dormitory had been woken, one of the more disturbed sleepers got out of his bunk and punched the offender.

Within hours the suitably bruised offender had reported the 'assault' to the membership committee. Instead of telling those involved to behave properly and get over it, 'membership' avoided the issue and convened an emergency meeting of the steering committee. The steering committee deliberated, issued a Kafkaesque decree that a crime had been committed, and expelled from the chorus the person who had lost his patience and delivered the punch.

News of this scandal spread like wild-fire, the significance of the unfortunate incident escalated and there was uproar in the ranks. Some pointed out quite rightly that 'the aggressor' was defending his personal space and the basic human rights of everyone else in the room, and that 'the alarm ringer' was being abusive and selfish. Others quite rightly countered that physical violence can never be condoned in any circumstances. The chorus email group was ablaze with anger. Members were threatening to resign, call an 'extraordinary general meeting' to depose the steering committee, go to court, go to the newspapers. At times it looked as if the whole organisation was going to blow itself apart. We were a group of indignant idealists whose very existence was based on the principles of right and wrong, justice and equality. In this case the facts were not complicated, but it still didn't help us decide exactly who was the victim, and of what?

By curious coincidence the media was gleefully reporting an equivalent incident which involved John Prescott, the Deputy Prime Minister. During a visit to North Wales an angry spectator had thrown an egg at him, and Prescott had swiftly retaliated with a well-aimed punch. The action had been caught on camera and was viewed as an amusingly undignified scuffle, rather than anything serious; most commentators seemed to say of both sides 'they got what they deserved'.

In the chorus however it took interventions from a previous chairman, appeal hearings and months of simmering discontent, before sanity and an uneasy peace were eventually restored. There were no winners; the steering committee wrote a guarded apology to the person who had been expelled, and their 'expulsion' verdict was downgraded to suspension till the end of that year. We carefully rewrote our 'code of conduct: policies and procedures' document to ensure that in the future both sides got a fair hearing, and belatedly learned that political correctness does not always equate with common sense.

There was one final, bitter-sweet post-script to the story. The chorus end-of-year parties are legendary, we often hire a gay pub for the evening, and the centrepiece of the event is the awards ceremony. In cruel mockery of the Oscars/ Emmies/ Golden Globes (and ourselves) the members submit nominations in such award categories as: 'Just one more' (drinker of the year) 'Prima Donna of the year' (for an overinflated ego), 'It's Primark' (fashion faux-pas) and 'The Goldfish' (lip-synching when not knowing the words). At the 2007 party, amidst some booing and somewhat louder cheering, I was presented with a 'Slapper of the Year' award, for it was I who had thoughtlessly delivered that notorious early morning punch. I tried to accept the cynical award with good humour, but it had not been funny and I knew I would never live it down. I was mortified that my quick-tempered response to somebody else's selfishness had been the cause of such disturbance. Perhaps it was some consolation to realise that the chorus reaction demonstrated just how much this organisation was not about 'a bunch of blokes having fun'; this was a group that cared about right and wrong.

It had been a turbulent and stressful year. 'Bad Boys' was the last concert we did with Charlie Beale as our musical director. The New York City Gay Men's Chorus had offered him a well-paid full-time job, and he just couldn't refuse. It was one of the dangers of participating in the international chorus festivals; everyone got to see who was at the top of their game, and would then adopt the best ideas. With the US economy in a bad way, the

New York Chorus had lost most of their private charitable funding and needed to up their stakes. For all the time that Charlie had been with us we had only ever paid him for two days of work per week, and they out-bid us. In a way we were flattered that such a prestigious outfit would want to poach our MD, but it would be difficult for us to fill the gap.

We were very fortunate that our Deputy MD and long-time accompanist Simon Sharp felt able to step forward and take on the larger role of Musical Director. He had been sitting behind the piano, occasionally conducting us, and at the heart of the chorus since the millennium; he knew exactly how things worked, has an encyclopaedic knowledge of musical theatre, and a fine instinct for the ways in which the chorus might develop. What could have been a traumatic upheaval was accomplished with minimum disruption.

The next concert was 'Accentuate the Positive', a fund raiser for the 25th anniversary of the Terrence Higgins Trust at the London Palladium. The production had been in development for at least the previous twelve months, and it proved a very efficient exercise in show business entertainment. The continuing importance of the 'safer sex' messages that were needed were delivered with a combination of both wit and sincerity. We more or less stuck to the tried and tested formula; didn't push any boundaries, and raised a lot of money for a very worthy cause.

The wonderfully strange show that we presented in the middle of 2008 called 'Songs of Innocence and

Experience', was a very different affair. The concept had been devised by one of our own members, Michael May, and as the title implied, was based around the ideas and philosophy of William Blake. Michael, Simon Sharp and other interested members assembled an eclectic jigsaw of musical pieces which spoke about the spirit and the body, the past and what might come to be, tradition, convention and contravention, optimism, disillusion and redemption. It was magnificently deep, puzzling and extraordinary, and I can't think any other group that could have pulled it off. Three new pieces were specially commissioned from Dan Gillingwater, an uncompromisingly modern composer, and we also included John Tavener, Kate Bush, Bernstein and Beethoven. There was electronic, flute and brass orchestration, and for some of the time the chorus stood in darkness, only dimly illuminated by abstracted photography, video and text projected onto a screen suspended above the stage. William Blake was amazingly advanced in his thinking, and deeply suspicious of anything that appeared to be a 'closed system of thought'. During that concert we felt that both he, and the angels, were at our side.

The previous two or three shows had been commercial, uncomplicated and loud. 'Songs of Innocence and Experience' was none of those things, and even amongst our own membership there had been some questions about why we were breaking away from such a winning formula. Initially not all the chorus members were enthusiastic, and many had not encouraged their friends and family to buy tickets; the sales had been OK, but it was not the sell-out we had come to expect. After the show the overwhelming consensus was that the concert had been a very rewarding experience and a significant creative success, but our accountant told us we had made a loss. Balancing the finances, fulfilling the aspirations of our members and also attempting to satisfy the expectations of an unknown audience, seemed like trying to walk a tight-rope whilst blindfold.

We would face the same problems later that summer; we had been invited to tour northern Spain. The autonomous government of the Catalonia region had organised an 'International Festival of Men's Choirs', and were willing to subsidise the chorus to participate. We would pay our own travel costs, and they would provide free board and lodging in a tourist hotel at a beach resort just north of Barcelona. It all seemed a bit unlikely but it was a very attractive proposition, and ninety of us jumped on board.

Although gay choirs did not exist in Catholic Spain, 'men's choirs' were very much part of the Catalan culture. Many had been started by workers' unions at the start of the industrial revolution; they sang in Catalan, celebrated regional identity and were of particular significance during the civil war when Barcelona became a republican stronghold. Under the Franco dictatorship the use of the language was suppressed and these groups were harshly treated. There remains a strong legacy of asserting your culture and expressing your identity through the use of song. Perhaps a somewhat subversive gay chorus from London was much more 'in tune' with the ethos of this festival than might at first appear. We would be ambassadors both for our sort of music and for our alternative lifestyle.

In any large chorus project the motives of those who chose to join in were mixed. Some of us were involved because we wanted to make a political point; others simply wanted to have a good time. Most of us were on the same early Saturday evening flight from Heathrow, and the party got started as soon as the seat belt sign went off. It must have been very surreal for the few other passengers, to realise the entire plane seemed to be full of happy middle-aged gay men who all knew each other.

After a brief interlude for luggage and passports, the party continued on the bus from Barcelona airport to the hotel, an hour long trip up the coast-road to the manufactured tourist resort of Santa Susanna. The Hotel Mercury was of the standard 3 star package style, had a funny shaped pool and was much favoured by German families on a budget. We really didn't fit in, but the weather was warm, the bar huge and we were on holiday; the party continued until late that night, and didn't seem to stop for the next week.

The extravagant atmosphere of that whole adventure was heightened by the presence of a film-crew. Caroline-the-camera was a creative and fun-loving young woman, and she and her sound-recordist had found a niche for themselves by documenting various fringe art and performance activities. We were a group of people who could be both spontaneously inventive, and wildly extrovert. She adopted the chorus as her special project for that year and followed us everywhere. Unusually the repertoire we had prepared for that season was dominated by serious and classical pieces, so she must have ended up trying to edit together a very odd mixture of sombre performance footage and exuberant off-stage material.

Our first concert took place in the Palau de la Musica Catalana in central Barcelona. This architectural masterpiece was built in the extreme high modernist ('Gaudi') style in 1905, and declared a world heritage building by UNESCO in 1997. Every square inch of the interior, including the stage itself, is covered by polychrome mosaic, stained glass or writhing, organic, allegorical sculpture. The glittering stage is overlooked by huge busts of Beethoven and Wagner, and it felt a very significant place to perform. There were four other international choirs in the festival, and we were by far the largest. The audience of 2000 must have wondered what a gay choir would look and sound like, and I should think they were surprised we appeared to be so disciplined, powerful, and polished. It has always been a paradoxical quality of the LGMC that although our image might seem frivolous, we have always had serious musical aspirations and practise the art of choral singing as well as we possibly can. Our final piece, 'Je ne regrette rien', with its moving and tumultuous climax, was received with a standing ovation, and we found that wherever we sang in Spain we were treated with the greatest respect.

This was especially apparent in the subsequent concerts. Over the next few days we were not going to be performing in the context of a sophisticated and cosmopolitan city, but many hours coach ride away, in little mountain villages to an audience of farmers and their families. Even though 10pm seemed to us a very late start for a concert, we would usually have to assemble in our Hotel Mercury foyer by 3pm for the coach to get us there on time. Twice we discovered the tiny roads of the destination village were so constricted that the big motorway touring coach had to drop us at the outskirts, and we walked the last bit.

On one occasion the concert venue anachronistically turned out to a newly built art gallery and cinema complex, but usually it was a platform in the market square. Our performance was always preceded by a few songs from the local men's choir, and it was rare to see any young people involved. These were severe, black-suited, elderly gentlemen who wore gallantry medals from the Spanish civil war and lined up on the platform as if on parade. None of us spoke Catalan, but we could tell they sang with conviction and sincerity; this was a serious business. We sat to one side and paid attention to their impressive presentation, and when our turn came to sing they did the same for us. There was one such evening that was particularly memorable. After the concert tables were set up round the square, and all the women appeared with trays of sandwiches and tapas. Initially the veterans from the village, and the gays from the city, stood slightly apart in awkward and separate groups, but then the singing began again, more informally now, and the local sherry in forked glass flasks was passed around.

We cheered and clapped as they skilfully shot thin streams of the amber liquor into their opened mouths, and they laughed with us as we soaked our chins and shirt-fronts.

No doubt a liberal supply of alcohol might have helped to initiate the thawing of international barriers, but under the surface there was a lot more going on than just a bunch of men getting a bit tipsy together. Before the tour began we had attempted to learn an old Catalan folk song, and that night we stood side by side with those people and all sang it together. Suddenly there was an extraordinarily intense feeling of brotherhood. We were such different groups of people, but had so many important things in common; our only communication was through the shared emotion of music and song. We were up in the wild mountains and a thousand miles from home, but it felt as if we were completely and utterly safe, and surrounded by our deepest, oldest and dearest friends.

None of us had set out that afternoon with the expectation of having a profound experience, but all of us felt it, and many commented and wondered at how it happened. The coach roared back down the empty motorways towards our 3 star package hotel.

Life in the London Gay Men's Chorus can really shake you up sometimes. Take you by surprise.

One of our own members took us all by surprise during the Spanish tour. He had spent most of his life in America, but his name was 'Soon', and he had the appearance of an inscrutable oriental villain straight out of a 1950s Hollywood B movie. It was apparent that he liked to dress well; even on a regular Monday night rehearsal he would sometimes chose to wear the sharpest of designer jackets. What none of us quite realised was that he had a serious uniform fetish, and the surprise was what he had packed in his suitcase for the tour.

At the beginning of the evening the hotel bar was usually pretty quiet. The Germans tourists occupied the main area and there was oomm pah pah music coming from the jukebox, but nothing too rowdy. The gay Brits were grouped at the tables to the back, or spilled outside on to the wide terrace of the funny-shaped pool. As the evening got late the gays tended to take over more and more, and the music got noticeably nancy. One evening Soon appeared in full camouflage kit dressed as some sort of drill sergeant, complete with an artful smudge of axle grease on one cheek. We all smirked approvingly, it was a standard look for a full-on inner-city gay bar, but the German mums and dads must have wondered if it was a gay thing, or was there a convoy in town?

Another night Soon transmogrified into a San Francisco motorcycle cop, with helmet, boots and shades (he always got the details right) it was so blatantly 'Village People' that even the most naïve tourist must have twigged.

Soon's piece-de-resistance had been saved for the end of the trip, and was an ambitious amalgam of all sorts of fetish wear; leather chaps, jock-strap, chains and studs. He had accessorised this outfit with a short whip and a wide leather collar, and Alisdair joined in the fun by squatting down, putting on the collar and playing doggy. Soon was now in the role of dominant sado-master, and much to everyone's delight the pair of them paraded provocatively round the pool. It was now late at night and all the German tourists had retired and left the bar, but the shouts of encouragement and whoops of laughter bought them out on to their balconies to see what on earth was going on beneath. Caroline-the-camera, with portable spot-light, was on hand to document all the depraved decadence and she finished the scene with a wickedly slow-motion pan across all the startled faces staring down from above. The ghosts of a Weimar Republic cabaret were returning to haunt them.

Things that happen by accident are perhaps more interesting than those which are planned. That spontaneous poolside performance was a strangely inverted mirror image of one that took place a couple of days before at the mountaintop monastery of Montserrat. It was the only organised group outing during the busy week, and since there were few seriously committed Christians in the chorus at that time, it can be assumed that most had gone along to see the magnificent scenery. Once there, however, the monastery and all that it represents is unavoidable; there were monks, nuns, choirboys and clerics wherever you looked, and although no performance was scheduled we all lined up in the quadrangle and sang some of the more gentle pieces in our set. It might have seemed on the surface to have been rather a reverential thing to do, but as a gay chorus in the very heart of a Catholic stronghold, we were being extremely subversive and challenging.

We seek to educate, and to entertain, but the difference between activism and hedonism is in the mind's eye of the observer, and sometimes when we do what we do none of us can ever be sure of which is what.

All sorts of odd things turn up on our events calendar. A few weeks after we got back from Spain there was an evening reception 'do' at the Museum of London in Docklands; then an invitation to sing at the opening ceremony for the International Gay and Lesbian Football Association World Championships. A football event at Shepherds Bush Empire might have been really important to some of us; publicity for international gay football teams and creating a bit of a fanfare for their competitions can be a significant political act. For others who don't follow the sport it was merely an obligation, and you do it because your mates are going and it might be fun. That opening ceremony involved many hundreds of people from all corners of Europe; it was an elaborately staged evening and it might just have changed someone's life, you can never tell. We don't accept every single invitation, but we try and do as much as we can.

'LGBT History Month' is always soon after the Christmas concert, and often our first event of the year. At the beginning of 2009 Mike, the youngest member of the chorus, organised an event for us at The North London International School where he was a final year student. Because it was mid-morning only about twenty of us were able to go along, and the entire school had been assembled before us in the main hall; it was quite daunting to be faced by all the staff and so many young people. The institution was a private school with high academic standards, and we suspected that all those 11 to 17 year old children were the off-spring of diplomats, politicians and top rank executives. The parents had been informed of the event, and 97% had given consent for their children to attend. The older students probably already understood what the word 'gay' meant, and the teachers must have attempted to provide some explanation for even the youngest; we were scrutinised with intense interest.

We sang for them, and a couple of us had prepared speeches about 'coming out', and how difficult the situation had been in 'the old days'. Some things might have changed but it's still difficult, that's why we were there, and several of the students were brave enough to stand up and make statements about their sexuality. Only a few years previously, before clause 28 was finally repealed, all that we said and did that morning would have been considered illegal. It was a privilege to be there, and it made me feel giddy to stand so close to the edge of all that was past, and so near to the start of so much future.

In May 2009 some seeds planted in April 2006 came to fruition. Much preparation had gone into the successful bid to hold an international festival of gay choirs in London, now a consortium of the three LGBT London choirs, Diversity, The Pink Singers and ourselves, took on the responsibility of ensuring the event ran like clock-work. Organising one concert can be a gargantuan task, and the 'Various Voices' project comprised about 50 different performances from 60 assorted lesbian and gay choirs from 14 countries.

The original proposal had events spread across several central London venues, but as the ideas were developed it became apparent that we had to focus and rationalise everything into one location. The South Bank Centre had the Royal Festival Hall, The Purcell Room, The Queen Elizabeth Hall, The Clore Ballroom and a multiplicity of other rooms, terraces, foyers and bars that were flexible enough to accommodate all our needs. To figure out how to make it all work there were ever-changing charts, grids and spread sheets. A project management system evolved, and all the individual elements were laid out and shuffled around until a workable structure was devised.

There were several large concerts which involved all the 2000 delegates, smaller show-case performance opportunities for individual choirs, grand communal warm-ups and sing-alongs, and many workshop sessions; each day and every evening was filled to the brim with the business of singing.

With so much going on it was sometimes difficult to figure out what to do and where to go to next. It was fascinating to see and hear so many choices of material and styles of presentation on the main stages, but many of the more experienced singers chose to concentrate on the more intimate workshop sessions. It was a rare opportunity to work with an unfamiliar conductor or someone who had trained in a different musical tradition. Everyone develops their own particular preferences and techniques, and as singing is just as subjective as listening, there is no universally correct way of doing it. Where one conductor might talk about relaxing the shoulders and straightening the spine to get a note or express some soaring emotion, another would recommend lifting the palette and expanding the resonance. It's important to see such things demonstrated, and then you can consider the options and decide what works best for you. Most successful choirs seem to operate on a timetable dominated by performances, and it's easy to forget the fundamentally important foundation lessons on practical technique.

I found it frustrating that the more interesting smaller workshops were often not well publicised, and it was difficult to find out when they were happening. Both the South Bank management and perhaps some of our own Various Voices team had decided that they wanted to sell the more expensive tickets for the big events, and the less spectacular free of charge fringe activities were neglected. During the development phase there had been enormous pressure from within the chorus to ensure that the event did not make a loss. When any chorus project becomes really big and really expensive, 'balancing the books' becomes a priority; it's a penalty that can't be avoided.

On those terms the huge Various Voices festival was successful, it didn't make a loss, and in spite of all that was available the registration fee for participation was less expensive than at previous Legato events. I enjoyed being there, and also felt some of the details could have been more developed; others don't share my opinions.

Since the LGMC began there are now gay choirs established in other British cities, and when I chance to reminisce with singers from Brighton, Reading or Birmingham, Leeds or Manchester, Edinburgh, Glasgow or Dublin, they invariably remember Various Voices as a seminal event which gave them confidence and expanded the horizon of possibilities. An unlooked for legacy of the festival was the complex and sophisticated project management system devised by Martin and his team of helpers. Their template has since been adopted by the American Gala organization and was used for Denver 2012 to deliver a successful and profitable event. In London 2009 over 10,000 people were estimated to have passed through the South Bank during those four days, and prior to the event in excess of £200,000 worth of support and sponsorship was raised. If a creative arts programme is to be taken seriously then financial forecasts and audited accounts have to be a part of the picture.

We had devised and rehearsed a repertoire of relevant 'London' themed music for the LGMC contribution to the festival, and at the end of June we took it to Helsinki and the Finnish Pride celebrations. It was yet another very busy long weekend, and this time it was significantly expensive. A chorus bursary scheme had been put in place for students and those on income support, but with travel costs and accommodation in the Radisson Hotel, and then the added cost of meals, drinks and club entrance, not everyone in the chorus was willing or able to participate.

The chorus flight left on a Thursday evening. Upon arrival in Helsinki there was a communal midnight meal arranged with 'Out 'N Loud', the local gay men's choir, then all but the most desperate retired to bed. The joint concert was scheduled for early Friday evening, so the 'tech run' in the theatre had to begin at 11.30 the next morning. The concert was at 6pm; the 'after-party' in the city sauna began at 9. That Friday night was the start of Pride weekend, so afterwards there were lots of other club events and parties happening. The Pride march through the crowded city centre happened next morning, and in the afternoon there was another joint performance with Out 'N Loud in the main park. The traditional Pride party kicked off at 9pm, and it went on traditionally late into the Saturday night. Sunday morning was free time, if anyone was awake, and assembly time for the flight back to London was 1.30pm. Sometimes a lightening tour with the LGMC is remarkably similar to being trapped in a rock 'n roll cliché.

Later that summer the 'London' package was also presented at The Shaw Theatre in Euston and the Museum of London. On those occasions everyone was able to join in, but not everyone chose to. The idea of opting in or out of an event was a significant development. Previously there had been an unspoken assumption that everyone should do everything; now the chorus seemed to acknowledge that different groups within the membership were able to pursue separate activities. Some were wealthy, others not. Some had relationships with partners to consider, or demanding jobs, others had no commitments and the luxury of spare time. As long as the music team kept track of overall numbers and the balance of voice parts, we were now large enough to subdivide without falling apart.

The first official 'small group' of 16 singers from the LGMC was formed in 2005. Initially they were our highly mobile and adaptable rapid-response unit, but it was soon realised they were being booked for events such as civil partnerships which demanded a different repertoire. The small group worked on a slightly different set of songs from the main chorus and began to develop their own musical identity. A dedicated name, 'Far from Kansas', soon followed (just after the hurricane at the start of the Wizard of Oz movie, Judy Garland says to her small dog "we're not in Kansas anymore Toto") but their name always appeared with the strap-line ' part of The London Gay Men's Chorus', so although they borrowed from our greater reputation, we all benefited from the added exposure. The extra commitment needed to become a member of the small group was huge; there were additional Wednesday evening rehearsals and much more frequent performances. All the revenue they raised was for the benefit of the main chorus, but in many ways these hard working members were participating in their own quite separate and equally extraordinary adventure; they were part of the larger organisation, but became an exclusive and tight-knit group in their own right.

In 2008 they devised their own show 'There's No Place Like Homo' which was a mixture of their own material and pieces from the main chorus. It was well received at the Edinburgh Fringe, and shortly after was presented at the King's Head Theatre in London. Encouraged by that success, in 2009 they put on the more ambitious 'Oklahomo'. The plot involved a gay cowboy's psychotherapy group and about 20 really good songs, and it was irresistibly described as 'where Brokeback meets Broadway'. Their production won The People's Choice Award at the Dublin Gay Arts Festival, and again went to the Edinburgh Fringe. 'Thoroughly Modern Willie', with a naughty and nostalgic school days theme, was the show for 2010. 'Little Shop of Homos' went to Edinburgh in 2011, and 'Hi-De-Homo', a farce set in a very 'camp' holiday-camp called Buttlands, followed in 2012. Their extraordinarily creative portfolio of shows is only the tip of an iceberg. In most years they clock up as many as 40 additional events compared to a main group average of 10 to 15 per annum; anything from a civil partnership at Brighton Racecourse to a guest-spot with Dolly Parton. Their exploits merit a book all their own.

TWENTY TWO
Sitting on the See-Saw

For the Christmas show in 2009 we attempted something we had never tried before, a no-holds-barred traditional British pantomime. Since the format should have suited us perfectly it was perhaps surprising our project turned into something of a tangled disaster.

We felt the need for some fresh input into our creative process, so before the start of the season an independent artistic director had been appointed. To ensure he didn't go completely off the rails and make demands we knew the chorus couldn't handle, he had been given the song list, together with a cleverly written script titled 'Singderella', and told he could interpret them however he chose.

The problems arose when one of our own members arrogantly thought he knew better than the team that had democratically devised the script and began to meddle. He privately told the innocent artistic director that he was an experienced professional and often acted as our production consultant. The original script which was in rhyming couplets, had made sure the audience was never more than a couple of minutes away from some singing. It was replaced by ponderous ten minute slabs of dodgy double-entendre. Members who had been auditioned to play the main speaking roles kept quiet about the new script so as not to 'spoil the surprise', and the songs we had all been rehearsing for the previous four months were now no longer relevant to any plot. Instead of the presence of a large chorus on stage being part of the story-line, we were reduced to an incongruous and superfluous embarrassment standing at the back. To make matters worse, the untried artistic director assigned the entire on-stage budget to costumes and left nothing for props. There would be no bling chandelier for the ballroom scene, no sparkly cut-out coach for the big arrival, no magical double-sided doorway to explain all the location changes, and no trees in the enchanted forest.

Chorus shows are big productions, and all the myriad tasks have to be divided between different individuals and teams. It's often not till near the end of the process that anyone other than the director gets to see the whole picture. In this case it was only a couple of weeks before the show that the 'improved arrangements' surfaced, by which time it was too late to attempt a rescue.

During three performances the wit and improvisation skills of the two ugly sisters, and Alisdair as the fairy godmother, went some way towards mitigating the situation, but for those of us who knew what it was supposed to have been like it was a painful experience. The size of the chorus can be a great bonus, it enables us to tackle projects that a smaller group couldn't consider, but it can also create problems. The Singderella pantomime was a sad casualty of impractical logistics and rampant egos, and afterwards we were all relieved to say "it's behind you".

December is always a busy month for the chorus, and after our collapsing pantomime there were many other events to distract us. We were invited to sing for a congregation including many significant local government people at the Mayor's Carol service in Southwark Cathedral, a small group of us performed at Tate Modern and again at the Clore Ballroom, and the season was rounded off with a guest spot on Sandi Toksvig's 'Christmas Cracker' variety show at the Royal Festival Hall. If we thought our show had run into a few problems, they paled into insignificance compared to this one. There were the same issues of lengthy blocks of unfunny dialogue as we had faced, but Sandi's show was compromised by an event no one could have controlled; on the 18th December the Arctic jet-stream shifted and it began to snow. Within hours the entire country was feet deep and it didn't stop; roads were closed, cars were immoveable and trains were cancelled. Even if the production had been a theatrical masterpiece attendance would have been poor, but its week-long run was savaged by the critics after the very first night. A group of about 20 of us had signed up and we were bound both by loyalty and by contract to struggle through the snow, but being on stage in such a big and half-empty venue as The Royal Festival Hall felt very flat. The potential audience stayed at home and watched a recording of the 'Christmas Cracker' show on Sky Arts and, ironically, there was a much better party happening back stage every night. It consisted of the anarchic folk-rock collective Bellowhead, who were the house-band for the run, Ronnie Corbett the co-host who was always up for a laugh, and Sandi herself who had previously been a guest at a sequence of our Barbican shows and enjoyed all the gay company; we were having a backstage ball.

After it finished, on Christmas Eve, we heard some ugly news that put the gay show-business glamour into a different perspective. One of our group had been homophobically abused and seriously assaulted after he left the dressing room. The attack occurred by a bar inside the Royal Festival Hall, and although there was no sound recording of the initial verbal abuse, the physical violence had been partially captured on a security camera. The management and the police both carried out investigations, but their only conclusion was that gay people were still in danger all the time and wherever they went. We knew that already; there was snow on the ground, the seasons turn, the world always goes around, tic, toc, tic, and we had been there before. Earlier that year a middle-aged gay man named Ian Baynham had been kicked to death by thugs in the middle of Trafalgar Square. We had sung at a sad and angry memorial vigil on 30th October, when Sandi Toksvig and Sue Perkins had read out a list of all those who had died as a result of hate crime in 2009.

One of the paradoxical things about being a gay person in a gay choir is that because everyone around you is also gay, it's no longer a topic of any significance or even much interest; outsiders are always more aware of the issue than we are. An individual from outside our community who noticed that large sections of the music business continue to have a problem with being gay was the New York based music producer Mark Ronson. It was he who pioneered the idea of 'retro-soul' and was responsible for the success of Amy Winehouse and many others. His work crossed genres and broke through cultural barriers, and for a track called 'The Business' on his album 'Record Collection' he wanted to mix together white English gay singers with a black American rapper named Pill.

The sheet music came through via e-mail, and a little group of us stayed behind after rehearsal and worked through it. A week later we went over to the Metropolis Studios in Hammersmith. All the famous people who had recorded there (Hendrix, Santana, Oasis, The Who, McCartney) ensured the place was a legend, but it wasn't till we got there that I realised the studios had that name because the building was a 1920s art-deco power station, and both inside and out it looked exactly like a monumental set from the 1927 Fritz Lang film 'Metropolis'.

Recording is an hypnotic and addictive activity; it's rare to have the luxury of endless repetitions until every detail is exactly right. In the studio you can nod along to the off-beat, sway in time or even just shut your eyes without any concerns that an audience might be watching. There are no inhibitions when you are aware that the engineer can transform the results, play them back and you can have another go. We spent all day getting five minutes of singing sounding perfect, and at the end of the session Mark came down from the control-room for a coffee break and group photo. The 'Record Collection' album was released at the end of September 2010, and when he and his band came over to London in February 2011 for a one-off publicity concert, we performed the song live on stage with him at the Camden Roundhouse.

The chorus had ambitious plans to present a big concert of our own at The Roundhouse in June 2010, but whilst we prepared for it there were constant distractions. As well as the Ronson recording we had a 'retreat weekend' in Winchester, and were asked to participate in the première of a new Orlando Gough piece at the National Portrait Gallery. There were also events at The South Bank, London Bridge and 'West End Live' in Leicester Square. In May our small group was asked at short notice to provide the entertainment for the inauguration celebrations of the new Mayor of Camden, Jonathan Simpson. Later that month we sang at a most moving memorial event for a TV celebrity Kristian Digby. It had originally been scheduled to happen in Southwark Cathedral, but at the last minute his family had objected to the presence of a gay chorus, and the bereaved partner had to rearrange everything for their own large private back-garden in Bromley. With all the couple's closest friends, a radiant sunset and hundreds of flickering night-lights, our singing made a far more meaningful memorial than any sad ceremony the disapproving 'blood-relative' family attended in Southwark.

We tried to remain focused on our own imminent

show, The Seven Deadly Sins. The concept had come from Stuart Burrows, an independent producer and choreographer who had been collaborating with us for about nine years. He knew our abilities exactly, and we had complete confidence in his taste and judgement, style and talent. He and the music team had devised a cross between a musical and a morality play that explored what are considered to be man's most objectionable vices: wrath, avarice, sloth, pride, lust, envy and gluttony. The challenging programme was exceptionally varied and included pieces from Britney Spears and Erasure to Verdi and Irving Berlin. We felt it was a great coup to be in the famous Camden Roundhouse, and spared no expense with the production. There was a twenty piece orchestra on stage and spectacular costumes, made by Mark and Mike, for all the actors who portrayed the 'sins'.

The sin of envy was represented by the John Lennon song 'Jealous Guy', and as if our show wasn't complicated enough already, we asked a group called 'DNAMIX' to join us. This band consisted of teenage white and black guys who had already become fathers, and were exploring film-making and the music business as a way out of their often deprived and difficult circumstances. Our show would give them some experience of recording and appearing on stage, and a chance to write for themselves some additional rap lyrics about their lives. The song was performed by four of them together with four chorus singers arranged in a tight half-circle at centre-stage. Although there were complicated issues with microphones every time it was done, the piece was an attention grabbing addition to the show.

The resident technical crew rigged up a custom-built multiple-level stage for us, and a gigantic, central, sloping ramp was incorporated for dramatic entrances. The positioning of musicians and singers on and around this structure was complex, since everyone had to be able to see the conductor and the audience at all times. Setting up the microphones and monitors proved even more so; before the first of the three shows we endured the tech-run from hell, and the chorus had to spend the entire day standing and singing whilst the sound system was reconfigured a dozen times.

The Roundhouse audience were seated at tables, each themed to represent a specific sin and decorated with relevant novelties and sinful treats. Ushers and attendants greeted the arrivals and teased and tricked people as they showed them to their seats; watching the show must have been an extraordinary experience. The sin actors were able to move right round the front of the stage, and singers moved to pre-set positions to make dazzling patterns with different colour shirts. At the beginning of the song 'Hit me Baby one more Time' we all outrageously applied thick red lip-stick, and as the final punch-line was delivered, smeared it slowly down our chins like blood stains. The effect was meant to shock, as was the confrontational power of Verdi's 'Dies Irae' with the volume going all the way from 0.5 to +11. The meaning of any piece is often subtly altered by the context in which it is presented. 'Carousel' by Jacques Brel was perhaps intended to provide an insight on relationships; when we did it with an ever escalating tempo, the song began as a hypnotic trance and became a frightening evocation of the mad pressures of twenty first century life and the human condition.

Seven Deadly Sins was an awesomely complicated creation, and in spite of all our careful preparation and a sequence of performances, we never did succeed in getting every last detail perfect, but it was a triumph. We made a charitable donation to the Albert Kennedy Trust, and we made a financial loss, and we would do it all over again. In one crazy season we had rediscovered self-worth, affirmed our artistic integrity and developed a rock-solid sense of stability and security.

TWENTY THREE
Marching the Rainbow Road

One hundred and fifteen of us went on the chorus trip to Poland, and what we experienced must have come as a shock to some of our newer members. The suburbs of Warsaw were built during the era of Soviet socialism and resembled the grimmer edges of Croydon. The modern business district at the centre was reminiscent of Toronto. The so-called 'old' city was 90% destroyed during the war and rebuilt as affluent, pastiche, rococo Vienna. In Warsaw the prevailing social and political attitude towards all things gay seemed to come from the middle-ages, and the ghastly and evocative remains of the ruined Jewish ghetto were only a hundred yards from our hotel.

The Palace of Culture is the largest, and often thought to be the ugliest landmark in the city. Legend has it that after the war Stalin asked the people if they wanted a tram system or a town hall, they chose the trams, and he built the Palace. It is still known as 'the gift from Uncle Joe' and widely disliked; now, unbelievably, we had flown over to do a 'Europride' concert there.

We shared the honour with a small gay choir from

Sweden called Gaykor. The capacity of the auditorium is 2600, but only about three hundred people turned up. The evening began with what felt like interminable speeches and presentations; 'Hyacinth' awards were given to all those who had been seen to promote tolerance and equality during the previous year. It was all very worthwhile, but by the time singing began the audience must have been feeling deflated. When we came on the reaction was enthusiastic, and it was a sobering thought to realise that the existence of our organisation represented a cultural freedom that was not yet possible here. The low attendance at the 'palace of culture' concert could have been due to lack of publicity, or sweltering heat, or fear of exposure and reprisal, or dislike of the venue, or a preoccupation with the big march happening the next day; whatever the cause, it was not encouraging. After the show I wandered off to explore the city. Most of what I saw was very familiar, wide straight roads, big name department stores, office blocks, side turnings inhabited by chic little restaurants or crowded pubs. It didn't look either significantly deprived or obviously ostentatious, but I suspect the economy of Warsaw bears little relationship to the realities of life in the rest of Poland.

At a crossroad somewhat removed from the commercial centre I came across what appeared to be a gay pub. There was a prominent rainbow flag displayed, it was buzzing with activity, and crowds of young people had spilled out on to the pavement. I went in and time seemed to slip backwards, it was just like the old London

Lesbian and Gay Centre I remembered from twenty five years ago. This was the city's main gay bar, and it had been designated as the centre of operations for the Pride march and rally. Three people had set up a trestle table against one wall, they had sheaves of paper, clipboards, lists of names and boxes of what might have been plastic security passes. In a corner was a group painting slogans on banners and large placards. I had taken part in just such workshops myself in the old days. On all sides the walls were covered with posters, and next to the door was a noticeboard with safer-sex leaflets, flyers and fluttering, hand-written notes pinned layers deep. There was a side bar serving vegetarian food where music was playing, and an outside courtyard full of people talking, eating, smoking and drinking. It had a great atmosphere, relaxed yet brimming with energy, earnest but easy. I cruised around for a while, and thought it was a shame there hadn't been a few more people like this at our concert earlier that evening. I realised it was late, so picked up a leaflet with a map of the march, and found my way back to the hotel.

The first faltering steps towards holding a Pride march in Poland occurred on 1st May 2001, when 300 people with a single rainbow flag walked down the streets of Warsaw. For the next couple of years numbers grew, but in 2004 the mayor banned the march to 'protect public morality'. In 2005 the mayor stated that such a parade would 'promote a homosexual lifestyle' and official permission was again refused. A lawsuit was filed against the Republic of Poland at the European Court of Human

Rights. Two years later Strasbourg passed a verdict stating that the Mayor had violated three articles of the Human Rights Act, and at last a Pride march was sanctioned.

By midday on 17th July 2010 the temperature was nearly 40 degrees. I made my way to the square where the march was due to start, and saw a row of empty coaches parked in a side street. There were many hundreds of people milling about, and dozens of police in hi-viz jackets on duty. I worked my way through the crowd and came to a heavy crash-barrier dividing the pavement from the road. The march was gathering in the road, and I gradually realised I was in the midst of the anti-gay protesters. There were now thousands of people, and many hundreds of police, and I pushed my way through until I found a gap at a road junction where I could cross to the other side of the barrier. Over the heads of all the people I could see the chorus banner at the far side of the square, and after more struggle through the stationary masses was greatly relieved to join the rest of our group. The start of the march was being held back whilst the authorities attempted to keep the protesters corralled in the side streets. This hostile crowd was an unholy alliance of fascists, neo-Nazis, Catholics and skinheads, and although I couldn't understand what was written on their banners, the meaning was clear. The graphic symbols depicted gay people as stick-figures in a circle with a diagonal red line through it; they didn't just want to restrict our rights, or refuse gay partnerships, they wanted gay people completely crossed out. Further on I could hear shouting; there was trouble ahead. Our ex-chairman Martin was on a float at the front of the march, and there they were being pelted with eggs, balloon bombs full of holy water and other missiles. The police were arresting some of the most blatantly violent, but they couldn't do anything about the people spitting and shouting at us except take photos. As the march was getting started Martin was hit on the head by a sharp chunk of cobble stone, and sustained a 4 cm gash which bled profusely. He attempted to mop up the mess of broken egg and blood with a white flannel, and this gory rag was later claimed by one of the march organisers who held it aloft for the news cameras like some iconic religious relic and declared angrily "this is what happens to our invited guests".

The progress of the march through the city streets was painfully slow, we kept coming to a halt and it was unbearably hot in the crowds. There were many thousands of police, some on horse-back, and military personnel armed with automatic weapons. At one point where the sound of chanting and disco-music bounced off the surrounding high buildings I heard loud bangs close by, and wasn't sure if it was gun shots or fire crackers; smoke drifted slowly across the scene of rainbow flags and rifles. The march seemed to be a conduit of bright colours and happy faces hemmed in by hatred.

Further on the road changed to a wide avenue lined with department stores. There were fewer hostile demonstrators and we sensed some support from the general public. When the march moved we sang our

Polish folk song, 'Hej Hej Hej' and as surprised spectators recognised it some cheered and waved encouragement. We were supposed to be giving a performance on a stage set up at the end of the route, but an anonymous authority decided to change plans and cut the march short so as to avoid confrontation with another anti-gay Christian rally. The ending was the most dangerous part of the event for us. Previously there had been some safety in numbers, but as everyone dispersed we were reduced to small groups or left on our own, and there were gangs of skinheads roaming about looking for trouble. We were advised to remove any recognisably gay T-shirts and stick to busy main roads. Later that night many of us gave worrying accounts of being spoken to with obvious aggression and feeling threatened as we made our way back to our hotels.

The chorus went to Warsaw and learned a lesson. History must be remembered, and freedom must be protected. After the Palace of Culture concert and troubled march, Polish gay people told us how inspiring it had been to witness our presence and the confidence with which we sang and expressed ourselves. In 1989 Lech Walesa and Solidarity reached their objectives, and the entire Soviet Union experienced a seismic shift. In 2010 it appeared that the Polish gay community still had a long and difficult journey to endure before achieving equality.

We returned to London and began the preparations for our winter concert. 'Make Your Own Kind Of Christmas' was all about friendships and families, and we realised the privilege of being able to make our own choices should not be taken for granted. In October there was another 'Say No to Hate Crime' vigil in Trafalgar Square, and the gathering was both a remembrance of victims and a demand for legislation to establish equal rights. The position in Great Britain may not be as extreme as that of the Catholic Church in Poland, but there are still many religious factions who assume it is reasonable to discriminate against gay minorities. For some, spiritual belief can bring great comfort and be the foundation for much good work, whilst for others such religious ideas cause distress. Christmas isn't always kind to everyone, and even for those of us who don't consider mid-winter to be a religious festival or suffer financial hardship, there may be tensions between spending time with friends and perceived family duties. When we devised our programme of songs for 'Make Your Own Kind of Christmas' we consciously included material that dealt with alienation and isolation. At the concert there was a speech from a Samaritans fund-raiser; Christmas is always the peak time for the Samaritans switchboard. We held a collection for them at the exit door, and also made a donation from our ticket sales.

Right from the very start the chorus simplistically sought to 'make the world a better place', and doing good work has always been at the top of our agenda. When we solicit cash from an audience or share our profits with another charity we make a simple gesture, but in some circumstances a less obvious course of action can be of greater value. History does not stop; we may be condemned to live in the sliding moment that is 'now', but if we seek change we should also attempt to reach forward and shape the future. As long as we take care not to proselytise, our gay chorus can mix education with entertainment.

During 2011 we continued an outreach programme of work with schools and young people. In February we spent an afternoon singing and talking at the Stoke Newington School in Hackney, and in March there was an anti-bullying seminar held at the William Ellis School in Highgate where we sang for both delegates and students. In May we participated with school choirs in a family day at the Southbank called 'Singing for Social Change'. So many day-time events whilst we were rehearsing for our summer concert were not always convenient for those with 9 to 5 employment, but attempting to initiate lasting social change demands a bit of effort.

One of our members works for Survivors UK, a charity that helps men who have been sexually abused. This is not an issue that commands popular appeal, and on a very limited budget they run a confidential helpline and arrange counselling. We helped Survivors UK to organise a fund-raising concert during May at the Cadogan Hall. The compère was rugby legend and broadcaster Brian Moore, and singers Lesley Garrett, Hannah Waddingham, David McAlmont and Ian Shaw all contributed to the first half of the show. It was inspiring to be able to share the stage with high-profile professionals; such people are celebrities for a reason, and you can learn a lot about singing just by looking and listening.

In addition to generating a significant amount of money for a good cause, singing can communicate ideas and emotions. The very act of singing was the subject our musical director Simon wanted to explore for the next show, 'Sound'. The vocal spectrum of the human voice and how it can be used is an ambitious remit for a two hour show, and it was daring to tackle such a boundless subject.

The concert took place in the Union Chapel, Islington, a large, octagonal, wood-panelled church building with a wonderful acoustic. For the traditional Celtic folk song 'Parting Glass' half the chorus encircled an upper gallery, and harmonic chords seemed to hang in the air like a synaesthetic sunset. An 'a capella' version of 'Good Vibrations' used counter-tenors instead of electronics, and became as multi-layered and rich as a symphony orchestra. We included a very peculiar 'sound-scape' by the Icelandic singer Bjork, where language was replaced by strange invented noises. There were songs in Latin, German, Bulgarian and French, a Zulu chant and an African-American spiritual. Perhaps most challenging of all was a choreographed Bollywood epic 'Jai Ho', sung in Hindi. We worked hard on this for six months, and the performance lasted only about six minutes, but all the effort was rewarded with a standing ovation from the astonished audience. For the 'Sound' concert both artistic and musical direction were masterminded by Simon, so inspiration and execution were perfectly integrated. The project was a uniquely satisfying experience, perhaps because both audience and chorus could sense a pure and original vision which had not been diluted or compromised in any way.

For the chorus to focus all its energy and effort on a single somewhat academic theme was a risk. We could have found the unusual repertoire prepared for 'Sound' un-useable in any other context, and would then have been unable to respond to any other opportunity or request. Luckily the next event on the schedule was a weekend of experimental and exploratory singing at the Barbican called 'Extraordinary Voices'. For two days in July the entire complex was filled with performers, artists, musicians and clamour. It included traditional Egyptian folk, klezmer, reggae, poetry, jazz improvisation and Mexican trumpet tunes. There was an Ottoman marching-band going up and down in one of the lifts, a chill-out trance experience in the basement and a sound-effects workshop on the terrace. We sang in several different locations and then just wandered round and listened, marvelling at the Barbican's bravery at putting on such an enlightened and adventurous event free of charge. The place was packed with people who no doubt spent a considerable amount in all the cafés, bars and restaurants, but nothing like it had ever been attempted before, and the board had undertaken considerable risk at a time of recession and budget cuts.

Events such as the 'Various Voices' festival, 'Sound' and 'Extraordinary Voices' become more feasible in a huge and multi-cultural city like London. The richness and availability of contemporary and historical culture is a great bonus to any arts organisation, and in the chorus we try to explore all possibilities. In early December there was an opportunity to sing at the launch of a 'Charles Dickens in London' exhibition to celebrate the bicentenary of his birth. Neither the repertoire of Sound nor the imminent Christmas concert were suitable, so a group of us revised some 'London' songs, added several Victorian carols and scheduled extra rehearsals. The launch was at the Museum of London, and the exhibition was fascinating. Dickens's writing encompassed all aspects of society from dockers to aristocracy and from prostitutes to poets; he might have been surprised at gay culture, but would probably have approved of our chorus's being such a melting-pot of international influences.

To add contrast to our somewhat intellectual year, the Christmas concert in 2011 was designed to be an undemanding and uninhibited party. There was a medley of Christmas number one pop songs, an audience participation quiz and a stripping Santa. It was called 'Make Mine a Snowball' and the weekend before we did the London shows we presented a polished 'dress rehearsal' of it at the amazing art-deco De la Warr Pavilion in Bexhill on Sea. For many of us it felt odd to be going to the seaside at Christmas, and the long train ride with the whole chorus added to the sense of adventure. Bexhill is branded as a retirement haven, and the sell-out audience included a very high percentage of widowed and elderly single women; a demographic that used to be celebrated as 'the blue rinse brigade'. They might not have been as gay or diverse as our usual crowd, and didn't all have tinted hair, but the night we were in town they were certainly celebrating. We all had a wonderful time, and regretted having to leave the after-show party to catch the last train back to London. One week later the London performances proved equally popular. The three shows generated enough profit to make a donation to 'Scope' the charity for cerebral palsy, and went a small way towards balancing the losses that are often incurred by our more adventurous summer seasons.

TWENTY FOUR
Coming of Age

New Year 2012 brought a surprise. An ex-member named Duncan had moved on from the chorus in about 1999 to pursue other interests in the music business and was now a notable keyboard player. He remembered us with affection, and more than a decade later recommended us to some film producers for a sound track recording. As soon as we heard their project was a spin-off from the Monty Python team involving all the remaining members, we readily agreed to take part. The film was to be an animated 3D interpretation of a notorious Graham Chapman diary and was called 'A Liar's Autobiography'. Since Graham Chapman had died in 1989 the project had taken nearly 23 years to come to fruition. The recording studio was a tiny suite of cluttered rooms in a Soho backstreet, with a maximum capacity of about twenty singers. We sang 'Sit on my Face' in multi-part harmony, a version of 'Silent Night' for a 'cold-turkey nightmare' sequence, and added various orgasmic 'oohhs, aahhs, and mms' (in B flat major triad) for a Biggles interlude. It was not a well-paid morning's work, but it was undeniably fascinating and fun. We didn't get to meet the Pythons that day, but when the film premiered on 16th October we did get to sing live at the Empire, Leicester Square. It was a preposterously whacky event. Roads were closed off, a 100 metre red carpet was rolled out and there were crowds of onlookers, crash-barriers and countless photographers. A troop of look-alike actors were enacting some classic Python sketches for the crowd and then for the audience inside. The crusader knight galloped around with cocoa-nut shells clopping behind, the sergeant-major didn't want anything silly, 'Brian' implored us not to worship because we are all different ("we are all different" we chanted in unison) In the cinema the chorus were seated incognito in the front two rows of the stalls. About 45 minutes in when our sequence appeared on screen, we all sprang up, spun round and sang to an audience entranced by the movie and glazed behind 3D glasses. By the time people understood we were real and began laughing, we were all sitting down again and acting as if nothing had happened. It was a wonderfully surreal bit of theatre, and afterwards Eric Idle and Michael Palin came to the front and thanked us for the contribution.

The year 2012 was the 21st anniversary of the founding of the London Gay Men's Chorus, and sometimes history and memory haunts us. In the same week as the Python recording another small group of us sang at the funeral of John Sparks, one of our dearly remembered early members. It was a cold, bright day when we gathered at Hither Green Crematorium with his friends and relatives. Several ex-members who had heard of John's death turned up. We met old friends and missed others, we celebrated and we were sad, we spoke, were silent and sang. We remembered; there were so many crowded years. One of the stories that were told came from the time of the turning of the century. A month or so before we sang at the opening of the Millennium Dome, John and some of his 'bear club' friends were talking in a gay pub called the Kings Arms in Poland Street. The chorus involvement in the pending Dome ceremony had been mentioned in a newspaper, and John laughed about it and referred to us as the 'domo-sexuals'. The label was so wickedly appropriate that they decided to coin a slogan and get a few T-shirts printed, which were worn at subsequent rehearsals. Much to everyone's delight, the irreverent T-shirts were spotted by a tabloid photographer and featured in a newspaper. We recalled the man we had known, his humour and his habits, his face and his voice, and realised none of us had ever known his family; although John had been more than a friend and member of our group for twelve years, he had deep connections with other history.

Some long-term chorus members have described the organisation as feeling like a secondary family, but if so, we have all sprung from different roots. There are sometimes parents, siblings and nephews and cousins and much more; we are all part of an extended network of relationships. When a gay man or woman experiences prejudice, intolerance or inequality an entire family is affected. We consider the primary victim and rarely think of the ripples of hurt and damage that spread far and wide. Support or even counselling is available for those who are seen to suffer, but second-hand hatred settles just as securely on those who are rarely acknowledged. Think of all the wounded mothers, remember the damaged partners. Ignorance and intolerance can ricochet through time and space as effectively as a lethal kicking or a thrown stone.

Our twenty first anniversary show at The Royal Festival Hall was called 'A Band of Brothers'. The title was obviously a declaration of the bonds of friendship and support that develop within our organisation, but for the concert we meant to encompass more than that. We chose repertoire that included our friends and families, and was also relevant to other groups who experience inequality and prejudice. The chorus has concerts at prestigious venues and we often receive media coverage, we have attained some visibility and feel a responsibility to share it with others who would also benefit from greater recognition. Disabled adults and children might have legal rights, but before the Paralympic Games of 2012 they were rarely regarded as equals with their own 'voices'. The disabled children who attend the Riverside Special School had been involved in our outreach programme, and all have direct experience of prejudice in their daily lives. Along with students from four other schools we invited them to share the stage with us at 'A Band of Brothers'.

The Royal Festival Hall has an auditorium capacity of over 2000 and a big stage. Our director Stuart wanted the show to be visually as well as musically entertaining, so in addition to a projection screen above the stage there were three costume changes, character actors, a guest choir of ex-members and a group of women singers from the Southbank 'Voicelab', lighting effects, choreography and performers moving to different positions. A new oratorio had been commissioned from composer Conor Mitchell with lyrics by Mark Ravenhill, the writer in residence at the Royal Shakespeare Company, and 'Shadow Time' proved to one of the most challenging works we have ever sung. The piece told of the dramatic changes in gay culture from the 1950s to the present, and at the end both the chorus and the audience were invited to turn and kiss the person next to them. The symbolic gesture was inspired by a gay pride 'kiss-in' that occurred in Hyde Park in 1971. Although much appears to have changed in terms of legislation and visibility since then, a same-sex kiss in a public place would still be seen as a provocative and dangerous thing to do. 'Shadow Time' was an ambitious idea, and unfortunately for the chorus creative composing does not always conform to a timetable. The completed sheet music wasn't delivered until long after the start of the season and rehearsals were rushed and felt tense. On the last weekend before the concert it was decided that some of the most difficult sections would have to be re-assigned to a professional soloist, and the chorus would need to have music scores with them on stage. The rescue plan worked; parts of it were underprepared and the performers may have felt apprehensive, but the results were impressive. The subtleties and complexities of that one piece made everything else seem simple.

There was much wonderful music in the concert;

Wagner's 'The Pilgrim's Chorus' appeared alongside 'The Trolley Song'. 'Love Don't Need A Reason', a poignant gay anthem from 20 years before was put with 'Make Our Garden Grow' an optimistic prophecy from Bernstein. Groups of school children joined us for 'Our Time', 'Electric Dreams' and 'Born This Way' and the emphasis was forced towards the future. During the run-up to the concert small groups of chorus members had rehearsed with the pupils at their schools. Over the course of months they had grown to accept the idea of gay men and were no longer inhibited at singing with us. It must have been startling to experience the power of the entire chorus in action only a few feet away. Some of the more autistic children from Riverside School turned their backs to the audience sitting beyond the footlights, and were far more interested in watching the brightly lit chorus moving and singing behind them. After the concert one of the Riverside parents wrote a most moving letter to the chorus saying their normally withdrawn child had become able to speak more freely, and how inspiring it had been to hear everyone singing 'Born This Way' together.

A month later we took 'A Band of Brothers' to Belfast without the school groups, and it then became apparent what a significant part of the event they had been. The production remained a dramatic and meaningful musical experience, but the emotional quality was completely altered. It was less obviously inclusive, optimistic and future-facing; the hardships and bitterness of the past became more prominent. We had visited Belfast before in

2003, and been greeted with a threatening demonstration outside the theatre and a small and very appreciative audience within. This time we were performing in the Grand Opera House, and found the reception less hostile. Andrew had done some preparatory publicity work and discovered radio stations were keen to arrange interviews. 'Gloria' the lesbian and gay choir from Dublin had been invited to perform, along with 'Quire' the Belfast based LGBT choir, who's formation had been partly inspired by our visit nine years before. Conor Mitchell, the composer of 'Shadow Time', is considered a local celebrity and has also written pieces about the dangers of a perceived return to violence in Belfast.

A picture of Northern Ireland is impossible to pin down. During the previous twelve months the entire 'Celtic Tiger' economy had undergone spectacular meltdown, and everyone was feeling the results. The population of Belfast seemed to be at peace for a month or two, but then some random event would spark troubles all over again. There was no stability; at first sight 'gay equality' issues might not appear that important, but ironically intolerance of others beliefs seemed to be the most intractable problem of all. Some of us went on a guided tour of the city during our visit, but instead of going to see the usual political murals we were taken to the remnants of the cotton industry. The guide told a fascinating story of how for religious reasons the 18th century trade unions opted out of any participation in the lucrative slave trade. In consequence the Belfast cotton mills had lost out to Liverpool and Manchester and there was great economic hardship. It's ironic that the same population subsequently rejected an influx of Catholics, again on religious grounds; their 'moral imperative' couldn't tolerate the idea. For all I knew the insight provided by our guide could have been perceptive truth or far-fetched fantasy. We are so hungry for any explanation of trouble some of us invent omnipotent gods and monsters, and then have to live our days according to their mythical lore. I'm told the sectarian divide permeates every aspect of life in Northern Ireland, and in 2016 research revealed that 95% of the schools in Derry are still Catholic/Protestant segregated. Unfamiliar individuals are subjected to an inquisition as to where they grew up or what school they went to, in an attempt to discover 'what side they are on'. Religious affiliation might be even more conflict-ridden than sexuality. When Conor Mitchell came on stage to introduce 'Shadow Time' he disclosed that until very recently in his home town he had to avoid frequent cross-examination about his sexuality; to be openly gay was to invite even more stringent persecution.

The resident technical team at the Belfast Grand Opera House anticipated that a one-off performance from a visiting choir would be straightforward production, but our 'Band of Brothers' show was not. It had been designed for the Royal Festival Hall and there were continuous entrances and exits, changes in lighting, microphones and stage lay-out. In the Opera House additional staging was installed early in the morning, and we started the technical run-through at mid-day.

Expecting a simple set-up, various vital staff had not come in. There were frequent interruptions whilst the sound-desk was reconfigured, lights were rehung and monitors repositioned. We had meal-breaks and rest periods in our timetable, but had to continue rehearsing right through till forty five minutes before the show began. As the evening started music-team, chorus and crew all felt shattered; it was an uncanny recreation of the scenario I remembered from the last time we had played Belfast. Just as before, there was an expectation of significance; both lightweight moments and darker passages seemed balanced on some indefinable edge. Past trauma and future tension jostled their way into the present. A month before in London this same set of songs and images had been an informal, confident and optimistic entertainment. Here the pressured attention of the audience seemed to be demanding a revelation from us, or an act of profound healing. As the house-lights dimmed the darkness in the auditorium was so tense it had density. For those on stage there was an extraordinary suspension of stretched time, and then it was over.

The applause at the end was not polite or well-mannered; it was a standing ovation that was like a breaking tidal-wave of relief and gratitude. Some nameless hope had been fulfilled, even if we hadn't understood the questioning. Potent music delivered with a purpose has the power to heal and provide something that feels like an answer; sound waves had swept the troubled surface smooth, a transient peace was revealed.

TWENTY FIVE
People Power

Time passes and facts erode and fade away. Half-memories, conjecture and the harder reality of the present moment is all that remains.

The group that formed in 1991 has vanished. It gradually evolved into something completely different. Each new person who joined it changed it, and step by step it transmuted into the organisation we have now, which will in its turn evolve. The original group was formed by radical, free-thinking people who wanted to make some alteration to the social structure and were prepared to stand up and be counted. The individuals involved had all gravitated towards the weekly gatherings at London Friend. Not only were we all gay outcasts who had rejected the current scene, but we also wanted to do more than be involved in the relatively comfortable alternative that London Friend provided; we felt a need to step outside that group of outsiders.

Ironically, and probably within a matter of months, that collection of individuals could have been perceived from the outside as having attained a coherent group identity; we had become 'a choir'. There were various reasons other people might have wanted to join us at that stage, and musical ambition might not have been their primary motivation; our choral activities had barely even begun. We had the reassuringly identifiable and conservative 'choir' label, the regularity of a weekly routine and the safety of a tightly-structured activity. New people would have been attracted to us because we resembled a little pretend family. The generations of gay men who had been born after the war, and realised their gender preferences or come of age between the late 1950s and early 1980s, had lived difficult and secretive lives in a very hostile environment. In all probability they had never had a family or a group of friends who would accept them unconditionally; the early chorus was a very attractive proposition to the insecure, the lonely and the needy, as well as those with political and musical aspirations.

The devastating effects of the AIDS epidemic had become apparent in the gay community during the 1980s, and it was inevitable that the songs a gay choir was most interested in singing were those concerned with loss and mourning. We desperately needed to grieve, but it was not as simple as mere communal lamentation, there were other significant needs. In addition to bereavement the early members had just experienced a decade of intense media hostility and social rejection; we needed to express our anger. As well as appealing to the needy, the chorus also appealed to those who were filled with fury and antagonism. Unrequited aggression sat alongside overwhelming grief and sorrow. The chemical formulation of the membership resembled a volatile and bitter brew bubbling inside a witch's cauldron.

It proved to be an astonishingly fertile mixture. If not for the fact that everyone was gay and had an instinctive distaste for intolerance, it might well have exploded. In spite of all our differences we had a common cause, and the forces that bound us together were more powerful than those that might have driven us apart. The character of the group was still young and unformed, as pliable as clay. Music bought us together, but if some of us needed the choir to be a psycho-therapeutic support network it could be. Others had simpler needs; maybe for them it was just a good bunch of mates to go to the pub with, or a nostalgic reminder of the company of intellectual equals remembered from school or university days. In reality there were still very few alternatives for out gay men. We needed each other and so we stuck together.

Whatever our ulterior and individual motives might have been, the common bond that cemented us was the music we aspired to make. Some of us had always had musical and creative ambitions, and right from the start we rehearsed our songs assiduously. Within a few months of beginning there were already opportunities for the group to perform; often these were in gay pubs for other people who were obviously like us, on other occasions we sang for a more public audience, and then we had little idea of how confrontational we were being or what the reception might be. It could be unnerving, not knowing if you would be clapped and cheered, or sneered at and mocked.

As well as learning how to sing, we also had to learn

how to insulate our vulnerability and put on a performance. As gay men some of us were already very familiar with the idea of concealing one's identity and living behind a protective shield, whilst others felt that was exactly the sort of mind-set we should be avoiding. Some would turn up for everything, regardless of how antagonistic or friendly the audience might turn out to be, but others would choose more warily. In 1992 when we first went to Manchester and facilitated the initial midnight vigil, the situation was a completely unknown scenario, none of us could predict what we might have to face, and only nine of the fifteen members chose to come along and leap into that darkness.

It wasn't long before we started to attract other people who specifically wanted to be performers; extroverts who relished the idea of being a centre of attention, gay men who felt they deserved to have an audience and needed their fifteen minutes of fame. In those days we certainly never experienced all the glittery show business paraphernalia that we now take for granted, but even then the early manifestations of the choir offered a modest echo of fleeting celebrity.

The extraordinary disparity of the different individuals who were participating in the choir might sound like a recipe for disasters, but it contributed to the richness of the group; I sometimes felt there was a palpable tension being played out on stage as we performed. Some would jostle to be in the front row, other chose to stand back. Right from the start our choice of material was eclectic and encompassed everything from the sincerely and genuinely tragic to the savagely angry. When a radio comedy script writer named Keith Parke joined and we knowingly started to exploit the 'camp' card, our productions became an authentically gay experience that was completely our own and unlike anything any choir had ever done before.

In the 1990s there was a fashion for manufactured 'boy bands'. The entrepreneurs who formed those bands deliberately selected different characters that could bounce off each other and appeal to a larger cross-section of the potential audience. The same broad spectrum of different personalities occurred in our group, but it happened as a natural consequence of whom we were, and the all-inclusive, politically correct, non-judgemental policies inherited from London Friend.

1993 slipped swiftly by, and the diversity of our membership continued to grow and deepen. Alisdair who was a qualified actor joined us in 1994, and we benefited considerably from his professional stage skills and his more objective feedback and positive criticism. Another new member, Martin McGonnigle, was undergoing religious training and about to be ordained as a priest. He was always aware of the on-going and occasionally rather subtle ethical implications of what we were doing, and he seemed to radiate a much needed calmness and balance during our sometimes fraught meetings.

It was a dynamic group, and the dominant characteristics changed unpredictably from one season to the next. Our awareness of the devastating effects of AIDS led some of us to a preference for seriously healthy living, early nights and moderation; others strayed into an arena where new-age meditations, healing crystals and tantric massage workshops were prevalent. For a few of the younger members this degenerated into an alarming celebration of the latest offerings in ecstasy culture, skin-tight t-shirts and remixed trance tracks. There were no rules and every life-style choice and experiment, however unreasonable it might appear, was accepted. New drugs, both HIV therapeutic and recreational, were often on the conversational agenda, but then so were the more mundane realities of mortgage options and employment opportunities. Radical politics and sex make fiery bedfellows, and relationships were constantly being discussed and dissected. The mid-rehearsal tea break sometimes felt like eavesdropping a rather far-fetched soap-opera script-writing session.

For a brief period the choir took on an unexpectedly religious aura. An older, gaunt looking man named Michael had joined us, and he was an authentic monk. He never proselytised his beliefs, and his religious order was liberal enough to not need to wear a hood and a habit, but for several of our concerts there were little groups of his friends and other monks and nuns present in our audience. On those occasions we were perhaps more cautious and self-conscious about exactly what we chose to mock. Eventually his vocation took him off to a mission in Africa, and we lost touch. He must have been a truly determined and self-aware person to have been able to accept and explore his own gay sensibilities in such circumstances.

Richard, the homo-hippy who lived in the back room at Voicespace, introduced a radical actor friend of his to the choir. Many years before this person had chosen to call himself Cloud, and he was the artistic director and leader of an anarchic little alternative-theatre group called Aldebaran. Cloud had trained with Lindsay Kemp, and then spent some time in Berlin during the seventies developing some rather advanced performance ideas. We shared our Voicespace shows with the Aldebaran company on several occasions, and were by turns both puzzled, encouraged and amazed at the poetic, scary and peculiar things they attempted to do.

The procession of people who passed through the choir was inspiring. Some stayed for years on end whilst others just brushed briefly past and moved on. Whatever skill or experience they could contribute was likely to be integrated; the choir made room for everyone. We needed to evolve a basic organisational strategy, as well as learn some theatrical technique, and as the numbers grew those with experience of administration, human resources and office management became more and more valuable.

The choir was expanding in many different directions, but the essence of the enterprise was always a group of people who wanted to sing together. As our musical proficiency grew we became involved with national choral competitions, and attracted more talented and ambitious singers. There was sometimes a tension between those who were motivated purely by singing, and others who wanted to develop in more theatrical directions. The pressure was by and large productive; our planning meetings went on late into the night and were exciting sessions that fizzed with passion and contradictory ideas.

As if on some astronomical star chart, the group of self-elected individuals that chose to meet and make plans was criss-crossed by potent force-fields in a constant state of flux. Alliances and attractions between factions were humming power lines, throbbing with energy and bouncing back and forth, breaking apart and reforming. By the time that evening's chairman called a halt, the collective had usually arrived at consensus and a light could be seen to shine on our next hesitant steps.

The choir had always had a mission. It was born from a desire to re-educate the society we lived in and promote a greater tolerance and understanding, both of ourselves and for other minority groups.

After a few years of singing together we realised that for our message to be heard more effectively we would have to become a larger and more significant organisation. Entertaining our friends and performing for our core audience was not fulfilling our real mission. We needed to put on bigger and better concerts, chase external funding, sometimes court publicity, appear on TV, sell CDs and go on tours. It was a risky road to travel, the stakes were going up and it was now necessary for us to gain a greater prominence.

The 'choir' part of our title sounded misleadingly ecclesiastical, so it was changed it to the more showbiz 'chorus'. We applied for official charitable status, reorganised our infrastructure and worked hard.

Every passing year brought with it a different set of problems and possibilities, and season by season the group was changing. The number of members grew, and that alone made us look and feel more noteworthy. There had never been any formal audition process for people who wanted to join, they just turned up and started singing. After they had been coming along for a few weeks, when it had become apparent that they were likely to stay, they were asked to pay the regular subscription, and at that point they 'joined the chorus'. We realised that it was difficult for new people, and disruptive for the group, if someone joined in the middle of a season. They either had to catch up with a whole set of new songs very quickly, or else miss out on their first concert. The solution was to start a waiting list so that anyone who applied to join had to wait until the start of a season, then two or three times a year a whole influx of new members began simultaneously; recruits were always welcomed and sometimes privately referred to as 'fresh meat'.

The chorus was an unusual opportunity for gay people, and London is a cosmopolitan city, so all sorts of adventurous and remarkable characters would turn up. You could meet a wild, hairy poet or a married policeman, a sexy banker from Glasgow and a boring ballet dancer from Canada, some were sad and romantic, some were attractive, some were performers and others were organisers. One person might be in search of adventure whilst another desperately craved stability. Many gay men seem to be constantly searching for a mythical Mr Right, and in the chorus there was a chance 'he' might materialize, you could never tell.

There was an ever-increasing percentage of people with musical experience, and the dynamic sound quality of the chorus changed noticeably from one season to the next. The escalation in numbers inevitably meant that our social structure also had to change. For the first few years everyone in the original little choir had known everyone else intimately. We shared in all the tribulations together and participated in each other's lives; it really was like being part of a surrogate family. When that family grew to sixty or seventy people it was no longer possible to be on such intimate terms with everyone. You certainly knew their names, but not where they lived, or what they did for a living.

Because the chorus had grown relatively slowly it still felt like a company of friends, and although many of us did find whatever intangible thing it was that we might have initially wanted, it did not always meet the needs of everyone. One evening Martin told us of a horrendous tragedy that had just overtaken one of our ex members. It was someone who had only been in the chorus for a short time and had then left quite suddenly and without much explanation. A few months after his departure he decided he could no longer continue with life; he went to Coventry Cathedral where he sat down in the middle of the concourse and poured petrol over himself. If there was anybody else around they couldn't have done anything, it was all premeditated, he struck a match and burned.

There was a brief mention in the newspaper, and speculation that his actions were some sort of political protest about military interventions in the Middle East, or possibly something to do with homophobia within the church. Although he had chosen to bring his very private despair to a very public arena, it was appalling that none of us would ever understand the message behind his motives. I recognised and now feared his photograph, but there was nothing more than that. I couldn't remember ever having spoken to him whilst he had been a member of the chorus. Some of the other people who had been in his voice section had got to know him better, and a month after the shocking news had come through Martin held a memorial ceremony one Saturday; a few people sang a couple of songs and we all felt helplessly and horribly inadequate.

By the turn of the millennium we had become a well organised assembly of about a hundred, we were frequently appearing in the media, and much to our surprise we even seemed to have earned a degree of respect from the musical establishment. The London Gay Men's Chorus had gained a certain status, and that eminence brought with it an intractable problem; we now began to attract frustrated individuals who were perhaps more interested in power and status than in music.

In any group of adult males, gay or straight, there is likely to be a degree of competitiveness. Those who feel a need to be in control constantly jockey for position and resolve their ranking by virtue of age or size, experience or appearance, income, talent, formal qualification or some other more indefinable quality. A measure of social ambition seems to be an unavoidable and natural state of affairs for all of Homo sapiens, but it can have unfortunate consequences.

Many gay men in the twentieth century were drip fed a message that they were inescapably inferior; they were excluded from society and could never succeed. Some unfortunate individuals never learned the trick of transcending this inheritance of inadequacy and continue to carry a huge chip on their shoulders; a sub-conscious inadequacy that poisons their lives. Gay men can be great fun, clever, compassionate and creative, but some of them can also be seriously screwed up.

Society is scattered with individuals who can't quite manage to fit in, who need more than anything to be part of a group, but can't bear to share their toys and are unable to interact as part of a team. They mostly exist in isolation and boil with frustration and depression, paradoxically both longing for acceptance and bitterly resenting anything that appears to be an integrated group.

In the general population such sociopaths come in all shapes, sizes and degrees of instability. They range from the overly aggressive motorist or bully at the supermarket checkout to serial killers; from sullen loners to megalomaniac dictators. In the chorus our misfits are able to exploit our ambition to succeed and our need for volunteers, and as in any large company, we have experienced the occasional inadequate individual who compulsively wanted to be in charge, excluded anyone else from participating, but then couldn't get the job done properly.

Genuine originality often seems to go hand in hand with a certain liberality of spirit and selflessness; creative people enjoy sharing the fruits of their inventiveness with others. If such qualities are appreciated and nurtured within a group, an entire culture can become enriched. Unfortunately it's sometimes the case that a greed for glory doesn't seem to be partnered by any generosity or openness. Insatiable control freaks are unlikely to be successfully altruistic.

The chorus has always had at its heart a brotherhood of volunteers who work tirelessly for the benefit of the whole chorus community, unsung heroes who get all the satisfaction they need from the knowledge that they are driving the enterprise onwards. It has always been recognised that not everyone is able to contribute time, inspiration and effort equally, but for the proactive few who choose to shoulder a greater load, that's never been a reason why we shouldn't all experience the adventure together.

It's a testament to our inclusiveness that nowadays we often seem to carry with us our own rotten apple, a poisonous malcontent who gains both satisfaction and notoriety from undermining the efforts of others. The group has attained some momentum, but that doesn't render it invulnerable to being damaged by a single wilful individual.

The power, and the problems, of the chorus now lie within its own membership. Throughout our history we have been unconsciously experimenting with all sorts of organisational arrangements, from primitive commune to utopian republic to elective dictatorship. The intimate brotherhood that was ideal for fifteen people didn't work for fifty; the social structure that suited seventy fell apart when we became a community of a hundred and twenty.

Human beings are social animals, and when we gather together different conventions and relationships develop in different size groups. Satisfactory codes of conduct encountered within a family differ from those found in a village, or a city, or a nation; each one evolves its own idiomatic structure. As far as we know there has never been a large community of gay people cooperating together, and such a group is not compelled to follow the same behavioural patterns, or adopt the same stratagems, as an equivalent heterosexual group. The chorus has no prescribed model to follow and I know of no other artistic enterprise that attempts to be quite so democratic. We also find creativity by committee can be impractical, and need to find alternatives.

The chorus developed because a few practical idealists devoted a lot of time, imagination and will-power to make it happen. It is now the largest gay arts organisation in Europe, but it still attempts to run on volunteer time, and the work load is impossible. Apart from a few who are motivated by ego, most of the members profess and even demonstrate loyalty, but they come along to sing, and because it feels like fun to paddle in the shallow end of show business. Few now follow any higher calling, or volunteer to organise our activities. The members willingly support the greater group, much as one would support the local independent greengrocer. One admires the shopkeeper's enterprise, and elects to buy ones potatoes there, but one doesn't choose to turn up after closing time and help scrub the floor.

In the year of our fifteenth anniversary, the chorus steering committee sought developmental guidance and advice from successful charities and other art and business organisations. A whole host of top-notch professionals were convened, and several all-day brainstorming workshops took place. The representatives we consulted tried to be helpful, but ultimately none of them could tell us what to do or how we might do it. Perhaps we had to try to reverse the clock and reduce our size and activities, maybe split up into a host of smaller units. The London Gay Men's Chorus could become The London Gay Men's Creative Co-operative. Government funding or private sector sponsorship would change the whole economic picture; we could then employ some full time administrative staff. If we relinquished our hard-won charitable status and became a profit making business, we might even earn wages or start a recording label. The possibilities were legion.

We even explored the idea that our job was done; a 'gay' chorus was no longer needed in the now more enlightened twenty-first century. We could abandon any political or social agenda, and simply relax into being a group of ordinary men who happened to sing well. That was a comforting idea, but it is a narrow view from a privileged part of London. Planet earth is a closed system, and the politics, ecology and economy of any one part of the world affects us all; there are still 7 countries where homosexuality carries a death sentence, and more than 80 which threaten life imprisonment. Perhaps it would be wiser, both for us and for the greater good, if the Gay Men's Chorus remained an organisation with political as well as musical sensibility.

Our forward planning remained haphazard, and regardless of what our more intellectual concerns might have been, the seasonal routine of rehearsals and shows rolled on. Sometimes the pattern was reassuringly familiar, and the 'old-timers' could relax and roll along the predictable paths, being entertained at the way the 'new boys' were so thrilled with the excitement of our activities. On other occasions we were all taken by surprise. In 2011 there was a confidential invitation for us to participate in a reception taking place in 10 Downing Street. The theme was 'homophobia in sport', and our small group went along and provided entertainment and inspiration to an extraordinary assemblage of politicians and sporting personalities. Some of us viewed it as a visit to the sunlit upper slopes of significance, others as an unavoidable duty to voyage into the heart of darkness. The diversity of our membership is one of the elements that make life interesting.

As the years march past incremental change continues to occur, and we regularly arrange an all-day work-shop for interested parties to indulge in crystal-gazing and discuss potential developments. A 'three (or even five) year plan' might sometimes prove useful, but there would be a downside to such long-term security. It could inhibit improvisation; life in the twenty first century moves fast, and if we were locked into a programme that left us unable to change and respond we would rapidly become irrelevant. Any truly creative enterprise that knows exactly what it will be doing for the foreseeable future is deluded and has fallen into a fatal trap. The past shows us that the future is not foreseeable; we need to maintain flexible plans which enable possibilities rather than confinement.

The history of the chorus is a text-book demonstration of chaos theory, how the wing beats of a butterfly on one side of the planet can produce a cyclone on the other. We have made many 'wing beats' during our existence, and might well claim some responsibility for the changes that have occurred in the last twenty five years, but the chorus itself is susceptible to apparently inconsequential occurrences. Market researchers note that gay men are 'early adopters' of the latest fashions and gadgets, but nobody was able to predict how successful the new communication technology would become. Within months of the introduction of any novel 'iPad', 'tablet' or smart-phone, the weekly rehearsal seems to be awash with them. A large proportion of the chorus no longer prints out sheet music; they download and read it off a screen. We all still attend a physical music rehearsal, but a great deal of homework is done by individuals on-line via our website. Chris Pethers, who stepped up to the rostrum and rescued us in San Francisco twelve years ago, is now our assistant musical director, and he pre-records rehearsal tracks for each individual voice-part before the start of the season. We practise repertoire plugged in to our MP3 players whilst we sit on the tube or wait at traffic lights. With the help of technology the chorus can now rehearse and polish eighteen or more new songs in a fourteen week season. New advances also create new problems; during the rehearsal some members with such technology at their finger-tips access their emails, text and tweet when they are supposed to be paying attention. It's no longer possible for singers to make lightning-fast pencil notes on their scores, e-mail updates have to be sent out long after the rehearsal 'moment' has passed. The pattern and practice of the learning process has been fundamentally altered; the steps may change, but the dance goes on.

Thinking about how to commemorate our anniversary was an opportunity for reflection; the changes that have occurred are startling, but the present is connected to the past and long-term members also notice a clear continuity. Alisdair Low joined the undeveloped 'Gay Men's Choir' in 1993, and in 2010 enjoyed a two year tenure as chairman. Paul Hawley also started in 1993 and was our musical director for a brief period. In recent years he has consistently sung with the 'small group' as well as the main chorus, and has now probably experienced more man-hours of membership than anybody else. Ray Frost found his way to the group when we moved from London Friend to The Holborn Centre for Performing Arts in 1992, and is still around. Our General Manager, photographer and office expert Michael Cheetham has changed employment, living arrangements, partner and roles, but been with the chorus from the very start. There are many champions in the chorus story, and some are rarely recognised. The succession of accountants who have kept the organisation solvent are doing an un-glamorous and lonely job, but we would have crashed into debt a dozen times without them. The member who volunteers to chair a committee is only noticeable for the duration of a monthly meeting, but their invisible duties need to be done most evenings. Perhaps it needs to be acknowledged that every single person who has ever played a part has had to overcome their own private adversity, and the head-count of heroes is then immeasurable.

When the original chorus members began their journey there was no fixed destination, but they knew they had to start. We continue the quest, and may even discover that such exploration has no ending.

This narrative which began with the phrase 'Once upon a time...' should perhaps end with '...happily ever after,' but foresight is fugitive.

What I do know is no matter what path is taken next, there is never going to be any map other than the one we make for ourselves. The seeds we have sown shall produce the future, and one day the future will become history.

The LGMC (nearly complete) Chronology

1991

Sep   LGMC officially started

Dec   Angel tube station and London Friend
performances

Not many records exist for **1992**

1993

3 Apr   'People of the Passion'

21 May   London Lighthouse performance

Aug   Choir does August bank holiday vigil in
            Manchester (later named Mardi Gras)

24 Oct   London Palladium with Pet Shop Boys

30 Oct   'Undying Heart' premiere in Free Trade   Hall,
            Manchester

1 Dec   World Aids Day, THT, St Martin in the Fields

13 Dec   Our first committee meeting, at Louis' flat in
            Finsbury Park.

1994

15 Apr	Lesbian/Gay Christian Movement
Jun (?)	Launch of Dr Elizabeth Stuart's book 'Daring to Speak Love's Name' Westminster Hall
15 Jul	'Love and Lust under the Library' concert at Voicespace
Aug	Manchester Mardi Gras
30 Sep	'Third Birthday Bash' cabaret concert at Voicespace
Oct	Perform at Middlesex Hospital Chapel (and carols in Dec)
9 Dec	'Fairies in the Grotto' cabaret concert in Voicespace

1995

28/29 Apr	'LGMC World Tour' multi concept concert in Voicespace
26 May	'World Tour' production at Central Station, Kings Cross
Aug	Manchester Mardi Gras
15/16 Sep	'Carry on up the Chorus' an audience with the LGMC, Voicespace
22 Oct	Equality Show, Royal Albert Hall with Elton

| 15 Dec | 'Herods (pre-season) Wassail' multi concept concert at Voicespace |
| Dec | 'Fireball' Andrew Logan performance party at the ICA |

1996

24 Feb	Hackney Pride benefit at Chats Palace (with Labi Siffre)
21-23 Mar	'Women and Children First' concert at Emery Theatre
26/27 Apr	'After Eight Mince' cabaret concert at Voicespace
11 May	Sainsbury's 'Choir of the Day' award at Westminster Methodist Hall
25 May	BBC World Service from Westminster Abbey
27 May	Pink Angel Weekend, Islington
Jun (?)	Rededication of London Lighthouse, Westminster Abbey
Aug	Manchester Mardi Gras
Oct (?)	'Dungeon in the Sky', ULU, Mallet St
1 Dec	World Aids Day, 'One World, One Hope', Gabriel's Wharf, South Bank
Dec	Christmas carols at St Botolphes, Bishopsgate

| 13 Dec | 'Eat Drink and be Mary' – the Voicespace concert that was busted! |
| 25 Dec | Big Breakfast with Vanessa Feltz, Channel 4 |

1997

16/17 May	'It's just not Cricket' concert at Oval House Theatre
May	Pink Angels Weekend, Islington
Jun (?)	'Pinknic', Crystal Palace Park
Jul	Pride with Toyah Wilcox and Donna Summer, Victoria Park
12 Jul	'Gala concert' with L.G. Symphony Orchestra, St James's, W2
2 Aug	'Out in the Open', open air concert, Blue Pool, Highgate
Aug	Manchester Mardi Gras
21 Sep	'Variety Night', Theatre Royal, Stratford East
6 Oct	Show with Jackie Dankworth at Clock house
Nov	Show with Lorraine Bowen at Duckie, Vauxhall Tavern
1 Dec	World Aids Day, St James's, Piccadilly
14 Dec	'Light up the Night', Union Chapel, Islington.

1998

31 Mar	Lorraine Bowen's Greatest Bits, Rheingold Club, W1
9 Apr	'Night of a Thousand Bunnies', Connaught Grand Hall, WC2
4 Jun	'Link Gala' with Susan Black, Camden
Jun (?)	Walk for Life
Jun (?)	Summer Rites
18 Jul	'In the Bushes with the LGMC' open air concert, Blue Pool, Highgate
27 Jul	'Blue Skies' with Sydney L&G choir, Hackney Empire
30 Aug	Manchester Mardi Gras
10 Oct	'Torch Songs', Croydon Clocktower
12 Nov	Launch of first CD 'Hear the Difference'
1 Dec	World Aids Day, St James's, Piccadilly
5 Dec	'Hear the Difference live', The Palace Theatre, WC1
17 Dec	TFI Friday, Channel 4
24 Dec	'Snow Graham Norton' Channel 4

1999

24 Jan	'Variety Night', Theatre Royal, Stratford East

Spring	Chorus retreat at UEA, Norwich
2 May	Soho nail bomb memorial event, Soho Square
15 May	'A Capital Evening', Beck Theatre, Hayes
3 Jul	Mardi Gras
6 Jul	'Pride and Prejudice', Museum of London
9 Jul	Torch Songs, Croydon Clocktower
17 Jul	'Loitering with Intent', Bloomsbury Theatre, WC1
Jul (?)	Hammicks Book Shop, Leytonstone (Jake Arnott launch)
23 Jul	'Voices Raised', with Joanne Pickins, All Hallows, NW3
28 Aug	'Lavender Ball', Manchester Town Hall
29 Aug	Vigil, Castlefields Arena, Manchester
1 Nov	'Farewell 20th Century' with Cleo Laine, Festival Hall
28 Nov	Equality Show, Royal Albert Hall
1 Dec	World Aids Day, St Pauls, Covent Garden
3/4 Dec	'It's about time', Palace Theatre WC1
31 Dec/1 Jan	'Millennium Choir', The Dome

2000

12 Feb	'Gay Day', The Dome

28 Mar	Record 'Jerusalem' at Air Studios, Hampstead
9 Apr	Retreat show, UEA, Norwich
16 Apr	Awarded Sainsbury's 'Choir of the Day', Guilford
20 Apr	Pride launch party, Swiss Centre, Leicester Square
1 May	Admiral Duncan bomb memorial event, St Anne's, Soho
29 May	BBC Music Live, South Bank
9 Jun	Top of the Pops, BBC Elstree Studios
11 Jun	Jerry Springer Show
Mid-Jun	Wembley Stadium
18 Jun	'West End Boys', Piccadilly Theatre
1 Jul	Mardi Gras, Finsbury Park
Jul	US Tour (21st Boston; 27th 'Afternoon Tea', San Jose; 30th Grace Cathedral, San Francisco)
26 Aug	'Lavender Ball', Manchester
7 Nov	Borders Bookshop, Oxford St
12 Nov	Buxton Opera House, Derbyshire

Record CD Nov/Dec/Jan, Release pinup calendar

2001

| 3 Mar | 'From the Ritz to the Anchor and Crown', |

Queen Elizabeth Hall. Official release of the second CD.

16 Mar	Comic Relief, BBC, White City
27 Mar	Record for Queen Mother obituary programme
25 Mar to 1 Apr	'Because I Sing', Roundhouse and Channel 4
17 Jun	Walk for Life show, London Bridge
6 Jul	'Surrey Harmony', Harlequin Theatre, Redhill
16 Jul	'Outreach', Cecil Sharp House, Camden
2 Aug	Record Jonathan Ross Show pilot, BBC, White City
5 Aug	Launch Gay Football Cup, Scala, Kings Cross
31 Aug	'Sing Out', UEA, Norwich
16 Sep	'Ballads for a Living Planet', South Bank
14 Oct	Equality Show, Royal Albert Hall
Oct	Awarded £5000 grant from 'Awards for All' programme
20 Nov	Bishop Johnson retirement evening, St Martin in the Fields
1 Dec	World Aids Day, St Pancras Church, Euston
4 Dec	A Winter Sparkler, St Martin-in-the-Fields
7 Dec	The Big Breakfast, live on Channel 4 TV

| 9 Dec | '10' Tenth anniversary show, Prince of Wales Theatre |
| 14 Dec | Carols in Trafalgar Sq. (also Euston, Kings Cross and City Farm) |

2002

2 Feb	Mike and William's partnership event, Spitz Club, E1
17 Feb	Ballads for a Living Planet, British Library
Mar	New Musical Director (Dr. Charles Beale) appointed.
30 Apr	'Opening Doors' Age Concern annual conference, Plaza Hotel, Victoria.
3 Jun	Jubilee street party, Royal Marsden Hospital.
3 Jun	'Command Performance' (Cruisaid), Comptons, Old Compton St.
23 Jun	Walk for Life, South Bank
29 Jun	'Straight from the Heart' Gatehouse Theatre, Highgate (with Heartland)
26 Jul	'A Golden Reign', Queen Elizabeth Hall (with Melo Men)
27 Jul	'A Golden Reign', Queen Elizabeth Hall (with Surrey Harmony)
18 Sep	Summer in the Square, Trafalgar Square
20 Oct	Cleo and Johnny's 50th, Royal Albert Hall

25 Oct to 9 Nov	Gay Games, Sydney, Australia
19 Dec	Vauxhall City Farm, SE11
20 Dec	Ruby Wax Show

2003

4 May	Showtime at The Stables, Milton Keynes
13-15 Jun	Sing Out at DCU, + National Concert Hall, Dublin
16 Jun	Showtime at The Waterfront, Belfast
21 Jun	Food Chain event, Covent Garden
22 Jun	Walk for Life, After Party, Thames Embankment
29 Jun	Midsummer Celebration, St James's, Piccadilly
18 Jul	Showtime/Tying the Knot, Queen Elizabeth Hall
26 Jul	Pride in the Park, Hyde Park
23 Aug	Showtime, Manchester Library Theatre
27 Sep	Loose Ends, BBC Radio 4
15 Nov	Lighting the Christmas Tree, Covent Garden Piazza
30 Nov	Showtime, Theatre Royal, Brighton
18 Dec	Carols for RNIB, Trafalgar Square

2004

29 May	Eclecsis, Adrian Boult Hall, Birmingham
8 Jun	Eclecsis, Queen Elizabeth Hall
Jun	(Brian Williamson) Protest at Jamaican High Commission
2 Jul	Pride Rally, Trafalgar Square
11 Jul	Cannizaro Park, Wimbledon, SW19
16 Jul	Kennedy Centre, Washington DC, USA
21 Jul	'Love in the Square', Trafalgar Square
17-25 Jul	GALA Festival, Montreal, Canada
10 Oct	For the Public Good, with ENO at London Coliseum
22-24 Oct	Retreat at Benslow Music Trust, Hertfordshire
5 Nov	Memorial for David Morley, St Anne's, Soho
27 Nov	A Little Christmas Right Now, St John's, Pinner
18 Dec	Make the Yuletide Gay, Barbican
19-24 Dec	Selfridges, Oxford St, W1

2005

| 19 Jan | Memorial for Philip Dewdney, St Joseph's, Bromley |

25 Jan	Holocaust Memorial for GLA at City Hall, SE1
17 Apr	Patrons launch, Victoria and Albert Museum
3-7 May	Various Voices, Paris
25 Jun	West End Live, Leicester Square
1 Jul	Dept. for Constitutional Affairs Conference, Earls Court Exhibition Centre
1 Jul	Gay Police Assn. Anniversary Dinner, Park Lane Hotel, W1
2 Jul	Pride march and rally, Trafalgar Square
10 Jul	Soho Festival, St Anne's, Soho
22-24 Jul	You'll do for Now, Cadogan Hall, SW1
8 Oct	St Luke's Music Society, SW12
14 Dec	Make the Yuletide Gay, Symphony Hall, Birmingham
17 Dec	Make the Yuletide Gay, Dome Theatre, Brighton
21/22 Dec	Make the Yuletide Gay, Barbican
18-24 Dec	Selfridges, Oxford St, W1
24 Dec	Carols in Trafalgar Square

2006

21 Jan	Winter Concert with Pink Singers, Royal Academy of Music, NW1

4 Feb	LGBT History Month launch, Museum of London, EC2
12 May	National Portrait Gallery, 150th Anniversary
29 Apr	The First Fifteen, Cadogan Hall, SW1
17 Jun	West End Live, Leicester Square
26 Jun	Europride Sings, Queen Elizabeth Hall
1 Jul	Pride March, Oxford St
2 Jul	Europride The Show, Royal Albert Hall
15 Jul	The First Fifteen, St David's Hall, Cardiff
27 Jul	Cabaret Party, Heaven, The Arches, Charing Cross Road
15 Sep	Settembremusica, Agnelli Auditorium, Turin, Italy
12 Nov	Dedication, Islington War Memorial, Islington Green, N1
1 Dec	World Aids Day, St Pancras Church
18-20 Dec	Selfridges, Oxford St, W1
20 Dec	Make the Yuletide Gay, Barbican
22 Dec	BBC Radio 1 Christmas Party
22 Dec	Club XXL Christmas fundraiser

2007

Feb	Voices of Refugees, Museum of London

15 Mar	100 Ideas – Radical Singing, Hayward Gallery, South Bank
20-21 May	Bad Boys, Cadogan Hall, SW1
26 May	Bad Boys, Usher Hall, Edinburgh
27 May	Bad Boys, Royal Concert Halls, Glasgow
8 Jun	Overture Weekend, reopening of Royal Festival Hall, South Bank
2 Dec	World Aids Day Benefit with Barbara Cook, London Coliseum
Dec	Christmas Carols in Covent Garden Piazza (x 3)
16 Dec	Accentuate the Positive, London Palladium

2008

25 Jan	Seduced: Art and Sex, Barbican Art Gallery
26 Feb	Cabaret, LGBT History Month, Henderson Ct, Camden
2 Mar	BBC Choir of the Year competition, Anvil, Basingstoke
6 Mar	Outside Edge, Museum of London, Docklands
21 Jun	West End Live, Leicester Square
4/5 Jul	Songs of Innocence and Experience, Cadogan Hall, SW1
13 Jul	Palau de Musica Catalana, Barcelona, Spain

16 Jul	Jardins de l'Ajuntament, Castellar del Valles, Spain
17 Jul	Municipal Theatre, La Garriga, Spain
18 Jul	Auditori Josep Carreras, Vila-Seca, Spain
21 Jul	There's no Place Like Homo, FFK at Kings Head Islington, N1
Aug	There's no Place Like Homo, FFK at Edinburgh Festival
24 Aug	Int G and L Football Assn. Opening, Shepherds Bush Empire, W12
Nov	Festive Songs, Museum of London, Docklands
19/20 Dec	For Christmas' Sake, Cadogan Hall, SW1

2009

17 Jan	Milk Watch – the movie, on location
Feb	LGBT History Month
19 Mar	The North London International School, Friern Barnet Lane, N11
1-4 May	Various Voices Festival, South Bank Centre, London
12 Jun	The Scoop at More London, City Hall, SE1
25-28 Jun	Helsinki, Finland
16 Jul	Songs of London, The Shaw Theatre, Euston Rd, NW1

13 Aug	Songs of London, Museum of London, EC2
11 Oct	Oklahomo by FFK, New Players Theatre, WC2
30 Oct	Say No To Hate Crime Vigil, Trafalgar Square
18 Nov	Museum of London, Docklands, West India Quay
4/5 Dec	Singderella, Cadogan Hall, SW1
10/7th Dec	Sing London, Tate Modern, Bankside
15 Dec	Mayor of London's Carol Service, Southwark Cathedral
20 Dec	Clore Ballroom, Southbank Centre.
20-22 Dec	Sandi Toksvig's Christmas Cracker, Royal Festival Hall

2010

12 Feb	Recording with Mark Ronson, Metropolis Studios, Chiswick High Road, W4
9-11 Apr	LGMC Retreat, Winchester University
7 May	National Portrait Gallery, 10th Anniversary Ondaatje Wing
9 May	'Chorus – Celebration' Clore Ballroom, Royal Festival Hall, Southbank
11 Jun	Scoop, City Hall
19 Jun	West End Live, Leicester Square
25/26 Jun	Seven Deadly Sins, The Roundhouse, Camden

16 Jul	Palace of Culture, Warsaw, Poland
17 Jul	Europride March, Warsaw, Poland
10 Oct	Thoroughly Modern Willie by FFK, Shaw Theatre, Euston Rd
23 Oct	Hate Crime Campaign, Trafalgar Square
10/11 Dec	Make Your Own Kind of Christmas, Cadogan Hall, SW1

2011

11 Feb	Dept. of Education, LGBT History Month, Westminster
11 Feb	Google LGBT Group, Westminster
16 Feb	Mark Ronson at the Roundhouse, Camden
8 Mar	William Ellis School, Highgate. Camden Anti-Bullying Seminar
15 May	Chorus: LGMC Showcase, Clore Ballroom, Royal Festival Hall, Southbank
22 May	Songs for Survivors UK, Cadogan Hall, SW1
5 Jun	Walk for Life Closing event, Potter's Field, London Bridge
18 Jun	West End Live, Trafalgar Square
24/25 Jun	Sound, Union Chapel, Union Terrace, Islington, N1
24 Jun	Extraordinary Voices, Barbican Centre, EC2

1 Dec	World Aids Day, Waterstones, Gower St, W1
9 Dec	Dickens and London, Museum of London
11 Dec	LGMC Christmas Cracker, De la Warr Pavilion, Bexhill-on-Sea
16/17 Dec	Make Mine a Snowball, Cadogan Hall, SW1

2012

14 Feb	John Sparks Memorial, Hither Green Crematorium
18 Feb	Monty Python recording, Redwood Studios, Chapel St, W1
24 Feb	Educate and Celebrate, Stoke Newington School
6 May	Band of Brothers, Royal Festival Hall, Southbank Centre
20 May	A Band of Brothers, Grand Opera House, Belfast
15-17 Jun	LGMC Retreat, Winchester
5 Jul	World Pride march, London
8 Jul	Ha Ha Hackney, Gayextravaganza, Hackney Empire, E8
21 Jul	'Big Gay Sing' Cultural Olympiad, Trafalgar Square
8 Aug	Showcase at Scoop, London Bridge

Aug	Hi De Homo, by LGMC ensemble at Edinburgh Festival
21 Sep	William Ellis School, Highgate
6 Oct	Hi De Homo by LGMC ensemble at Shaw Theatre, Euston Rd
9 Oct	William Ellis School, Anti-Bullying Seminar, Highgate
11 Oct	Ackland Burghley School, London, NW5, Equality workshop

PRINTED AND BOUND BY:

Copytech (UK) Limited trading as Printondemand-
worldwide,
9 Culley Court, Bakewell Road, Orton Southgate.
Peterborough, PE2 6XD, United Kingdom.